IDEOLOGY AND METHOD
IN ECONOMICS

GIFT OF

JIM BECKER

© DEMCO, INC.—Archive Safe

Ideology and Method in Economics

Homa Katouzian

94-790

New York University Press
New York *and* London

Library of Congress Cataloging in Publication Data

Katouzian, Homa.
Ideology and method in economics.

Bibliography: p.
Includes index.
1. Economics. I. Title.
HB71.K33   330   79–3301
ISBN 0–8147–4574–1
ISBN 0–8147–4575–X pbk.

Manufactured in Great Britain

TO THE MEMORY OF KHALIL MALEKI,
who was *never* 'led into temptation'

ACKNOWLEDGEMENTS

The author and publishers wish to thank the following, who have kindly given permission for the use of copyright material:

Journal of Economic Theory, for extracts from 'Optimal Economic Growth and Uncertainty: the discounted case', by W. A. Brock and L. T. Mirman.

Review of Economic Studies, for extracts from 'Incentives and share Cropping', by J. E. Stiglitz.

CONTENTS

. . . carrying a few books like a beast.

SA'ADI

One knows so much and comprehends so little.

EINSTEIN

PREFACE

This book is a product of many years of reading and reflection on methods of understanding social and economic questions; on efforts to find intellectual solutions to these questions; and on practical attempts to resolve the problems whence they arise – that is, on philosophy, the social sciences and history. For this reason it may appear to be 'too philosophical' to some economists, even though I have *never* had – and I would repudiate – any interest in 'philosophising' about social and economic problems: in general, it is the problem itself which gives rise to the philosophy – not the other way around; in particular, a serious inquiry into the relevance and significance of our methods of understanding and solving economic and social problems would be incomplete (and often worthless) in total oblivion of their historical and philosophical contexts. It has been necessary both to present and discuss relevant philosophical concepts and theories, and to compare them with methods of socio-economic discovery by means of illustrative examples from the theories and methods of economic science, past and present. In Chapters 1 to 7 I have given examples from the theory and practice of economics (and, sometimes, other social sciences); and in Chapter 8 I have presented a sample of modern theories and approaches to our subject, as a summary illustration for the critical remarks of the preceding chapters. Yet I have kept down the number of such examples, and the space devoted to each, to a minimum which in my judgement has been compatible both with economy and with clarity. And I have left the reader to supply countless other examples which are available from textbooks – not to mention the innumerable current publications which threaten to bury us all under their dead weight. I have intended to solve problems not to sell products. Whether or not my arguments are judged to be 'too philosophical', 'too economic', 'too radical', 'too moderate' – all of which appellations, and others besides, can be conceivably attached to this essay, by readers of different persuasions or specialisations – I would happily agree that my general approach is *unprofessional* in a sociological sense of this term which I have discussed in Chapter 5 of this work.

It is a product of many years and, indeed, its origins are shrouded in unclear memories from my childhood. It therefore owes a great deal to many who – either by their wisdom or by their follies – have made indispensable contributions to my intellectual development. If I cannot name them all here it is not because the value of their teachings have been overlooked or forgotten. Some of them are among us no longer: for example my father, who – apart from his generous and unselfish material support – taught me (both in conversation and in conduct) the value of a love for truth; the ethic of a regard for the freedom and welfare of others; and the excellence of a restless, but dignified, life over a peaceful, but servile, existence. I cherish their memories dead or alive, and I acknowledge my debt to them wherever they may be.

Happily the number of those who have had a direct and immediate share in this piece of work is not too large to forbid explicit acknowledgements. Professor T. W. Hutchison – to whose learned lectures I owe my introduction to the history of economic thought – read the entire manuscript in draft and offered valuable comments and criticisms. Likewise, Professor Joan Robinson (who is not in need of witnesses for her analytical powers) read and criticised the whole of the material with characteristic generosity, efficiency and candour. Professor Syed Ahmad's and Professor Peter Victor's selfless encouragements as well as their suggestions, and reassurances, on certain important points, were very helpful. Professor Sir Karl Popper, though not directly involved in this particular project, has made an important (indirect) contribution to it, both by what I have learned from the spirit (in spite of my occasional disagreement with the letter) of his ideas, and by his distant encouragements, including his frequent gifts of offprints from his (relevant) publications. I have also benefited from suggestions for improvement by two anonymous readers, the standard of whose scholarship is reflected in their acute observations on form and content, and in the generous spirit of their assessments. None of these, known and unknown, critics would necessarily agree with all my descriptions, analyses or prescriptions. And, on occasion, I have retained my own views or style of presentation, in spite of their contrary, and no less reasonable, suggestions. They all share in the credit (if any), and none in the blame.

The work was completed in the academic year 1977–8 when I had the pleasure of living in Canada, and the privilege of serving McMaster University. In the same year I was libelled in England, and I lost a brother in Persia. Yet the openness of space and society in Canada, the amiable environment of the Department of Economics at McMaster, and the moral and material generosities of my colleagues were such as to mitigate the grief caused by those catastrophes, and generate enthusiasm for life and work, none the less. It is difficult to know whether the delightful combination of efficiency and humanity with which the departmental secretaries fulfil their tasks is a cause or a consequence of this congenial social and intellectual atmosphere. However that may be, Mrs Ruth Nicholson's general supervision of my works and duties, and Ms Debbie Sanché's highly skilful and conscientious typing of the manuscript had a significant share in the outcome. The contributions of Miss Monique Raitchey, Mrs Sharon Ciraolo and Miss Elvia Horvath may have been less direct, but no less valuable . . . I thank them all for a debt which can never be fully repaid.

Finally – and in spite of all its limitations – this work may not have been realised without the moral support of my wife and the wonderful gift of our children. Efforts of this kind may not justify their costs, and especially those which are inflicted on others. Yet this imbalance between their real costs and their hypothetical benefits may be rendered less drastic when we remember that men die but ideas remain.

M. A. Homayoun Katouzian

University of Kent at Canterbury
September 1978

1

ECONOMICS AND PHILOSOPHY OF SOCIAL SCIENCE: THE TASK AND ITS SCOPE

Philosophy, science and society are all indispensable features of human life. Society cannot dispense with either philosophy or science; nor can science and philosophy dispense with each other. Without philosophy, science loses its social direction; without science, philosophy ceases to be socially relevant. The philosophy and the science which are alive are – like life itself – not only analysable but also indivisible. And like life itself, neither is entirely concrete nor entirely abstract; exclusively material or exclusively intellectual; totally practical or totally theoretical. Such rigid lines of demarcation are false: they have no counterparts in the realm of reality. Only that 'usefulness' can be opposed to truth which is no more than a lie; that is, one man's usefulness at the expense of another. Otherwise, truth itself is useful, just as well as usefulness is true. Both a soulless technology and an immaterial piety have destroyed themselves in the past. They may do the same in the future.

Philosophy, science and society will live – or die – together; and that includes the Great Technological Civilisation.

OF THE TASKS OF THE SOCIAL SCIENCES AND THEIR PHILOSOPHY

In principle the social sciences would have to fulfil two major tasks: explanatory and prescriptive. Both these tasks involve solutions to well-defined scientific social problems. They both require an accurate description of the relevant events and phenomena, and a precise analysis of their interdependence. The explanatory task further demands a study of the broader (dynamic) tendencies in the evolution of social and economic entities. Apart from this, the main tasks of the social sciences are prescriptive, and they necessitate the formulation of clear policy statements for the fulfilment of the major aims and objectives of the society: for example, theories which state the required conditions for a democratic government, or social progress, or the efficient allocation of economic resources. We have discussed the essentially prescriptive nature of economic science in Chapter 6, where we have also emphasised that this fact has no bearing on the issue of the scientificity of economics. The arguments are generally applicable to the other social sciences.

Philosophy of social science is neither abstract nor useless. Or, it is as 'abstract' and 'useless' as a critical guide-book to a big city – addressed, in the first place, to its citizens – which reviews the layout and architectural pattern of the city in a historical perspective; discusses the policies of the civic authorities in this and other regards; detects the sources of pollution and waste; emphasises the interdependence between the welfare of the various districts; and maps the most efficient routes within and between those districts. They need not specialise in such knowledge, but they do need to have a basic grasp of it. Those who would deny such a basic necessity would still have some, haphazard, idea of the relevant issues, but they are more likely to get lost in a road, or to have an ill-informed knowledge of other localities. To drop the metaphor, philosophy of social science discusses the logic and the methods of social and economic inquiry against their historical background. It discusses their development, their present state and their future prospects, both in theory and in practice; that is, both as they are theoretically intended by the social sciences, and as they are actually applied by them. Furthermore, it can investigate the social and institutional characteristics of the mode or scientific behaviour in general. In the latter role it functions as the social philosophy or sociology of science, or the scientist (including the social scientist). Value judgements and ideological prejudices are not, strictly speaking, problems which concern a descriptive sociology of the scientist. Or, at least they can be treated separately.

If a philosophy of social science is successful in fulfilling the above functions, it would automatically achieve two further objectives. First, it would make it clear that methods and results, means and ends, routes and destinations are inalienable from each other. That it is nonsense to say, either in science or in society, that we have obtained, and we can obtain, the *desired* results without regard to the means for obtaining them. Every activity leads to *some* objective; but this is unlikely to be the *desired* objective unless appropriate methods have been used in reaching that objective. The road to Cambridge takes us somewhere, to Cambridge perhaps, but not to Oxford; or if it eventually does, it would be a more costly journey, both in time and in money. The seizure of political power is *possible* by *any* means; but the establishment of a definite political system would be possible only by the means appropriate to it: Jacobinism often ends up with Robespierre at the guillotine – and Bonaparte at the helm! . . . A social theory would provide some information about some social problem; but it may be the wrong information or the wrong problem, unless the approach and methods have been carefully selected, and revised in the process of discovery. The end may or may not justify the means; but the means are certain to influence – if not completely determine – the end.

Second, that social and economic problems are indivisible. That it is possible to provide a 'purely' economic, sociological, political, etc., analysis of given socio-economic phenomena; but it is impossible to suggest 'purely' economic, etc., solutions to real social problems. Both in its functionings, and in its disorder, the liver does not distinguish between 'purely' chemical, 'purely' physical or 'purely' psychological factors; nor can a *solution* to its malfunctionings – assuming of course that the aim is not solely to publish a paper on the 'purely' chemical features of a certain liver disease; it is also to cure the patient! Obviously, this is not to say that as social scientists, or even as economists or sociologists, we should know and consider every conceivable method, theory and fact (concerning a given problem) in our science, or even our discipline. That is neither possible nor useful. It means that, as much as possible, we should consciously try to acquire a broader vision of the various aspects and dimensions of the problem, the subject, the discipline and the science; and, moreover, that we should stop deluding ourselves that our methods and subject of interest, say in economics, are 'the most useful' or 'the most high-powered'; or, that among the social sciences, economics is 'the most important' or 'the most scientific': that we should, all of us, begin to become less intellectually chauvinistic and more tolerant, if not more modest. In fact such a state of intellectual self-satisfaction or narcissism – though it can be highly destructive – has little to do with the method and substance of social inquiry. It is most likely to be a by-product of an upbringing, and an approach to culture and history, which have convinced almost every single race and nation on this earth that – for some real or imaginary reasons – they alone are a gift to humanity. At times even the height of mountains, the size of deserts and the depth of oceans are cited as evidence for such grotesque proclamations. It is time that at least intellectuals avoided the extension and application of such perfect irrationalities (of which we are all victims) to their pursuit of knowledge.

OF THE SCOPE AND RELEVANCE OF THIS ESSAY

'Economics is in crisis'; every economist, or almost every economist, knows and agrees with that statement, even though they may disagree on the precise diagnosis or an effective prescription for the crisis itself. As a matter of fact, the view has become so widespread that it is embarrassing to cite the usual evidence, or references to it. Indeed in the past decade we have witnessed a situation where such pillars of the economics establishment as Sir John Hicks, Professor Leontief and Sir Henry Phelps-Brown have joined the historical heterodoxy of distinguished economists like Professor Galbraith, Lord Kaldor and Professor Joan Robinson in discussing different aspects of this crisis. Dr Guy Routh's *The Origin of Economic Ideas* contains an excellent summary presentation of the issues and the references. And, as Professor Thomas Kuhn has noted, when a science is in crisis it usually resorts to a philosophical analysis of its own foundations. Hence a relative rise in interest, among some economists, in matter pertaining to the philosophy of economic science.

The crisis is as certain as the absence of a generally accepted solution to it. Yet – we assert – the issue is incorrectly envisioned: it is a mistake to believe that economic science had been capable of an adequate analysis of – and prescription for – economic problems until there suddenly appeared a seemingly inexplicable crisis! If a sudden heart seizure must have a latent history behind it, so must a social or intellectual crisis. In particular, the unwarranted optimism with which we viewed our theories and methods in the 1950s and 1960s – the high tide of Positive Economics – is no evidence for our success at the time; on the contrary, it is evidence for our socio-psychological weaknesses, our intellectual complacency, which have now led us into the present bewilderment. It is unlikely to be an accident of history that the same decades witnessed a similar socio-psychological state among other social scientists; when the End of Ideology was proclaimed; when Behavioural (Social) Psychology was invented; when Functionalist Sociology reigned supreme; when the Science of Politics began to discover how to be politically scientific, or scientifically political; when a knowledge of the history of ideas and events became a liability, a source of intellectual embarrassment.

This state of general intellectual self-satisfaction reflected the broader socio-economic optimism of the period of full employment, high consumption, trade liberalisation, consensus politics, etc., echoed by the famous (British) political slogan 'You never had it so good!' It is well beyond the scope of this book to enter a discussion of the nature and causes of that incredible state of social and economic optimism. It is, however, very likely that, both then and now, the socio-economic environment has had a greater role in causing the boom and the slump in the status of orthodox social and economic theories – their erstwhile 'success' and their present 'crisis' – than any other factor; and certainly, more so than any sudden or continuous intellectual issue. The relatively smooth and buoyant social and economic functioning of the West had had little to do with the truth or falsehood of existing social and economic theories. It was no evidence that these theories were 'working'; it simply did not call upon them to explain any serious problems, or prescribe solutions to them. It left them to indulge in cultivating their back-gardens, to invent and then solve 'scientific puzzles'.

Let us examine this argument at its weakest point; that is, with reference to the case of economics where it could be argued that our post-war 'success' was a direct consequence of the Keynesian theories. No one would deny that John Maynard Keynes proposed a satisfactory theory of demand-deficiency unemployment which was largely responsible for the development and use of the techniques of demand management in a capitalist society. But that should not give us much cause for self-congratulation. First, the idea that public expenditure could help establish some sort of full macro-economic equilibrium in the economy (indeed, promote economic growth) had had many precedents both in theory and in application. Take the case of the German and the Japanese industrialisation policies. If those neo-classical economists had been right who argued that a pound's worth of *public* investment would merely replace a pound's worth of *private* investment (hence resulting in no net increase in *aggregate* investment) then those of their compatriots who had had their guts torn out by the German bayonets (in the First World War) must have been experiencing a nightmare of fantasy; for the bayonets, and the economic power behind them, had been the direct consequences of the active intervention of the state in the German economy. At any rate, many political parties, intellectuals and activists in Western Europe had advocated public intervention in the 1920s. In Britain Keynes, Lloyd George and Mosley, among others, had put their signature to a document demanding some such intervention as 'early' as 1929. The roots of the conflict within the Labour Party, which finally ripped it apart in 1931, must surely be found in differences of opinion on these issues. The Nazi take-over of Germany (1933), and the services rendered to them by such brilliant intellectual gangsters as Dr Schacht (their finance minister) had – by the time *The General Theory* was published – left little room for argument. Even the comparatively meekish new deal policy of F. D. Roosevelt had been prior to *The General Theory*. Keynes's success in adapting the use of such policies to the orthodox framework of economic theory (though not without precedent) was a significant intellectual achievement. But these policies had 'worked', and would still 'work', in complete absence of any notion of 'the marginal propensity to save', 'the marginal efficiency of capital' or 'the speculative demand for money'. In any case a war economy (which was rendered inevitable three years later) would hardly have needed a theory of full employment. And the task of reconstruction after the war – by the 'victors' and the vanquished alike – would automatically result in the full employment of resources. Yet, *The General Theory* had been written, and it should perhaps be given some credit even for these practical events. But, in the decades which followed, what exactly was the 'Keynesian lesson' by public decision-makers and their professional economic advisers: very briefly, public *spending* is the panacea for everything at all times and in all situations – for party political success, for social welfare, for economic growth, etc. It may seem incredible but, at least in practice, no great distinction was made between investment and consumption expenditure; between long-term full employment and prosperity achieved by the renovation and the accumulation of capital, and the 'get-rich-quick' policies of 'never-had-it-so-good' – let us relax and enjoy ourselves because we now have theoretical proof that 'saving is passive'. Is this evidence of success either of the theories of Consensus Politics or of Positive Economics? Any village shopkeeper would know that he can live off his capital and credit, and face the consequences afterwards. . . . And what exactly was the contribution of professional Positive Economists to this great triumph of wisdom: (i) to solve Keynesian 'puzzles' (e.g. the linearity or non-linearity of the long-term consumption function and the 'theories' it gave rise to (ii) to construct the neo-classical synthesis – i.e. in plain language, to prove that Keynes was one of our boys without knowing it himself. In fact as early as the late 1930s it had been predicted that Keynesian policies would have inflationary consequences. Here was a *problem* which (in place of so many puzzles) could have been attacked much sooner and much more seriously, instead of catching us all by surprise, if not bewilderment.

Therefore, it is a mistake to believe that the present intellectual crisis is mainly because orthodox social and economic theories have *stopped* 'working'. This is where the mistake lies. The real crisis is that intellectuals and scientists have been, both then and later, merely reflecting the immediate socio-economic mood and environment; merely conforming or adjusting to them. For all we know the present socio-economic disequilibria may subside without the slightest effort on our part as social scientists: the wounds of the adventure in Vietnam may be finally healed, and their pains buried in a corner of 'the collective unconscious'; the oil-producing countries may become 'kinder' or less powerful; the western societies may settle for a slower increase in their affluence – and their effluence. It would then be relatively easy to procure some kind of posthumous explanation of the intellectual crisis of the social sciences, and, once again, begin to delude ourselves that our theories 'work'. This would be a great tragedy. Yet it is very likely to happen, as long as we regard the present intellectual crisis more as a localised malfunctioning than as the symptom of a widespread and chronic malady. We would then condemn ourselves to a succession of psychological booms and slumps parallel to their social counterparts. This is the real crisis of the social – perhaps all – sciences in our time, when the academic profession in general is neither a leader nor a (constructive) critic of the society, willing to expose its latent problems in periods of boom, and anticipate the subsequent slumps if those problems are ignored – and, instead, it is, at best, its uncritical follower or servant, and at worst its retainer and apologist.

The present study is a modest piece of intellectual effort in its own right; it is also a response to the real crisis of economics and the social sciences in the above sense. In its narrower objective it presents a comprehensive and critical study of the logic and methods of economic science, and the moral, ideological and sociological characteristics of its progress, or stagnation. In its broader aim it suggests a framework within which the roots of the real crisis of economic science may be discovered. There is no naïve presupposition that the limited efforts of an unknown writer would have any significant impact on men's ideas or the course of their change. Very likely they will be dismissed with contempt, as has happened time and again. In this respect it is no more than an attempt to fulfil that social and intellectual responsibility, which in a Persian expression, obliges 'the messenger to deliver his message' – regardless of its consequences for himself or its recipients.

Many of the issues of economic philosophy have been subject to a fairly considerable amount of misunderstanding and confusion Some of these must be due to the fact that in general economists do not take the subject very seriously, but do not refrain from pro-nouncing judgements upon its various problems. Some others arise from the frequent abstraction of these issues from their historical perspectives, or from their origins and status in the disciplines whence they have been borrowed. Chapter 2 provides a brief revision of the development of economic ideas *and* methods in connection with the most fundamental developments in philosophy of science and in social history. It therefore sets the background to the arguments of the succeeding chapters. Chapter 3 examines the criteria and the status of Positive Economics in relation to the logical positivist and Popperian philosophies of science. It ends with a brief appendix on Popper's critique of historicism. In Chapter 4 the modern trends in philosophy of science – specifically, those associated with the names of Professor Kuhn and the late Dr Lakatos – are critically discussed, both within their own contexts and in their application to the history and methods of economics. Chapter 5 suggests a relatively novel, but basic, approach to the explanation of the (contemporary) mode of professional academic behaviour, and its social and institutional origins. It is hoped to be applicable to *all* academic disciplines, subject to the necessary that it should be also useful in explaining the broader professional academic tendencies in economics and the other social sciences. Chapter 6 contains a critical discussion of various concepts of value judgement and ideology, and it assesses their relevance to scientific knowledge in general, and economic knowledge in particular. Chapter 7 examines the scope and limits of abstraction and generalisation – and the relevance and status of their techniques – in economic theory. Chapter 8 is exclusively devoted to a discussion of a sample of contemporary models, theories and approaches as further evidence for the claims and arguments of the preceding chapters (that is, in addition to the cases which have been cited in these chapters). Chapter 9 summarises and concludes the arguments.

The whole programme is part of an effort to find the limits to our knowledge by discovering the scope of our ignorance.

2

HISTORICAL PERSPECTIVES: FROM POLITICAL ECONOMY TO POSITIVE ECONOMICS

THE PROGRESS OF ECONOMIC IDEAS

When the dawn of classical political economy broke on the horizon of history human civilisation was on the verge of a great transformation. Only two centuries earlier the European feudal system – described by Adam Smith as a catastrophe which had befallen Europe since the fall of the Roman Empire[1] – had finally begun to collapse under the pressure of domestic and external forces. The gradual development of technology and the expansion of foreign trade had been accompanied by the accumulation of financial capital and the growth – and increasing political autonomy – of townships typified by the establishment of burghs or 'boroughs': hence the term 'bourgeoisie'. Whatever the direction of causation might have been, these developments were paralleled by a rapid increase in the functions and power of the state which – in the countries of northern Europe – received spiritual legitimacy by the collapse of the authority of the Roman Church. The intellectual revolution which concurrently unfolded marked the return of scientific speculation and artistic creation from other-worldly to this-worldly problems: a movement away from metaphysics to physics – from God to man – both in substance and in method.

These events attracted attention to the study of the economic problems of a predominantly rural and commercial society. For over two centuries a growing number of men concentrated on the study of these problems. Later in history they became collectively known as the Mercantilists – a misleading term, especially as it gives the wrong impression that their ideas had developed into a coherent and systematic body of economic thought. Adam Smith and other classical political economists claimed that the Mercantilists were indeed guilty of many 'mistakes': for example, they sometimes confused income with money, and money with capital.

On reflection, however, in an economy dominated by the commercial and 'circulating' forms of capital they were probably not too wrong in confusing capital with money; likewise, in an economy in which the *aggregate* velocity of circulation (per annum) was perhaps insignificantly greater than unity, they were probably not too stupid in identifying national income with the stock of money in circulation.[2] Even their preoccupation with a balance-of-trade surplus was not all that unintelligent. For free trade cannot be a *unilateral* policy and when all the national economies protect their home markets it would be folly for only one of them to engage in free trade. Therefore, a critique of Mercantilist *ideas* cannot be wholly abstracted from the Mercantilist *problems* as they emerged from their social and economic framework. (See further 'Of Ideology in Economic Science' in Chapter 6, pp. 153 ff.).

Meanwhile European economies had grown in prosperity and complexity. There had been a sustained increase in commercial activities and the accumulation of capital. Merchants and capitalists had already begun to extend their interest to agricultural production. The development of new productive methods and implements – mainly in agriculture – was slowly channelling some of the accumulated capital into fixed investment. In England the Civil War marked the arrival of an era in which the 'new' class of urban proprietors and gentleman farmers would play a more important economic and political role. There was a noticeable change in the scope and nature of economic problems, which encouraged a shift of emphasis from the explanation of exchange, the balance of trade, maxims of public policy, etc., to the analysis of value, production and distribution. This was the dawn of classical political economy illuminated by a line of writers stretching from Sir William Petty, John Locke and Charles d'Avenant in the latter half of the seventeenth century, to David Hume, Richard Cantillon and the French Physiocrats in the first half of the next.

These forerunners of classical political economy managed between them to touch on nearly every aspect of the economic problem and every concept of economic theory which until now has occupied economists of various generations. In retrospect their most important achievements were the formulation of a crude labour theory of value, the discovery (or invention) of the concept of equilibrium, its determination by the forces of supply and demand, the quantity theory of money and its implications for

foreign trade. This collective achievement was undoubtedly substantial and impressive. Yet, it did not amount to the construction
of a system of economic thought. Clarence Ayres (the founder of
the American Neo-Institutionalist School) had once suggested that
there had been no substantial change in economic ideas since this
period, and even before that. His evidence is based on the fact that
economic theorists have been mainly – Ayres would say exclusively – interested in the relations of exchange, and (therefore) the
determination of equilibrium prices.[3] More recently Guy Routh has
(independently) produced a much more substantial and sophisticated version of the Ayres thesis, which he supports with a great
deal more of historical evidence. Very briefly Routh argues that
almost all the important concepts and theories developed in the past
two centuries had been already discovered by the forerunners of
classical political economy, beginning with Sir William Petty. Using
a Kuhnian approach and terminology he asserts that the 'paradigm'
which was developed by these writers has dominated economic
thought down to the present time.[4] Routh's idea is interesting and
he has presented his case most forcefully. There is much to be
learned from his argument both by the self-satisfied and by the
confused. Yet his thesis is not entirely acceptable. To criticise it
satisfactorily one would need to examine the evidence together with
the Kuhnian framework within which it is presented. This is something which we shall take up in some detail in Chapter 4. For the
time being we should merely observe that, although Routh's
evidence is indisputable, he overlooks the fact that the collection of
ideas developed by the pioneers did not make up a system of
thought. The ideas were there, but the system was missing. The
hypotheses existed but the 'paradigm' was lacking. Or – to use an
alternative Kuhnian terminology – the 'elements' had been
developed, but a 'disciplinary matrix' was non-existent. The
emergence of a *dominant* 'paradigm' is associated with the appearance of a basic 'textbook'. This, in some sense, was the distinctive
achievement of Adam Smith.

Adam Smith lived through an age which gave birth to two successful revolutions: the industrial revolution in England and the
socio-political revolution in France. He befriended the French
Physiocrats, who had in turn befriended the Irish Richard
Cantillon. The *Wealth of Nations* was the ultimate fruit of this
liberal interaction between the Gallics and the Scotsman. For the

first time problems of value, distribution, economic progress, international trade, public finance and economic policy were discussed and analysed within an interdependent and systematic body of thought. The classical political economists, with occasional deviations, determined value with reference to the cost of production, which in most cases was identified with labour alone. Even Adam Smith, who started with a labour theory of value but is claimed to have abandoned it, was no exception to this general rule. This mistaken claim originated with Ricardo, and it was repeated by a distinguished line of economists, with the exception of Marx but, curiously enough, not Marxist economists.[5] It is of course true that none of them succeeded in formulating a complete labour theory of value until Marx, who bequeathed the problems of 'the transformation of values into prices' to posterity. Ricardo attempted to construct a consistent theory of distribution but he soon realised that this was impossible without a satisfactory theory of value. To this day the problem of the interdependence between production and distribution has been haunting economic theory. For Adam Smith the long-run wage rate was equal to the price of the environmentally determined level of subsistence. In the hands of Malthus this became a powerful weapon for the justification of the poverty of the working class and the prediction of its immutability. Ricardo, who accepted this theory of population, forecast an even gloomier prospect for humanity by his theory of the falling rate of profit (based on his theory of differential rent) which would end in an eternal 'stationary state'. John Stuart Mill took over the concept of the stationary state and – by a twist of psychology rather than logic – turned it from permanent gloom into permanent bliss. Economic development, through the division of labour, required accumulation which presumed saving. Turgot and Adam Smith had argued this case forcefully, according to the latter of whom it was 'parsimony' not 'industry' which was the main motive power of economic progress. This view was generally accepted. In vain did Malthus try to argue with Ricardo and Say that, given the existing theoretical premises, there could be excess saving resulting in a production glut. There were others, notably Sismondi, who took the same line, but they were, and remained, outside the main stream of theoretical debate. Ricardo and Say were quite right in dismissing Malthus, even though their own arguments were based on a 'defective telescopic faculty' (see, further, Chapter 7: the theoretical basis of his argument was weak, and his ideological motive in wanting to prove the necessity of an unproductive class (of landlords and their retainers) for a workable capitalist system was all too apparent. Besides, casual evidence from the *developing* economies of France and Britain seemed to be consistent with the orthodox opinion. Ricardo triumphed, but the problem failed to be subjected to critical discussion in the annals of the *dominant* economic literature. Keynes was later to describe this failure by saying that 'Ricardo conquered England as completely as the Holy Inquisition conquered Spain'.[6] He was right, but one would hardly expect Ricardo to take the blame for it. The blame must be taken by that destructive lack of critical attitude which in every context abstracts the economic problem from its dynamic social framework and turns it into an immutable metaphysic. Keynes himself succeeded in reviving the notion of Effective Demand where many, including Marx, Tugan-Baranovsky and Hobson had failed. But history is full of ironies, and where moral justice fails poetical justice knocks at its doors. For Keynes – who had blamed Ricardo for the dogmatic attitude of his followers – did not anticipate that his own theory would be vulgarised into a fantastic notion that saving did not matter. This is yet another example of how faith in an economic theory can easily transcend economic reality. It is now argued by many that a cause of the slow growth of the British economy – and the associated problems – has been a low rate of investment; 'without a smile on the face' as Keynes would have put it. For, given full employment of resources (which existed in the decades of the 1940s and 1950s) how is investment to be financed but by the difference between output and consumption and/or a foreign trade deficit. We shall pass in silence over the case of the underdeveloped countries. To return to our brief review of classical theories, the benefits arising from the domestic division of labour were found to be easily extendable to the sphere of international economic relations. Ricardo produced a simple logical formula and all was explained. Thenceforth the beneficence of free trade became a logical necessity which reinforced its power as an ideological creed.

Not long after J. S. Mill had claimed that there were no more important problems to be solved by the science of political economy Karl Marx offered a satisfactory solution to the classical problem of value and distribution, although he left it unfinished. His theoretical apparatus was almost entirely classical, and his solution impeccably consistent: whatever we may think of the labour theory of value itself, Marx's formulation was the most consistent and complete version of it. However, shortly after the publication of the first volume of *Capital*, W. Stanley Jevons, Karl Menger and Léon Walras shifted the basis of value theory from objective labour to subjective utility which was accompanied by the application of marginal analysis to economic theory. The concept of the 'margin' had been implicitly discovered by Ricardo in his theory of rent. The subjective theory of value had been earlier proposed, in some form, by some economists including Nassau Senior. The use of mathematical symbols had had a precedent in the writings of Cournot. The 'marginalist revolution' brought all these elements together in a new theoretical framework. Relative prices were determined by marginal utilities, on the demand side, and marginal costs, on the supply side. Wages and profits were equal to the marginal contributions of labour and capital to output. The magic formula of the marginal value seemed to have resolved all the major economic questions. Yet, neo-classical economists soon divided into two fairly distinct traditions in approach and degree of realism: the Walrasian (or Lausanne) School emphasised 'general equilibrium' with an apparently tighter analytical network, a greater use of mathematics and less of economics; the Marshallian (or Cambridge) School had a more partial and piecemeal approach, combining (speculative) marginalism and (empirical) supply and demand analysis, with an implicit acknowledgement of a host of problems in footnotes and appendixes. Generally speaking, the Cambridge approach tended to dominate until the end of the Second World War, since when the Walrasian tradition began to take over.[7] This was accompanied by an artificial split of the subject in micro- and macro-economics. In the meantime the basic marginalist framework had been extended to such issues as the inter-temporal allocation of resources, the determination of optimum 'welfare' criteria and the reformation of the Ricardian theory of international trade. And this was the age of stability, Empire and optimism.

The First World War upset the applecart and a decade after its conclusion the industrial world faced economic depression and massive unemployment. Keynes's *General Theory* is a symbol, not of the discovery of the ultimate universal truth, but of this change in the structural and empirical reality of the capitalist system. Inevitably, there was not much 'news' in it. The concept of 'Effective

Demand' had been as old, if not older, than Mandeville's *Fable of the Bees,* and this was acknowledged by Keynes himself (although this does not mean that Keynes's *specific* approach was the same as Mandeville's or anyone else's). The consumption function was no more than a generalisation of the classical view that capitalists saved and workers subsisted. The determination of the rate of interest by the interaction of the supply and demand for money had its roots in Mercantilist thought and the *Wealth of Nations.* The marginal efficiency of capital, although somewhat different in interpretation, was akin to Fisher's internal rate of return. Intervention in trade also had its origin in the Mercantilists and the socialist critics of orthodox economics. The 'euthanasia of the rentier' was a colourful description of the stationary state. The role of expectations implied the rejection of the silliest assumption of perfect competition, i.e. perfect knowledge and forecast. F. H. Knight had already drawn attention to this issue by his important distinction between risk and uncertainty. Keynes had two really great achievments: in practice, he proposed a workable solution to a certain type of unemployment; and, in theory, he destroyed the metaphysic of a self-adjusting mechanism in a capitalist society. Earlier, an unsuccessful attack on this metaphysic had been launched by Sraffa, Harrod, Joan Robinson and Chamberlin, with the theories of imperfect or monopolistic competition.[8] But neo-classical equilibrium had survived that assault through the skin of its teeth. However, Keynes was quickly turned into an extensive industry in much the same way as Marx has suffered that fate. But this refers to the sociological aspects of the growth of economic and social knowledge which we shall discuss in Chapters 4 and 5.

Post-war developments saw a return to the classical interest in economic dynamics. There was a predictable search for the *equilibrium* rate of growth and the conditions for its *stability.* The Keynesian approach discovered the conditions of equilibrium growth in a 'steady state' – where the rate of growth in income per head is equal to the rate of increase of productivity – but it turned out to be highly unstable: there could be under-utilisation of capacity and/or demand-deficiency unemployment without a self-correcting mechanism. The neo-classical theorists stepped in and, by altering the assumption of a permanently fixed capital–output ratio, saved the world from theoretical chaos. Interest in the development of the Third World gave rise to a voluminous literature – most of it restatement of old theories – the thickness of which may be contrasted to the thinness of its real achievements. Pure economic theory took off to an even higher level of abstraction, in spite of rapid developments in the arts of economic statistics and econometrics, or, perhaps, because of the frequent indeterminacy of their results in application. Piero Sraffa's reconstruction of the Ricardo–Marxian pure theory of value opened new channels for abstract speculation. Some neo-classical theorists began to read Marx, and at least one of them discovered that the differences between the Marxian and the neo-classical systems were insignificant so long, of course, as we put aside the labour theory of value![9] These developments ran parallel to the controversy over the theory of capital, subsequently known as the two-Cambridges controversy. Theorists in Cambridge, England, pointed out that the concept of an aggregate production function was circular because capital had to be measured by its marginal product and the latter could not be known without a knowledge of the output. The problem is basically due to the dichotomy of capital, as physical products and capital as finance, which had been originally posed by Veblen's critique of 'Professor Clark's Economics'.[10] The world still awaits a satisfactory solution to this problem by Cambridge, Massachusetts. The other great debate, with more relevance to economic policy, is on the role and significance of changes in the money supply. The controversy would be settled if the relevant 'identification problem' could be resolved – i.e. whether in fact increases in the money supply *cause* an increase in demand, or the other way around. That resolution, however, is unlikely to materialise. Meantime, the Phillips Curve describing a trade-off between unemployment and inflation provided a new opening for the exercise of the *productive* hands.[11] Suddenly, however, the real world started misbehaving – i.e. unemployment and inflation *both* increased together – and the Phillips Curve began to 'break down'. There was a great concern at this puzzling situation until some economists discovered the real 'cause' for it: the Phillips Curve had been shifting outwards because the expected rate of inflation had been higher than the actual rate. Few economists (if any) may have voiced that this argument is not much more than a tautology: we have no real evidence that 'the curve has been shifting'; and the *expected* rate of inflation is almost impossible to know. Yet we assume that this (unknown) expected rate has been different from the actual, and so we leave the curve no choice but to shift. However, this so-called 'explanation' increased the socio-economic stock of 'natural' concepts by one more; namely, the *empirically indeterminate* concept of the 'natural' rate of unemployment: this is the rate of unemployment at which that (unknown and, perhaps, unknowable) 'expected' rate of inflation equals the actual rate. Thus, almost any rate of unemployment would conceivably qualify for being 'natural'.

THE EVOLUTION OF ECONOMIC METHOD

The progress of economic ideas was accompanied by a gradual evolution in the methods of economic analysis, broadly speaking, from a partial, concrete and *casually* empirical, to a general, abstract and deductive approach. The Mercantilists generally tackled their problems with piecemeal and partial discussions based on casual observation, though this does not mean that they generalised from 'directly observed' facts. Apart from that, although their postulates were more of an aggregative, 'macro', variety, they did not normally indulge in universal generalisations in the sense of proposing 'laws' of economic 'behaviour'. Sometimes they even overlooked the interdependence between many of their own postulates.

The seventeenth century experienced a rapid growth and spread of modern science and philosophy. Galileo lost the battle and won the war. Modern physics and astronomy increased in scope and complexity mainly as a result of theoretical analysis, even though they did have a solid foundation in empirical reality. Descartes finally delivered philosophical speculation from medieval pre-occupation with the proof of the reality of the objective world by the simple formula 'I think, therefore I am'. This formula is generally known as the Cartesian *cogito*.[12] It was simple and concise but it went much further than its immediate purpose. If I know I exist *because* I think, then I can also know of the existence of all others because I think. Hence, the *cogito* not only elevated human reason to a supreme position for the proof of the external world, it also tended to make all knowledge of it *subjective* and *a priori*. Other – mainly British — philosophers reacted to this Cartesian subjectivism (sometimes called Idealism) by emphasising the primacy of sense-experience and, hence, observation of the external world, in arriving at a certain knowledge of it. They regarded the human mind not as a source but as a store of knowledge which had been primarily acquired by sense-experience and subsequently systematised by the faculty of reason. Francis Bacon told the parable of the farrier who had failed in persuading an assembly of learned men to 'go to the horse's mouth' (instead of searching in the speculative writings of great philosophers) in order to discover the number of a horse's teeth. John Locke likened the mind of a new-born infant to a blank tablet (*tabula rasa*) which would be filled in by learning and experience alone. This is how the two great traditions in modern philosophy, respectively known as Rationalism and Empiricism, were founded. On the whole, the former tradition tended to dominate in the continent of Europe, and the latter in Britain and (later) North America. To prevent confusion it must be emphasised that the Empiricists were not *irrationalists*. Irrationalism (or romanticism) mainly developed in the nineteenth and twentieth centuries; in principle it rejects both the Cartesian and the Empiricist traditions.

The progress of scientific knowledge was in general undisturbed by these philosophical debates. The scientists speculated by the process of logical deduction, and tested the resulting theories by experimentation and (aided) observation. This procedure appreciably made it possible for 'universal laws' to be discovered, which laid bare the *casual* relationship between natural phenomena and their changes. These achievements made a great impression on social philosophers and induced them to search for similar laws governing individual behaviour and its interaction in society. Thomas Hobbes's theory of human psychology was perhaps the crudest example of this methodological emulation: the human individual was no more than an engine whose actions and reactions were determined by the forces of 'appetite' and 'aversion', or pleasure and pain. He based his explanation of the emergence of civil society, 'the great leviathan', on this theory. The pioneers of classical political economy likewise began to formulate theories which were, to some extent, speculative, abstract and general. But they did not advance too far in this approach. Sir William Petty's elementary labour theory of value was by no means purely speculative. He observed that men were engaged in different occupations, and he conjectured that the value of their products, for the same amount of time spent in producing them, must be equal. His own example tends to confirm this claim, for he compared a year's production of corn by a farmer to a year's production of silver by a miner: both activities were labour intensive and involved comparable skills. Locke's labour theory was also formulated with a similar methodological spirit – apart, that is, from its ideological justification of bourgeois property and its implication for the illegitimacy of historically inherited property in land.[13] Again, Locke's supply and demand analysis was basically empirical not speculative. Petty's theory of 'absolute advantage' in trade – and his anticipation of the Fisher–Clark stage theory of economic progress – was also based on purely factual knowledge. He observed that in Holland the share of trade in output was high and that the Dutch relied on the 'Danes and the Polanders' for much of their agricultural needs. He thought that if the relative costs of production were different in England the same pattern would be likely to emerge.[14] In general, while there was a noticeable shift towards greater abstraction and generalisation, the forerunners of classical political economy did not establish a definitely deductive and speculative method of analysis. And this was consistent with the fact that they did not succeed in erecting a system of economic thought.

Classical political economy marked the arrival of a new era in the philosophy and method of economic discovery. At no time perhaps has nature exercised a greater hold over the minds of thinking men than it did in the eighteenth century. It became the absolute standard by which the truth, goodness, inviolability and purity of all phenomena were measured. We are still prisoners of that age, at least in our daily usage of adjectives and adverbs such as 'natural' and 'naturally'. What was good, just or right was also natural, and vice versa. Newtonian physics had discovered an apparently permanent *order* in the natural world which was independent of the will of men. If there was an order in nature in general there had to be an order in the human existence as a part of it, and in human society as an extension of the human individual. Therefore, there had to be such things as 'human nature', 'natural rights', etc. which were also permanent and inviolable. The concept of the state of nature – the notion of the prehistoric man all to himself – had already been invented in the previous century. Hobbes's concept of the state of nature was frightening – he was a realist. Locke's vision of that state was more pleasant but fairly nondescript. Rousseau's – in the eighteenth century – was no less than 'paradise lost'.

Rousseau realised that private property was unnatural since it did not, and could not, exist in 'the state of nature'. Liberal economists took the same view, but their concepts and theories made *feudal* property along unnatural, since all other property was the product of past or present labour. Adam Smith, who described a man's property as being vested in his labour and, *therefore,* 'sacred and inviolable',[15] also placed the origin of European feudalism in expropriation and 'usurpation'. He observed that without the (unnatural) laws of entail and primogeniture this 'catastrophe' might soon have come to an end.[16] The Physiocrats – the champions of 'laws of nature' *par excellence* – were apparently not anti-feudal. Rural activity was productive because it gave rise to a *physical surplus*; urban activity unproductive because it did not. But what about the landlords who did not produce *anything* at all? Besides, the Physiocrats' insistence on the great merits of capitalist farming tended to pull the rug from under the feet of the archaic French feudal system.

The liberal economists sought to restore 'the natural order' in society. In the words of Dugald Stewart, Adam Smith's friend and admirer, the latter's main objective had been the establishment of 'that order of things which nature has pointed out'.[17] It was therefore necessary to determine laws governing the economy in the absence of unnatural restraints, and demonstrate its superiority over the prevailing system. And since there was to be no restraint (perhaps apart from 'the constable') it had to be shown that the unrestrained (natural) system was workable in practice. In modern terminology this amounts to the discovers of the conditions of *equilibrium* and its *stability*. But if men were to seek their personal interests without economic restraints 'the simple system of natural liberty' could conceivably lead to conflict and disorder, reminiscent of Hobbes's state of nature. Therefore there had to be some other *natural* force in addition to the force of self-interest which would *naturally* restrain the latter. Adam Smith discovered this force in the concept of 'sympathy' or 'fellow feeling' which interacted with the motive of self-interest and created a state of unrestrained social harmony.[18] It was a dialectical synthesis which Rousseau had sought to achieve by uniting 'utility' (self-interest) with 'justice' (sympathy).[19] Now, although physics had discovered an *order* in nature, it had not necessarily established *harmony* in that order. The fact is that the concept of natural or social harmony transcends the rise of modern physics: it has been with us since the Fall of Adam! Plato's Republic, St Augustine's City of God, Al-Farabi's The Excellent City and Thomas More's Utopia are but a few well-known examples of presumed or predicted states of social harmony – i.e. the quest of man for perfect knowledge and certainty.

The philosophical schema, developed comprehensively in Smith's *The Theory of Moral Sentiments,* was debatable but consistent. Predictably, however, its consistent application to a system of political economy proved to be difficult. It may even be conjectured that this was a reason why Smith delayed the publication of the *Wealth of Nations* for so long. For in the latter book he had to acknowledge the existence of conflict even in the absence of restraint – a tribute to his intellectual honesty to which he always gave priority over logical mystification. Later in history this difficulty was described as 'The Adam Smith Problem'; and it was analysed as an 'inconsistency' between the two books. Jacob Viner accepted this view but he argued that the *Wealth of Nations* was so much the better for it.[20] He was mistaken, however, for even a cursory study of *Wealth* would reveal indispensability of the 'invisible hand' to its main arguments. A. L. Macfie, on the other hand, rightly rejected Viner's view, but he implied that there was nothing to explain.[21] The fact is that there is some inconsistency; but the inconsistency is *within the 'Wealth of Nations' itself.* Moreover, the inconsistency neatly divides the theory of production and the theory of distribution: The absence of restraint uniformly promotes the good of the society in all aspects of production; but conflicts arise when the product is to be shared out.

Adam Smith was not a pure speculator. He built up a system of economic thought, but not a completely *logical* one. He was content to face a conflict between fact and theory and leave it at that, without suppressing either. Nowhere is this methodological eclecticism more apparent than in his theory of value. He speculated that in the state of nature goods exchanged for each other according to the ratio of their labour content: if it took one day to 'kill' a beaver or two deers, then one beaver exchanged for two deers. He *measured* the value of each product by the amount of labour which it would 'purchase or command'. In the state of nature the amount of labour 'embodied' in a good and the amount of labour 'commanded' by it were necessarily equal. But he realised that where there was private ownership of land and capital these two notions of value were no longer the same: workers received a subsistence wage and rent and profit were 'deducted' from the value of the product.[22] He had no problem explaining rent – the return to feudal property, itself founded on 'usurpation' – which he described as a 'monopoly price'. There remained the problem of profit and within his scheme there could be no explanation for it. He dropped the matter.[23] This has given rise to the universal myth that Smith had *replaced* his labour theory by a 'cost-of-production' or 'adding-up' theory of value.[24] In fact, the labour theory was retained but it was accompanied by a 'dividing-up theory of distribution' – i.e. a purely factual statement that the value of the product was divided between rent, profit and wages. This was certainly *logically* inconsistent. But that was Smith. Ricardo, who discovered similar inconsistencies between his theories of value and distribution, worried where Smith would have left off. But this was Ricardo.

Malthus, Say and Ricardo revolutionised the economic method, though Ricardo's contribution to this was the most important. Malthus's theory of population was the first major step in this direction. Where Adam Smith had made some casual remarks on the possible link between standards of living and the birth rate, Malthus produced what would now be called an abstract model which was totally self-contained and which defied empirical refutation. He even *speculated* about the exact *quantitative* relations: i.e. the claim that the supply of food increases at an *arithmetic rate* while population increases at a *geometric rate*. What was true in his theory was not new; and what was new could not be shown to be untrue. Yet generations of men suffered in consequence of this 'abstract truth' which had a clear political purpose. Ricardo fully concurred both in the abstraction and in its politics: the theory of population was calculated to turn private charity into a sin and public assistance to the poor into an anti-social policy. Ricardo's cold-blooded parliamentary speech against the Poor Laws (1819) provides independent proof for his intentions. The Poor Law Reform of 1836 – largely drafted by his faithful followers led by Edwin Chadwick — was the most tangible outcome of this deadly campaign against the poor, the sick and the hungry. But Ricardo's own share in the promotion of the purely speculative *method* of analysis was by far the greatest. It may even be argued that, in terms of its impact on later economists down to the present day, it was the greatest single 'contribution' to the history of economic knowledge. He was the founder of 'pure economic theory' as an almost autonomous exercise in pure logic. All that was needed was a few assumptions and the rest would follow. If the resulting theories were logically consistent they would be true and acceptable; if not they would be false and should be rejected. This became the only test of success for a theory. It was an entirely Cartesian approach. These observations do not deny the value of his intuitions or his theoretical contributions; they merely serve to put them in balance.

Ricardo discovered 'the laws governing the distribution' of the product in the context of a simple and abstract model. He then tried to extend them to a more complex, but still abstract, economy. Here he ran into serious problems because different goods were produced in unequal time-periods, and more or less capital was used in their production. This appeared to make the determination of a *uniform* rate of profit for the whole of the economy impossible, and hence there would be no general equilibrium (a term which he did not use). Sraffa has now succeeded in solving this Ricardian problem. But for Ricardo himself it remained a great source of concern until his (untimely) death. There are different ways of interpreting Ricardo's personal dilemma, and there must be some truth in all of them. One interpretation which – to our knowledge – has not yet been suggested is that Ricardo's greatest source of worry was the fact that he had failed to determine the *equilibrium conditions*. Ricardo was not a philosopher but he accepted the basic philosophical background of the *Wealth of Nations* – i.e. the search for harmony in the absence of political restraint. The fact that he acknowledged, and engaged in, the conflict with the landlords was not inconsistent with this vision. His theory of international trade, or 'comparative advantage' (initially due to James Mill), is a monumental synthesis of this philosophy with his own economic method. By assuming differences in technology and nothing else he reached the conclusion that free trade would promote the welfare of *all* societies. The scenario is a textbook favourite: two countries, two products, constant returns, etc. However, the assumptions which are *not* normally mentioned are: no history, no institutions, no technological rigidities, no transfer of resources, no unemployment, no exercise of unequal political power, free trade between and perfect competition (i.e. 'the natural state') *within* each country! It is a tribute to the power of both Adam Smith's philosophy and Ricardo's method that this museum piece of theoretical curiosity (and another one with even more remarkable qualities of unrealism) is generally regarded by economists as a satisfactory explanation of international trade. But it also says something for the level of genuine intellectual curiosity enjoyed (or tolerated) by economists: Ricardo did his best, but what can we say for ourselves?

Classical political economy essentially carried on in the Ricardian tradition until Marx and the Marginalists. Senior, Lauderdale and Longfield had their differences with Ricardo but their method was not substantially different from his. John Stuart Mill, who took over the mantle of Ricardo in his political economy and that of Bentham in his social philosophy, did not innovate much in economic theory or in economic method. His major distinction is in the fact that – apart from Marx – he is the last great economist who combined a vast knowledge of social, political and economic theory in his approach to social problems. The source of the conflict in the *Wealth of Nations* – i.e. the clash of political freedom and social harmony – became increasingly obvious to him and he made an honest and admirable effort to face up to it. But, on the death of Ricardo, classical political economy had already produced its own critics. Godwin had already inaugurated philosophical anarchism by pointing out that the system of natural liberty did not lead to harmony and social justice. Indeed one of the motives of Malthus in proposing his theory of population was to teach an economic lesson to the likes of Godwin. The critics in the main divided between the Austro-German (reactionary) romantics and the Franco-British (radical) socialists. Of the latter, Sismondi, Fourier and Proudhon (from France), and Thompson, Hodgskin, Gray, Bray and Owen (from Britain) are the best-known. They were the first to formulate, explicitly, the concept of the exploitation of labour by capital. However, there was not a great departure in their method of argument and analysis from the broad Ricardian framework. What makes them particularly interesting is that they were the first group of political economists who recognised the absence of socio-economic harmony in the industrial system of production which had been (at least implicitly) promised by the earlier writers. In such an event there would normally be four possible reactions. One, to assume that it exists, or it would exist upon certain changes, even if in fact it does not; two, to deny completely that economic theory is dependent on any such assumption; three, to recognise conflict and analyse its properties; four, to recognise conflict and propose methods for its abolition. In general, orthodox economists have taken either the first or the second view, while the early socialists took the fourth. Marx combined the third view with the fourth.

It would be difficult both to do justice to Marx's philosophy and method and to avoid misunderstanding by the reader in a brief review of this kind. This is so because Marx is a particularly prolific writer, a particularly diverse thinker, and a particularly controversial figure. For the same reasons he is also seldom read. Many of those who call themselves Marxists either do not read Marx himself, or they concentrate their readings of Marx within the discipline (economics, sociology, etc.) with which they are most familiar; therefore it becomes difficult even for the latter to assess Marx's ideas and method comprehensively. Those who are opposed to Marxism perhaps read him even less. In fact, it turns out that many of their criticisms are of the ideas and interpretaions put out by the 'Marxists', rather than by Marx himself. Marx was an open critic of the capitalist society in all of its aspects. He was interested in discovering how the capitalist system worked and especially how it was likely to change and be changed. It is therefore impossible to extricate a 'pure' economist, a 'pure' sociologist, etc., out of the single person of Marx. Like many thinkers of the previous century – and particularly Adam Smith – he recognised that the social problem was indivisible into 'purely' economic or whatever, and he attacked the problems in which he was interested with this implicit conception. In one word, he would have been a source of embarrassment for many Faculties of Social Sciences in our contemporary world, for no specific discipline could have made him wear the right hat, or show the right flag. The labour theory of value which he took over from Ricardo and developed further was intended to add rigour to two other concepts (which he had already developed independently) in relation to the position of wage-labour in capitalist society: first, the concept of exploitation, or the fact that labour power produces a surplus over and above the cost of production; second, the concept of alienation, or the fact that division of labour *based on wage contracts* reduces labour to a commodity and alienates the labourer from the fruit of his effort. Both these ideas had existed in the works of his predecessors including Adam Smith.[25] Marx was not a pure speculator; if anything he put more emphasis on facts – i.e. empirical and historical knowledge – than on 'pure' theory. His interest in social dynamics led him to a study of change both *within* and *between* social systems. He anticipated macro-economic instability and the growth of concentration in production where all the harmony theories, before and after, had denied it. This is one evidence for his sense of realism which was basically because he took note of social conflict in his scheme of analysis. He has been much criticised for his model of historical development mainly on account of method. This is something which is worth investigating in greater detail and we shall postpone a discussion of it until the next chapter. The only occasion – an admittedly important one – on which Marx lapsed into *pure* abstraction and speculation was when he tried to develop his labour theory of value into a 'general equilibrium model' – i.e. his insistence on the determination of a uniform rate of profit in *all* the sectors of the economy, and 'the transformation of values into prices'. This was the legacy of Ricardo, and it may be conjectured that Marx felt impelled to provide a solution in order to make his general argument credible by contemporary economists. Whatever his motive, however, it was the desire to provide an equilibrium solution for the determination of the uniform rate of profit which led him to the invention of the concept of 'absolute rent' which is no more than a figment of imagination.[26] Depending on our predilections, we may like or dislike Marx's venture into abstract 'general equilibrium analysis'. The point being made here is that such a venture was neither a part of Marx's purpose nor characteristic of his method. Marx's method was a combination of theory and fact; logic and history. He was neither a pure speculator nor a pure empiricist.

Marginalism, if anything, tended to enhance the Ricardian method of purely logical speculation. This is most pronounced in the Walrasian tradition, but, as we have seen, less in the Marshallian approach. The early Marginalists regarded utility as measurable. This was the philosophy of Jeremy Bentham which had not been previously incorporated into the body of economic theory by a combination of two miracles: the first miracle was that Bentham himself did not take a serious interest in economic theory, though he did in economic policy; the second miracle was that in spite of Bentham's great intellectual hold over James Mill and his son, John Stuart, the latter two did not apply the philosophy of utilitarianism to *economic* theorising. According to Jeremy Bentham it was conceivable to produce a quantitative 'calculus of pleasure and pain' in an attempt to produce 'the greatest happiness of the greatest number'. The Marginalist transformation of this social philosophy into a body of economic theory was based on the classical notions of individual behaviour and social conditions in the absence of restraint: i.e. individuals seeking their self-interest in the system of natural liberty (which was reworded as 'perfect competition'). Each consumer would seek to maximise his utility (pleasure) and minimise his pain ('disutility' or cost). The process of perfect competition (i.e. 'the invisible hand') will mean that such maximisations and minimisations would optimise consumption, investment and output, assuming that tastes, techniques *and* the distribution of wealth remain unchanged. In fact the latter issue, of the distribution of wealth (and income), has remained the thorn in the thigh of neo-classical theory. Even the general equilibrium model developed by Walras – which does *not* involve the aggregation of inputs – could not escape circularity on account of this problem. Walras starts by assuming *a given quantity* of capital goods, and he determines a unique price for capital (the rate of interest equal to the marginal product of capital) as well as other goods. But if the system was not in equilibrium, such that there were different rates of return on different types of capital, then equilibrium could be restored only by a rise in the production of the more expensive capital goods and a fall in the production of the cheaper. This, however, would contradict the assumption of a given quantity of capital inputs! We are back to the Ricardian problem of determining 'the uniform rate of profit' without circularity or self-contradiction. What is most conspicuously absent from the Walrasian system is history, and indeed human society itself. The 'invisible hand' is converted into 'the invisible auctioneer'. If one were to visualise the system at work, one would have to imagine a group of faceless and unrelated individuals – even without a personal history except for what they own – gathering in a market-place occasionally nodding their heads and vanishing into the thin air. There is no yesterday and, apparently, 'tomorrow never comes'. It may be a fair description of a primitive market-place where goods are exchanged; it is hardly a meaningful abstraction of a complex industrial economy where goods are produced and distributed. It may be an elegant, though not perfect, logical system; but it is hardly a description (even though a simple one) of the processes of production and distribution in human society. We shall discuss this problem in more general terms in Chapter 7.

In an obvious sense utility is a subjective concept. But if – as it was held at the time – utility and 'disutility' were *measurable* then at least the subjective could be 'objectified'. To say that ten homogeneous 'units' of utility are greater than eight is no less objective a statement than to say five hours of homogeneous labour are more than four. This is all right so far as utility is measurable in standard units; but who can measure utility in any units at all. This was one of the major criticisms hurled at neo-classical theory by its critics, and its acceptance would have made nonsense of the entire system which was based on utility analysis. The 'solution' to this problem was later discovered in the ordinal concept of utility and its use in 'indifference curve analysis'. However, this new approach made 'preferences' purely subjective and gave rise to the charge of 'psychologism'. The 'solution' to the latter problem was discovered in the concept of 'revealed preference'. Neither the first nor the second 'solutions' are ultimately satisfactory, and we shall try to demonstrate this in the next chapter. It is significant to note that for as long as the 'ordinal' concept of utility (and, with it, indifference curve analysis) had not been proposed, neo-classical economists refused to agree that immeasurability of utility posed any serious problem for their theories. But once this was done every single textbook in micro-economics did not fail to note that 'of course a cardinal concept of utility is meaningless'. This says something for the sociology (and psychology) of the economic profession which we shall discuss in Chapter 5.

Neo-classical economics combined the social philosophy of Adam Smith and the moral and psychic philosophy of Jeremy Bentham with the abstract and speculative method of Ricardo. The product was 'news from nowhere'. This was particularly true of the Lausanne – as opposed to the Austrian and Cambridge – school which is now the dominant tendency among the neo-classical theorists. The Marshallian spirit was different from this but the problem with Marshall was that he wanted both to produce abstract and mechanistic models (however cautiously done) and at the same time keep an eye on reality. Keynes's method was not significantly different from the neo-classical tradition; his attitude and philosophy were: he combined practice (not 'consultancy' but participation) with theory, and this alone gave him the additional dimension which others lacked in reconciling theory with reality, rather than the other way around.

THE DEBATE ON METHOD

Ricardo's death left economists divided into an orthodox and a critical school. The differences were on the benevolence and stability, or cruelty and instability of the capitalist order, giving rise to opposing economic theories which were often based on the same fundamental postulates, although not the same philosophical vision. In retrospect it would seem predictable that these differences in theory and philosophy should quickly lead to methodological arguments. At any rate, this is exactly what happened. The first bone of contention was the question of morals and values in economic theorising. Since economists were reaching opposite conclusions in analyses which were based almost on the same set of basic theoretical concepts, it was tempting to conclude that their differences arose mainly from their incompatible value systems. This, in turn, threatened not only classical political economy but the very existence of any unique body of economic thought capable of general application. If we make of the world what we would like to believe, then we cannot claim to have a general theory even in the weakest possible sense of this term. Let us emphasise that, in its narrowest interpretation, this problem transcends the issue of scientificity: you do not have to believe that economics is a science comparable with the natural sciences (and it is doubtful if the earlier political economists held such a view) in order to be worried about the charge that its conclusions ultimately depend on personal or collective *opinion*. Political historians have no such claim of scientificity for their discipline, and they do have their differences in the interpretation of historical events, but would they ever accept that all knowledge of history is a matter of personal interpretation, and, therefore, no objective agreement could be reached between different claimants? It is a common mistake to say that a body of thought is based on a given value system would *merely* mean that it is not as scientific as the physical sciences. It is even a more common mistake to claim that the reverse would make the subject scientific. These are issues which we hope to discuss at greater length in the forthcoming chapters.

The orthodox economists responded to this challenge denying the charge. In particular, both J. S. Mill and Nassau Senior emphasised the neutrality of political economy. The elder Mill had already pointed out that 'Political Economy is to the State [i.e. society] what domestic economy is to the family', their respective aims being 'the consumption and the supply of the family (and) the Community'.[27] Somehow, the issue of distribution is lost in this description, since distribution among members of the family is arbitrarily determined. His son, John Stuart, almost repeated the title of Adam Smith's book when he said that the subject of political economy was 'Wealth . . . the nature of Wealth . . . including . . . the operation of all causes by which the condition of mankind . . . is made prosperous or reverse'.[28] It is clear from this – as it is implicit in the whole of classical and neo-classical theory – that the goal of economics is to lay bare the conditions for greater prosperity, or 'maximum welfare' as it would now be called. '*Whose* prosperity' is, however, a question which has engaged many a thinking mind not excluding J. S. Mill's. Thus we are pushed back to the issue of distribution, not surprisingly since this was (and perhaps still is) all that was at issue between the orthodox and their critics. Nassau Senior insisted that 'the political economist, as such, has nothing to do with any other physical or moral sciences . . . excepting so far as they affect the production or distribution of wealth'.[29] This was probably the first time that the well-known and ill-conceived phrase 'the economist as such' was invoked in an argument of this kind. Furthermore, Senior distinguished between pure analysis and political advice, the former being 'positive' and the latter 'normative'. This distinction has been reasserted by many later writers including Robbins, and it has now become almost a compromise formula for the status of economics. (In Chapter 6 we shall argue that such a distinction is logically untenable, and it is due to a simple but basic confusion about the nature of 'normative statements'.) Meantime the ground of methodological debate shifted to higher levels of philosophical disagreement.

The dress-rehearsal for the *faith* in reason and science – which is still, to some extent, with us – was performed in the eighteenth century. As men's faith in the supernatural and its propagandists weakened so their hopes in the ultimate delivery by reason and science strengthened. The intellectuals of that age tended to identify progressive social and political ideas with the application of scientific method for the discovery of truths. In France, leading intellectuals like Voltaire and his disciples ('the Encyclopedists') regarded the British political system as a model for social change in the continent of Europe. The British system of government was a direct outcome of the Civil War, its complete triumph through the Glorious Revolution, and the succession of the House of Orange to the English throne. It was not a disposition towards flattery which made John Locke dedicate his *magnum opus* on the theory of government to the new English monarchy. For he was body and soul in favour of the new system. The French philosophers on the whole identified Locke's brand of individualist political philosophy with his Empiricist theory of scientific discovery. Locke's democratic individualism was in marked contrast to the aristocrat and oppressive political system in France; and his objectivist philosophy of knowledge was in direct opposition to the official philosophy of the Catholic Church which used logical deduction from metaphysical axioms in arriving at truths about the real world. The two aspects – the political and the epistemological – seemed to go together. Hence – for the first and last time in history – facts and empirical evidence became the most cherished criteria of scientific truths for nearly all French philosophers other than Rousseau. That was perhaps why none of them except Rousseau attempted to build up a comprehensive system of thought. However, the original regard for factual knowledge and empirical evidence gradually developed into a new, 'rational' faith; a complete faith in the powers of natural science, the possibility of reducing all other phenomena to their nature elements or at least to their 'counterparts' in the world of nature. It was a misconception on two major grounds. First, because it implied that human action and social interaction could be reduced to pure mechanics; second, because it assumed that scientific discovery was based on generalisations from massive data without *a priori* hypotheses. Condorcet was one of the leading lights in this field. Later, in the Napoleonic era, such ideas gained so much ground that Laplace – the famous mathematician – claimed that, given an appropriate computing machine and sufficient data, he could tell the entire history of the universe in detail, and foretell what was to come. We may now laugh at the simplicity of his belief, but the idea is not too far removed from the popular contemporary views of the potential and prospects of computers. Let us note in passing, however, that if such a thing were possible it would be certain that human individuals and the human society are nothing but victims in a preordained process in which their own thoughts and actions play no part at all. In such a case such concepts as freedom, responsibility and morality (of whatever kind) would be meaningless noises. This view is often described as determinism, of which fatalism is an ancient variety. Henri de Saint-Simon founded something like a religious order based on the faith in reason and science. Thomas Carlyle – the well-known Scottish romantic to whom nothing was quite so odious as rationalism and scientific method – was pleasantly surprised to discover that the Saint-Simonians were after all not too different from himself in their basic sentiment.[30] However, it fell on the person of Auguste Comte – Saint-Simon's faithful disciple – to found a coherent and comprehensive school of thought in this tradition.[31].

Comte takes the credit for the invention of two terms which are still part of our daily intellectual vocabulary: 'positivism' and 'sociology'. Sociology was the science of society and positivism was its method. Very briefly, Comte's positivism had two main components: one, that the science of society could be, and indeed should be, studied on the basis of reason alone without the intrusion of moral, metaphysical or artistic prejudices; two, that the correct procedure for discovering scientific truths about society – i.e. the correct method for the social sciences – was to generalise from factual data which he (wrongly) thought to be the unique method of the natural sciences. Natural sciences formulated laws about the world of physical reality by the inductive method of accumulating empirical data for given problems, and inferring or 'deriving' general laws from them. We are already familiar with this view of scientific method from the English Empiricists of the seventeenth century, and especially Francis Bacon. It is a mistake which still bedevils many a social scientist – in particular all the contemporary 'behaviourists' in sociology, psychology, political science and economics – although it has been corrected long ago (both in theory and in practice) in science and in philosophy. However, Comte's 'original' contribution to this old legacy was his specific application of it to the social sciences: since this was the correct scientific method for sociology, then the social scientist should strive for discovering general laws about social problems by the use of 'observed' factual data from social events – i.e. history.[32] History became 'the horse's mouth' for social studies. To summarise: (i) the natural sciences are value-free; (ii) so could, and should, be the social sciences; (iii) the theories of natural sciences are the results of direct generalisations from facts, empirical observations and data; (iv) so could, and should, be the theories of social sciences; (v) history is the source of factual data for formulating laws about society; (vi) there-fore social sciences should construct scientific laws by generalising from historical data; (vii) such laws would be relevant only to that stage of history from which the data were obtained.

The impact of Comtean ideas on methodological thinking in the nineteenth, and even twentieth, century has been very great. In one sweep he managed to mislead a large number of historians and social scientists of diverse persuasions: from conservative and nationalist thinkers such as Roscher, List and Schmöller (of the German Historical School of Economics) to Friedrich Engels of the revolutionary internationalist tradition. John Stuart Mill fell under the Comtean spell only with respect to his insistence on the clear distinction between fact and value in social studies. But he did not accept the Comtean inductivist method, even though he went some way to meet its implications. Thus, Cunningham, the English historian, could later claim that:

> Economic 'generalisations' must necessarily be relative to a given form of civilisation and a given stage of social develop-ment. This, according to Mr J. S. Mill 'is what no political economist would deny'. . . . we have to thank the Comtist criti-cism for forcing us to remember that the material truth of economic principles depends on complicated social conditions, and that they have no independent validity.[33]

However, the Comtean philosophy opened a Pandora's box of argument and debate which, even at present, is not completely shut.

Complaints about the hyper-speculative method of political economy – established, as we have seen, by the authority of David Ricardo – had already begun to be heard in the first half of the nineteenth century. Richard Jones had repudiated the exclusively theoretical approach of Ricardian political economy; instead he proposed a method which a contemporary writer has summarised as 'look and see'.[34] There is no doubt that this emphasis on factual and historical knowledge as a reaction to the pure logicalism of the Ricardian method was both courageous and commendable; certainly one from which some contemporary economist may learn a very useful lesson. But this is a far cry from accepting the 'look-and-see' method as the correct procedure for social and economic investigation: look and see *what*? Man has 'looked' and 'seen' from

time immemorial but this has hardly led him to an intelligent formulation of scientific theories. Even although one may have a fairly
well-defined problem to begin with, little progress will be made
towards its solution by a random procedure of looking and seeing.
Suppose an economist wished to discover the relationship between
the demand for commodities and their prices. He then proceeded
by 'looking' and 'seeing' what actually happens in various markets
for different goods. Assuming that he goes about his work
meticulously, he would end up by such conclusions as the following:
over a certain period of time the demand for commodity *A* varied
inversely with its price by *X* per cent, commodity *B* by *Y* per cent,
etc. But what can we learn about the relation between demand and
price from anything like this statement *apart from what is stated.*
Still, Richard Jones was not a Comtean; he was more of a historical/
empirical economist. Later British critics, and especially John
Ingram, Leslie and W. J. Ashley advanced much further in this
direction. Their approach is the nearest to what may be described as
a Comtean or 'historicist' method among the English methodological critics of classical political economy, and neo-classical
economics. But not completely so. Schumpeter is quite right in
drawing a line between these English critics, Comte and the
founders of the German Historical School.

The scene is Germany, the age is what can be best described as
the Bismarck Era. These two simple facts go a long way in explaining certain aspects of the theme of our discussion. Until the acces-
sion of Bismarck to power – if not quite to the Prussian throne –
Germany was economically underdeveloped and politically dis-
united. The fires of German nationalism had been constantly
fanned – by romantics and radicals alike – at least since the French
Revolution. Parallel to this political ideal ran the economic objective of closing the technological and production gap between
Germany, on the one hand, and France and England, on the other.
The more distant future promised the possibility of a united and
industrialised Germany breaking into the Anglo-French monopoly
of overseas imperialism. Some of the origins of the First World War
must be sought in these ideas and events. It was in this socio-
economic environment that the German economists launched their
attack on classical political economy, neo-classical economics and
their methods. There are many names associated with this school,
those of Roscher, List and Schmöller, Hildebrand, Bücher and,

to some extent, Sombart, being the most well-known among them.
They came in different generations. They had their own differences
in substance and method, but it would be neither possible nor
indeed desirable to examine the specific theories and approaches of
each of them separately. For they shared sufficient methodological
views to make a brief and general description and assessment of
their approach possible. The main points of the Historical School
may be summarised as follows. First, they argued that economics
was, by its very nature, incapable of formulating abstract and
general hypotheses; second, that the correct procedure for the
study of economic problems was by means of historical investigation; third, that such historical investigation would in time lead to
the formulation of 'general laws' through the process of induction;
fourth, that such general inductive laws would be nevertheless
specific to certain stages of history, precisely because the data on
which they are based would be different from one stage to another;
finally, it is implicit in the foregoing that there can be differences in
policy conclusions according to the various socio-cultural frameworks in which the subject-matter is being studied. For example,
they regarded *laissez-faire* and free trade of possible – perhaps even
beneficial – relevance to England, but not to Germany. This last
point did not quite mean that values and facts were not distinguishable (which would have been an anti-Comtean position); it did
mean, however, that the adoption of appropriate economic policies
was largely a function of the specific stage of socio-economic
development. In one word, the German Historical approach was
world's apart from the neo-classical method. Schumpeter seems to
be missing the crucial point when – in an attempt to discover some
common grounds between the two sides – he argues that the differences between Schmöller and Menger were exaggerated, because Schmöller had admitted that the discovery of general
laws in economics was possible.[35] For, what was at stake was not so
much the possibility but *the way in which* and *the extent to which*
such generalisations were possible.

The German Historical School had the better of the argument in
at least three ways. First, their nationalist instinct proved to have
been correct, and the German economy succeeded in economic
development through interventionist *and* protectionist policies. This
was later reaffirmed by the experience of Japan, and there now exist
neo-classical arguments which could explain such an achievement.

Second, their emphasis on the relevance and usefulness of historical knowledge, and the role of cultural and institutional factors was well-founded; it is enough for one to have some general knowledge of the problems of the contemporary developing economies to appreciate this point, although the matter is by no means confined to those economies alone. Third, their attack on the purely logical and deductive method of Ricardian and neo-classical theory was justified; the same point was put by later critics when they poked fun at the 'empty economic boxes', constructed by assumptions 'plucked up from the air'. The German position also implied the indivisibility of socio-economic problems and the usefulness of a multi-disciplinary approach for their solutions. Nearly a century later, a president of the Royal Economic Society was to echo some such view in the simple slogan 'Down with economics as such'.[36] However – and to put it mildly – the defects in the views of the German Historical School were no less than their merits. The biggest mistake of the Historical School was their belief in socio-economic studies by *direct* observation – involving a detailed study of history and not much besides – and the inference of 'general laws' through such a procedure. To put their weakness and strength in one sentence, the Germans were wrong in general and right in particular: they were wrong to advocate direct generalisations from historical knowledge, but right in indicating the relevance of such knowledge to social theory, and pointing out the limits to generalisation whether by deductive or inductive methods. It was the weakness in their approach which limited their useful contribution to the content of socio-economic knowledge. The stage-theories of economic progress formulated by List, Hildebrand, Bücher, Sombart, etc., were of some value and, as a matter of fact, theoretical analysis – i.e. the method which they rejected – can be used to explain (that is, establish tentative casual relations for) these basically 'empirical laws'. For example, List's descriptive scheme of Agricultural, Agricultural-and-Manufacturing, and Agricultural-Manufacturing-and-Commercial stages of economic development can now be explained in terms of the Primary, Secondary, Tertiary stages associated with the names of Allan G. Fisher, Colin Clark and Simon Kuznets.[37] But even in such cases of relative success the ideas of the German Historical School suffered from the absence of a reasonable analytical base. To follow up our example of List, his explanation for social progress beyond the Agricultural stage to the

Agricultural-and-Manufacturing stage, was almost entirely based on the peculiarity of 'the European soul', which itself was a function of the European climate.[38] Likewise, Werner Sombart – the thickness of whose *Der Moderne Kapitalismus* was almost perfectly matched by the thinness of its analytical content – basically identified industrialisation with European specialness, Schmöller himself amassed a great deal of historical data without producing a clear framework for the study of socio-economic problems.

The neo-classical economists resisted the methodological critique of the Historical School. They stood fast by their own deductive and *a priori* approach and – while paying some lip-service to the usefulness of factual and historical knowledge in the course of the debate – in practice, they did not effect the slightest change in their basic methodology. Marshall, who cannot be regarded as an orthodox defender of pure speculation, attacked the Historical School at one of their weakest points in terms which, as far as they go, are unexceptionable:

> Experience . . . teaches that the most reckless and treacherous of all theorists is he who professes to let facts and figures speak for themselves, who keeps in the background the part he has played, perhaps unconsciously, in selecting and grouping them, and in suggesting the argument *post hoc ergo propter hoc*.[39]

Notice the emphasis in this statement on the role of personal values and preferences in the selection of facts and figures – something which, among others, may help modify an uncritical attitude to the application of statistical and econometric methods in the contemporary era. Karl Menger went some way to meet the Historical School by making some concessions on the scope of generalisation, and the usefulness of historical knowledge.[40] But there was no concession in practice and, moreover, once the main debate was over, the neo-classical attitude had hardened into an incredibly orthodox, inflexible and complacent set of methodological criteria.

The scenario may be described in the following steps. First, the neo-classical economists by and large uncritically accepted the claim of Comte and the Historical School that the method of natural sciences was inductive. Second, they rejected the view that such a procedure (*which they thought to be the correct method for natural science*) was applicable to economics. Third, they themselves divided into two groups: the first group – whose most dogmatic expositor was Ludwig von Mises – believed that, even though *the* methodology of natural science was inapplicable to economics, economic theory could nevertheless be completely value-free; the second group, notably Frank Knight and Friedrich von Hayek, rejected the neutrality of economic theory as well. The arguments of both groups, however, helped create no less than an atmosphere of figure-phobia and fear of historical knowledge. They attacked the use of statistics and history in one and the same breath as being both dangerous and irrelevant. It was their uncritical acceptance of the (mistaken) Comtean/Historical description of *the* method of natural sciences which gave rise to lasting confusions in the realm of social and economic method – for example the confusion of what they called historism (later described as historicism) with the use and relevance of historical knowledge for social study. They were as mistaken as their adversaries, with the difference that they carried the day and caused disastrous damage to the method and substance of social and economic inquiry.

There are some arguments in von Mises – regarding matters like the use of mathematics and statistics in economic theory – which are of sensible critical relevance to contemporary issues. Here, however, we are concerned with those of his arguments which are most relevant to the debate between German historicism and neo-classical *a priorism* (the term is von Mises's). He begins by noting that social and economic theory 'is not derived from experience; it is prior to experience'.[41] This, in our view, is a perfectly valid statement. However, he goes on to argue at length that therefore 'no kind of experience can ever force us to discard or modify a priori theorems; they are logically prior to it and cannot be either proved by corroborative experience or disproved by experience to the contrary . . .'.[42] And if this does not do sufficient justice to a full exposition of the phantasmagoria of von Mises's *a priorism*, the reader may take some joy (or horror) from the following statement:

> If a contradiction appears between a theory and experience, *we must always assume* that a condition pre-supposed by the theory was not present, or else that there is some error in our observation. The disagreement between the theory and the facts of experience frequently forces us to think through the problems of the theory again. *But so long as a rethinking of the theory*

*uncovers no errors in our thinking, we are not entitled to doubt its
truth* [emphasis added]. [43]

In other words, if reality is in conflict with your ideas, do not adjust
your views because reality must be at fault! Marx – the greatest
single target of attack by men like von Mises – has been quite
unfairly claimed to have held such views as the above. For Marx was
certainly not an *'a priorist'*. But even certain schools of Marxism
which have interpreted Marx's method in terms resembling the
above statement would be ashamed to express themselves with such
dogmatic and perfect disregard for empirical reality. Let us also
emphasise the fact that *in practice* many modern economic theorists
totally adhere to this piece of methodological precept, although
nowadays one would seldom find anyone who would openly confess
to it. One important implication of the German Historical – and
certainly the Comtean – approach was the concept of historical
inevitability or historical determinism, i.e. the claim that there was
a general order and pattern of historical development in which
human action could have no real influence. Critics like von Mises
rejected this claim and, although their extreme *a priorism* was not
wholly consistent with this rejection, they described social and
economic theory as *the science of human action*. One would therefore expect them to believe that human action could at least influence the direction and pattern of social change. Yet von Mises
argued that no such thing was possible and that societies were
condemned to the same social and institutional arrangements
regardless of any conscious attempt at social and economic reform.
Let us quote his own words on the subject:

> Scarcely anyone interests himself in social problems without
> being led to do so by the desire to see reforms enacted. . . . Only a
> few have the strength to accept the knowledge that these reforms
> are impracticable and to draw all the inferences from it. Most
> men endure the sacrifice of the intellect more easily than the
> sacrifice of their daydreams. [44]

Hayek's position on the subject was in line with that of von Mises
at least in two important respects. First, he fell into the same trap of
regarding Comtean positivism as *the* method of natural sciences; he

therefore attacked the desire for 'the slavish imitation' of 'the scientific method' by students of social problems – a prejudice which he (correctly) described as 'scientism'. Second, he rejected the relevance of statistical and historical knowledge to social theory. However, unlike von Mises, he did not draw a sharp distinction between fact and value; and, in connection with that, he was consistent with his indeterministic outlook when he wrote:

> It is probably true that economic analysis has never been the product of detached intellectual curiosity about the *why* of social phenomena, but of an intense urge to reconstruct a world which gives rise to profound dissatisfaction.[45]

A statement which curiously reminds the reader of another, well-known, statement put out by Karl Marx and Friedrich Engels almost a century earlier: 'hitherto philosophers have interpreted the world, the point however is to change it'.

Robbins's contribution to this debate is more widely known.[46] It was certainly more elegant, more comprehensive and less dogmatic than von Mises's, although it is not difficult to trace the latter's influence in Robbins's views. Where von Mises had spoken of '*a priorism*' Robbins described the method of economic theory as 'hypothetico-deductive'. And where von Mises had regarded economic theories as 'universally valid knowledge', Robbins argued that to claim 'that generalisations of Political Economy were applicable to the state of England in the early part of the reign of Queen Victoria, and suchlike contentions . . . is clearly misleading'. Robbins, however, introduced a new dimension to the twin problem of the universality of economic knowledge, and the relevance of empirical data to it, in his discussion of the significance of theoretical assumptions. According to von Mises, the assumptions of a plausible theory had to be both 'self-evident' and 'logically necessary'.[47] In an attempt to prove both the empirical realism and the universal applicability of economic theories, Robbins divided the assumptions of the neo-classical system into two basic categories: 'the fundamental assumptions' and 'the auxiliary assumptions'. He then claimed that the truth of the assumptions falling in the first category was self-evident (and, therefore, *universally valid*) although those in the second category might not be of universal validity.[48] We shall postpone a criticism of this argument to the next chapter solely because it gave rise to a controversy in the 1950s which must be discussed comprehensively.

While 'a priorism', 'hypothetico-deductivism', 'anti-scientism', etc., were making their own contributions to the time-honoured tradition of figure-phobia in the (dominant) Ricardian–Walrasian methodology, certain events were quietly moving in the opposite direction. The older practice of collecting census data by the state had gradually spread to the collection of similar data in other major fields of concern to public administration. Applied economists such as Arthur Bowley and, later, Sir William Beveridge and Colin Clark began to collect and manipulate statistical figures in the course of their economic studies. Influential critics such as Sir John Clapham – who could not be denounced as a follower of German historicism – described economic theories as 'empty boxes'. In the field of scientific method and social philosophy logical positivism – with its emphasis on empirical verification of theories – had begun to dominate Western thought. In fact, so attractive was the new school of logical positivism that over a certain period it tended to engage the minds of men as diverse in their socio-political views as Bertrand Russell, Rudolph Carnap and Harold Laski, although some of them (notably Russell) later repented. Meanwhile the Soviet attempt to develop her economy through comprehensive planning had shown that at least this was not an impossibility; and it was clear that some extensive use of statistical data and analysis was indispensable to its success. Keynes used a basically theoretical approach, but he proposed concepts which were not only quantifiable but had to be quantified if they were to be used in the formulation of public policy. Indeed, a quick look at the contributions of A. J. Brown, E. H. Phelps-Brown and others to the first volume of Oxford Economic Papers (1938–40) would reveal the extent and speed with which Keynes's ideas encouraged empirical research. T. W. Hutchison's departure from the orthodox methodological view was thus both timely and novel.[49] He was not a logical positivist. But the indirect influence of logical positivism may be detected in his methodological ideas – an influence which at that time was quite new and highly unorthodox. He attacked 'armchair theorising' and advocated the use of statistical evidence. The orthodox ('a priorist') economists reacted, more or less, in horror to Hutchison's criticism, whereas the more critical economists greeted it with applause: he was congratulated by Maurice Dobb and denounced by Frank Knight.[50] Some students of the history and philosophy of economics may be puzzled by these facts, although the source of their puzzlement must be sought in their own confusion of issues. At any rate, when the last guns of the Second World War were silenced, Positive Economics began to emerge as the new dogma.

CONCLUDING REMARKS

We have come a long way through a short route. The purpose of this chapter was not to present a detailed or comprehensive account of the history of economic thought and method. There are excellent treatises in the history of economic ideas already in existence; and a history of economic method should fill in many more pages and attract fewer readers. Rather, the intention was to provide a background knowledge to the evolution of both substance and method in economic theorising, such that ideas and the methods by which they were formulated would appear as an integrated whole. This was an indispensable task for our later discussion of the more contemporary issues, which are often discussed without due regard for their roots in history. In this connection, it was also intended to get rid of several conceptual and historical confusions which constantly bedevil methodological argument in the social sciences. The main points of clarification may be summarised as follows. The Ricardian method was logical, deductive and *a priori* and it dominated both classical and neo-classical theory since its inception. Comtean positivism – to be distinguished from the twentieth-century philosophy of logical positivism – had two *main* elements. One, that there should be a clear distinction between fact and value in social analysis; two, that social and economic theory should be derived from empirical (i.e. historical) generalisations. Generally, economists accepted the first element and rejected the second. The debate between the German Historical School and neo-classical economists led to some (insignificant) verbal compromise by the latter. However, the aftermath of that debate saw a hardening of the orthodox line to such an extent that at least one of its leading spokesmen regarded *no* empirical knowledge of *any* relevance to economic theory. Although the substance of neo-classical theory remained largely intact after the War, its *purported* method – i.e. Positive Economics – was a radical departure from its past history. If we refer to possible confusions it is because even scholarly and voluminous studies of the subject do not seem to have been immune from them. The recent volume by Hollis and Nell, entitled *Rational Economic Man,* is a case in point.[51] There are many good things to be said about this book not least its evident frustration with the present state of affairs in economic knowledge which we fully share with its authors. Yet, it would be dishonest and complacent not to speak out against some of its puzzling features. It draws a sharp distinction between the Ricardian and the Walrasian methods, the latter of which it describes as 'empiricist'! There may be problems of semantics in any field of inquiry, but it would be stretching it too far to blame such a confusion on semantics. It presents an admirable critique of the concept of the 'rational economic man' pointing out that 'all concepts are culture-bound';[52] yet it beats the drum of Ricardo's *method* with its incredible scope of abstraction and universal generalisation. It implies that the *methodology* of Positive Economics has been dominant since the rise of neo-classical theory, when even Logical Positivism – from which Positive Economics is supposed to have received its philosophical credentials – had not yet appeared.[53] It argues – although not consistently – that neo-classical theory and method have always been empiricist, and it ends by offering a 'proof' of the existence and superiority of *purely a priori* knowledge. Yet, it seems to overlook the fact that in doing so it is in good company both with the methodology of von Mises before the War, and with the attitude of mathematical economists afterwards. The very last comment, however, must await discussion in Chapters 7 and 8.

3

POSITIVE ECONOMICS: THE *LOGIC* OF NEO-CLASSICAL ECONOMIC THEORY

THE ADVENT OF POSITIVE ECONOMICS

Positive Economics, as a theory of the logic of neo-classical economic theory, was a post-war invention. By then the claim that economic theory is a positive, as opposed to normative, field of inquiry was already well-established. But this claim is neither the sole methodological criterion, nor the exclusive distinguishing feature of Positive Economics, even though some of its adherents (and critics) seem to believe that a mere distinction between fact and value is sufficient for its methodological requirements. The situation is further complicated by the fact that Positive Economics has now come to connote both the method and the substance of economic theory. In fact, it is intended as a logical positivist interpretation of the method of neo-classical theory. Nevertheless, it has partially confused the criteria of logical positivism in theory; and it has seldom adhered to them in practice. In retrospect this post-war marriage of neo-classical theory with logical positivist philosophy seems somewhat strange. For, if interpreted consistently, the methodology of Positive Economics stands the *pre-war* theory of economic method on its head. Yet it does so with little or no change in the content and analytical procedure of neo-classical theory which *both* these views have claimed to describe. More explicitly, if economic method was what von Mises and Robbins had described it to be (although, to Robbins's credit, the two views were not entirely identical), then it would not be strictly consistent with the rules of logical positivism. This inconsistency between the two views would become very pronounced if we add the rejection by Hayek and Knight of the distinction between fact and value in social and economic knowledge.

The problem is this. Both of these methodological views have *dominated* orthodox thinking in economics in two successive periods of time; both of them have been successively accepted as the correct description of – and prescription for – the method of neo-classical economics. Yet the basic content and analytical procedure of neo-classical theory has remained unchanged, even though the theorists – sometimes even the same individuals – accepted these conflicting views at different points in time. The question is, Why? A logical solution to this problem could run along the following lines. It is true that there is a basic conflict between the two methodo-logical views which have been dominant before and after the War; but this simply means that economists discovered that the previous view was mistaken, and so they corrected their mistake. Yet an argument of this kind is unacceptable at least on two grounds. First, if the pre-war *description* of neo-classical method had been contrary to facts, it should have been very easy to criticise and correct it immediately; why did practising economists have to accept an incorrect description of how they proceeded in their work? Second, when a new theory is proposed which is in conflict with an old, accepted, theory, it would normally succeed in displacing the older theory as a result of an open debate between the two parties; but the methodology of Positive Economics swept aside the '*a prioristic*' approach in no time, and with hardly a shot being fired! Indeed this is probably one reason why so many adherents and critics of Positive Economics (mistakenly) believe that the *methodology* of Positive Economics has been dominant since the rise of neo-classical theory itself.

A satisfactory solution to this problem may be more readily discovered from the realm of sociology (and/or psychology) rather than logic. It looks as if the '*a prioristic*' explanation was accepted at the time because it tended to *justify* 'how we do things' in economics; and Positive Economics was subsequently accepted, without argument, also because, this time, *it* appeared to justify 'how we do things in economics'.[1] Although they conflicted in their respective logic they both served the same 'useful' socio-psycho-logical purpose of reassuring us that what we do is right. Therefore the logical conflict (in so far as we have any awareness of its existence) should not disturb us at all, because both sets of criteria served not to attack, but to defend us; not to criticise, but to comfort us; not to refute, but to confirm our theories and methods. We shall postpone a more general discussion of the socio-psychology of the economic profession to Chapter 5.

A piece of independent evidence for this complacent approach to dominant methodological views is that economists often do not bother to find out the meaning and significance of the methodology which they themselves claim to uphold – much less, to discover the meaning and status of their purported methodology in the field of philosophy of science. Often, an impressionistic knowledge of the fashionable trend in the latter field – assuming that it is *not* dangerous – would be sufficient for them to piece together a superficial version of the real theory, and seek comfort from the conclusion that, even according to the new gospel, economics is a scientific discipline. Provided that a theory of scientific knowledge is both fashionable and (at least apparently) not critical of our unchanging ideas and methods, then it would automatically qualify for acceptance almost without argument. For these reasons an evaluation of the methodology of Positive Economics would require a brief discussion and appraisal of the philosophy of logical positivism on which it is *supposed to be* based.

THE ORIGINS AND STATUS OF LOGICAL POSITIVISM

Logical positivism is a product of the twentieth century, even though it has had its roots in the history of philosophy. Its rejection of value statements as unscientific – and even meaningless – is not unfamiliar from the history of philosophy. Its advocacy of the uniqueness and universality of *the* method of natural sciences – sometimes called naturalism, physicalism or scientism – has had important historical precedents. Its (rather qualified) approval of theoretical analysis is nothing new; its (rather unqualified) emphasis on empirical 'observation' is quite old. Its opposition to irrationalism is shared by all except the irrationalists; its repudiation of metaphysics is not exclusive; and its restriction of rational inquiry to a description of the observable phenomena – usually described as phenomenalism and nominalism – is familiar from age-old controversies. Yet logical positivism is a distinct product of our century, and its origins and characteristics are best discovered in a certain set of intellectual and social problems of our age and their developments.

The elements of logical positivism were developed by a number of philosophers and scientists many of whom cannot be accurately described as logical positivists. Mach's philosophy, sometimes called the philosophy of empirico-criticism, has provided some of the original elements of logical positivism; but it is, nevertheless, distinct from the latter. G. E. Moore's analytical philosophy was consistent with logical positivism but only up to the point where it regarded ethical categories or 'value judgements' as being neither tautological nor meaningless. Russell's and Whitehead's contribution to the philosophy of mathematics and their extension of mathematical tools and concepts to the task of logical analysis was helpful to the development of logical positivism. Yet Russell rejected some important aspects of logical positivism and Whitehead almost all of them. Wittgenstein's *Tractatus Logico-Philosophicus* (1922) was probably the first complete statement of the philosophy of logical positivism; but he later radicalised his own views and laid the foundations of what is now known as linguistic philosophy. In retrospect the origin and development of logical positivism is more closely associated with a group of philosophers – subsequently known as the Vienna Circle – which was dominated by Moritz Schlick and included younger talents such as Rudolph Carnap, who became one of its well-known exponents in years to come. The influence of the Vienna Circle in spreading the news may be discerned from the fact that A. J. Ayer's popular *Language, Truth and Logic* (1936) opens with an explicit statement that the ideas proposed in the book are in line with those of the 'Viennese Circle'.[2]

Logical positivism has had many adherents some of whom have left a personal impression on its doctrine. In addition, throughout its development for over half a century, it has faced difficulties and criticisms which have made it necessary to reformulate, amend or replace some of its principles. It is not possible in this essay either to do justice to those individual contributions or to these finer points of adjustment. Fortunately, neither is necessary for our purpose, and it would be sufficient to present a brief description and assessment of its fundamental tenets. We may begin by reminding the reader of the competitive claims of Rationalism and Empiricism in the history of philosophy. The Rationalist approach was deductive and *a priori*; the Empiricist, inductive and empirical. The former proceeded to generalise by a deductive *analysis* of *a priori* hypothesis; the latter by inductive *inferences* from 'direct' observation. In modern terminology the Rationalist method may be described as purely theoretical; the Empiricist as purely statistical. Logical positivism claimed to produce a synthesis between these two procedures, although it did not quite succeed in that part of its programme. It based this claim on the fact that, in principle, logical positivism regarded both logical analysis and empirical observation as necessary components of the method of scientific discovery.

The main principles of logical positivism may be described as follows: The process of scientific discovery begins by partial observation or sense-experience. Such observations are formulated into primary hypotheses which through logical analysis give rise to general theories. These theories are then put to test by an appropriate method of observation (or experimentation) in order to *verify* their implications. If the tests succeed in *verifying* a theory then it should be accepted; otherwise it should be discarded. It follows that if a theory is to claim scientific status it must be verifiable. Hence, all statements and theories which are *not* verifiable are nothing but 'meaningless noises'. They are words or sounds without rational meaning because they do not pass the test of rationality as defined by the verifiability of propositions. This is at once a rejection of metaphysics and a definition for it: Metaphysical statements are those which defy empirical verification; they are therefore *meaningless*. The same goes for normative statements, value judgements or ethical categories. To say that something is 'good' is at best to produce a tautological statement, for the quality of 'goodness' in that thing cannot be 'objectively' (i.e. empirically) verified; it can only refer to an axiomatic definition of goodness and that makes it tautological. Now if metaphysical statements are meaningless and value judgements are tautological it would follow at once that all *rational* inquiries about the world of reality should share the same method. That is to say, the scientific method, as described by the logical positivists, must be unique and universal: in particular, it would be applicable both to the natural and the social sciences. To summarise, a statement is rational (and therefore scientific) if and only if it is verifiable; it would be acceptable if and only if it was verified by empirical observation or experimentation; metaphysical statements and value judgements are meaningless and tautological; the method of scientific discovery is unique and universal.

Let us distinguish between the two central propositions of logical positivism: One, that a scientific statement must be *verifiable*; two, that it should be tested by the process of empirical *verification*.

Suppose a statement was *inherently verifiable,* but there were no available means of testing it; are we therefore to conclude that it is not a scientific statement? Many logical positivists would probably now maintain that such a statement is scientific even though it may not be possible to test it immediately. This would make the criterion of verifiability the most distinguishing feature of scientific propositions. But the matter does not end here. It would be reasonable to say that a class of statements such as medicine X is an effective cure for disease Y is scientific even though the means of its empirical verification were not immediately available. But – within the terms of reference of logical positivism – it would be *un*reasonable to maintain that a class of (logical) predictions such as the Earth will be destroyed in the year 2000 is also a scientific statement. Yet there is no clear logical distinction between these two classes of statement: neither is inherently unverifiable and neither is amenable to immediate empirical tests. If this interpretation is correct then lack of insistence on the immediate possibility of verification should force logical positivists to include (at least some) 'metaphysical' statements in the category of (as yet unverified) scientific propositions. It may be retorted that our interpretation is incorrect since one should also examine the basis for such statements and the contexts in which they occur. This may indeed be a sound argument, but one which is not reasonably available to logical positivists: as long as there is no analytical fault in a proposition and it is not inherently unverifiable, it should meet the logical positivist rules unless it is further insisted that means of verification must be immediately available. And many logical positivists realise that they cannot insist on this condition as, for example, it would mean that Einstein's theory was – until 1919 when it was empirically tested – *unscientific.* It is clear that this problem exists because logical positivism regards analytical consistency and empirical observation as the *exclusive* means of testing a statement.

A well-known criticism of the criterion of confirmation by verification is that it does not specify the number of successful tests which would be sufficient for the acceptance of an hypothesis. Apart from that, problems would arise when an analytically sound statement which has been consistently 'verified' by a series of empirical tests begins to be falsified by further tests. More important is the logical positivists' insistence on the formulation of primary hypotheses by immediate sense-experience or sense-perception. That is to say, according to the rules of logical positivism a scientific hypothesis is, *in the first instance,* formulated as a result of direct contact with the empirical world – for example 'direct observation'. This is well within the old Empiricist tradition, for it intends to locate all knowledge of reality ultimately in the external, empirical world: there is nothing within the human mind whatsoever which is capable of arriving at elementary truths; on the contrary even the most elementary objective truth is imposed upon the mind from the world of empirical reality. This position can be attacked from various angles; the simplest and most decisive argument against it is that there is no such thing as *passive* 'direct' observations. Indeed 'direct' observation is no observation at all except in the most literal sense of that term. A man sitting in a train and watching the landscape while thinking about his own problems is not observing anything except in so far as he cannot help but see the external world. On the other hand, if he was consciously *looking* for something this would mean that he had already formulated a problem *prior* to his attempt at observation. Besides, no two men observe the same phenomenon in exactly the same way, unless *at least* they are both looking for the same thing. Therefore to define a knowledge of objective reality as something which is wholly independent of the human mind – i.e. of *a priori* theories – is logically untenable.

It is not clear whether the criteria of logical positivism are intended as *normative* prescriptions or *positive* descriptions. Let us take the case of the verification of scientific statements first. The question is this. When we claim that scientific statements are tested for empirical verification, do we mean that this *is* a matter of fact, or that it is what scientists *ought to* do? Suppose we mean that it is a matter of fact. If so, it immediately prompts the question: How do you know? The answer would have to be something like the following: We have tested this hypothesis by empirical observation and discovered that it is true. Yet the results of no such empirical tests have been made publicly available by any logical positivist. However, suppose such a 'test' was conducted and it was discovered that some problem-solving disciplines (perhaps in the natural sciences) verify their hypotheses while others (for example the social sciences) do not.[3] The logical positivists may then claim that the former disciplines are scientific, whereas the latter are not. But this would beg the original question: if the rule of verification itself must be a positive, factual and empirically verified procedure, then it would not be verified by the results of the above test, and it would leave us with no *positive* criterion for determining the scientificity of different disciplines. It follows that the rule of empirical verification must be *prescriptive* as opposed to *descriptive*; normative, as opposed to positive. The same argument applies to the criterion of the empirical *verifiability* of scientific statements.

We have reached two important conclusions. First, that the rule of empirical verification is not a positive but a normative category, because it has not been rigorously tested and verified within the natural sciences, and that it is very likely to be refuted if it were tested within the social sciences. Since logical positivism insists on the uniqueness of the scientific method, it would then have to regard social sciences as unscientific (and, by logical positivist standards, irrational), but this would imply a circular argument – i.e. social sciences are unscientific because they do not generally follow a methodological procedure which is – by assumption – followed in the natural sciences. However, if the test of scientificity is purely empirical and descriptive, then why should be believe that it is the 'empirically observed' method of natural sciences which would qualify for our *description* of the scientific method? Second, that the argument can be extended to the criterion of verifiability. *Therefore, these two most important criteria of logical positivism – i.e. verifiability and verification — themselves turn out to be value judgements. But, according to those same criteria value judgements are (at best) no more than tautologies.* The position may be summarised in the following statement: according to the criteria of logical positivism value judgements are (at best) tautological; these criteria are themselves value judgements; therefore, they are tautological; hence the logical positivist claim that value judgements are tautological is itself not scientific but tautological . . . and we may run around the circle *ad infinitum*. This is the heavy penalty which logical positivism must pay for its insistence that verifiability and verification would have to be exclusively empirical; and that empirically unverifiable statements are either meaningless noises or tautological fantasies. In some ways it is a historical tragedy. Logical positivism developed in an environment in which wild and dogmatic claims to the possession of all knowledge and total truths were threatening to halt the progress of rational inquiry; and in fact they managed to cause a great deal of human suffering or at least act as an 'intellectual' justification for those who inflicted them. It could have been a limited but worthy line of defence for human reason and human dignity.

But, in no time, it degenerated into a body of dogmatic belief of its own, inhibiting the growth of knowledge and serving the interest of the *status quo* by effectively prohibiting criticism and the emergence of bold and new ideas. Every time a truly original idea is put forward, the followers of logical positivism cry out for 'empirical evidence', knowing full well that, for many ideas, hard empirical evidence is difficult to come by, and these include some of their own beliefs! Indeed, our brief description of the social origins of logical positivism – which is almost all that can be said in its favour – should be denounced by logical positivists as 'meaningless noises'. Logical positivism severed its radical and critical roots and became an ideology.

Voluminous books are still appearing in order to refute the philosophy of logical positivism by curiously complicated and roundabout methods; by attempts to refute its nominalism; by arguments to disprove its claim to offer an empirical solution to the problem of knowledge; by efforts to 'demonstrate' the existence of *purely a priori* knowledge. They often involve the use of either obscure, almost mystifying arguments; or abstract, 'learned' and 'sophisticated' discussions. Normally the two go together. Unfortunately, brevity, clarity and simplicity are not characteristic of a lot of intellectual effort in our contemporary era when they seem to be needed more than ever. Yet, even though flogging a dead horse by all (efficient and inefficient) means may be harmless, killing a fly with a hammer could still be dangerous; for the fly may evade the hammer and/or the hammer may crush life and property for which it had not been intended.

THE METHODOLOGY OF POSITIVE ECONOMICS IN THEORY

Positive Economics depends heavily on the philosophy of logical positivism, though not without a certain amount of confusion. Positive Economists draw a clear line of demarcation between statements of fact and statements of value; indeed, some of them regard this distinction as the necessary and sufficient condition for 'the scientific method'. Some would go even further and identify the distinction of fact and value with a parallel distinction between the quantitative and qualitative methods of assessment. For example, a distinguished Positive Economist once described the work of two economic historians (who had argued that the treatment of black slaves in the United States had been better than was generally believed) as scientific, *merely* because they had used quantitative methods in obtaining their results. Curiously enough, his own contribution to the debate was that the authors must be right for, as everyone knows, copulation with one's secretary would lead to a break-down of discipline.[4] Such confusions are even more evident among other Positive Social Scientists whose knowledge of 'the scientific method' is often acquired at second hand from Positive Economists. For example, after spending two hours trying to convince an adherent of the Science of Politics that collecting election data for Britain and Nigeria and comparing them in a diagram is not necessarily a scientific pursuit, an economist was once asked: 'so you think we should go back to the old normative stuff?' At any rate the simple distinction between positive and normative economics involves other important issues which we shall discuss in Chapter 6, below.

Positive Economics also insists that economic hypotheses and theories must be empirically testable, and tested against empirical evidence. At this point there is an important divergence of opinion which has never been explicitly debated. Some Positive Economists define testability as *verifiability*, and regard empirical tests as empirical *verifications*; others define them respectively, as *falsifiability* and *falsifications*. This divergence of views has rarely been acknowledged, but it has existed. The latter terminology and criteria belong to Popper not to logical positivists. The fact that there has never been a civil war among Positive Economists on this issue is explained partly by their lack of full regard for the philosophical background and implications of their own methodology, and partly by the popular mistake – reaching far beyond the ranks of Positive Economists – that Popper is a logical positivist. In a later section we shall present a brief critical exposition of Popper's philosophy of science, its relevance to the natural and social sciences, and its implications for a comprehensive critique of Positive Economics.

The 'Popperian' interpretation of Positive Economics runs along the following lines. Positive Economics studies problems which pertain to matters of fact, not value. Solutions to economic problems begin by *a priori* 'hunches', 'guesses' or 'conjectures' which are falsifiable and are subjected to tests aimed at falsification. When such (empirical) tests repeatedly fail to falsify a hypothesis, it is then tentatively accepted as a theory until such time as it *is* falsified by further evidence, and/or replaced by a better theory.[5] The logical positivist interpretation of Positive Economics retains the distinction of fact from value, but it claims that the initial hypotheses themselves are *empirical* – i.e. they are 'derived' from 'immediate' sense-experience and, particularly, 'direct' observation. This, as we have seen, is logically impossible. In addition, the criteria of verifiability and verification face the kind of logical and methodological problems which we have already discussed.[6] Furthermore, it is clearly more difficult to demonstrate that a statement is verified than simply to show that it has *not* been falsified: a statement which has *not* been falsified cannot be claimed to have been verified. Such a statement must be retained by the rule of falsification, but it may not be retained by the rule of verification. Therefore, the criterion of falsification offers a greater scope for the growth of scientific knowledge.

If our earlier (general) critique of logical positivist philosophy is correct, then it follows that a logical positivist interpretation of economic knowledge is untenable even prior to an examination of the record of Positive Economics. But this line of argument would overlook the 'Popperian' element in the methodology of Positive Economics. Moreover, it may disappoint the Positive Economist looking for a direct and specific critique of their method. Let us therefore put aside our general critique of logical positivism altogether. Let us assume that logical positivism offers a unique and faultless description of *the* scientific method, and try to discover the extent to which its rules are respected by Positive Economists.

THE METHODOLOGY OF POSITIVE ECONOMICS IN PRACTICE: I. THE CASE OF BASIC TAUTOLOGIES

To summarise, the minimum requirements of Positive Economics are as follows: one, economic hypotheses must be *inherently* testable; two, if the results of the tests are negative they should be rejected or (at most) be held in 'reserve'. One of the most fundamental economic theories – and one on which many other major theories depend – is the well-known Law of Diminishing Returns. The Law states that, given a fixed productive input, the application of a variable input to that fixed input would *eventually* result in additions to output in *decreasing* quantities.[7] This proposition sounds so reasonable that generations of students have understood and accepted it as a matter of 'common sense'. Yet it is *inherently* untestable, because it claims to be 'eventually' true without specifying the conditions of that 'eventuality'. The reason is this: suppose that the Law was empirically tested for an arbitrary period of time; if the test was successful then we would congratulate ourselves; if it was unsuccessful then we could always argue that the arbitrary time-period had not been 'long enough', for, according to the Law, marginal (and average) returns would diminish – *eventually*. The position is rather reminiscent of a story told by Alexandre Dumas the elder, the famous French novelist. A butcher once displayed a sign which read: 'From tomorrow, meat will be cheaper in this shop.' But, next day, when customers came to buy cheaper meat, he reminded them that it *would* be cheaper *from tomorrow*. An important implication of the Law of Diminishing Returns is that 'short-run' marginal and average cost curves would be U-shaped. Without it, it would be impossible to determine the 'short-run' *equilibrium* output of the firm. The latter theories were tested, in the 1950s, by statistical and econometric techniques, with unfavourable results. But, predictably, the general reaction to these results was to use various (reasonable and unreasonable) theoretical arguments in order to defend the theories.

The 'long-run' counterpart to the Law of Diminishing Returns is the theory of (eventually) decreasing returns to scale. When a firm expands it is likely that it would benefit from economies of scale; that is to say output would increase *more than* proportionately than inputs. It is nevertheless possible for output to increase *equiproportionately* with inputs, in which case there would be constant returns to scale. But, eventually, output would increase *less proportionately* than inputs, because of diseconomies of scale. Hence the 'long-run' average cost curve would rise, and this would set a limit to the expansion of the firm, i.e. it would determine the 'long-run' size of the firm and its 'long-run' *equilibrium* output. Now, this hypothesis is a much weaker proposition than its 'short-run' counterpart, both on theoretical and on empirical grounds. *Theoretically,* the logic of decreasing returns to scale is very weak, almost a flight of fancy: the firm gets so large (*how* large?) that its management becomes inefficient (why?), and it would have to pay higher prices for its inputs (what if it takes over other existing firms?) This prediction lacks even that element of 'common sense' which the Law of Diminishing Returns enjoys. Why can a large firm not go on having access to better management, better technology, cheaper markets for its inputs, greater credit facilities with more favourable terms and a better reputation among the consumers? *Empirically,* casual observation has demonstrated the continuous growth of market concentration in the past hundred years; and statistical and econometric tests have indicated that the 'long-run' average cost curves are at best L-shaped: i.e. firms experience economies of scale and end up with constant (not decreasing) returns to scale. In this case, there cannot even be much argument about the arbitrary selection of the time-period for, by definition, the 'long run' is a period long enough for the firm to be able to expand: i.e. we are already in the 'long run'. Unless of course it is further argued that the 'long run' in the 'long run' itself is a period long enough for the firm to experience decreasing returns to scale! Now, it is always possible in social and economic science to find fault with empirical tests on grounds of impurity of the data, ambiguity or downright poverty of techniques. But if this is what we believe, why do we insist so much on 'empirical tests', and, apart from that, why do we not react with the same degree of cautiousness and criticism when an empirical test seems to confirm our views?[8]

Neo-classical theory, especially in the context of *general* equilibrium, is dependent on the concept of the 'long run'. The Marshallian concept of the long run, as defined above, is circular but unambiguous – it is a period long enough for the firm to alter its scale of production. But this is only one of the many long-run concepts used in economic theory. For example, when it is claimed that in the 'long run' investment would be interest-elastic, then – although this is still a circular concept – it is not the same (and it would not necessarily involve the same 'length of time') as the Marshallian concept. And when it is argued that 'the long-run saving and consumption functions are linear and proportional', then we are introducing a third (circular) definition of the long run. And when it is said that in the long run smooth and infinitesimal substitution between productive inputs is possible we are talking about yet another (circular) concept of the long run. . . . It is clear that even on purely logical grounds the whole thing collapses, since the long-run *general* equilibrium is dependent on the simultaneous fulfilment of all such 'long-run' conditions which, by definition, do not coincide with one another. Apart from that, how can theories which depend on such unspecified conditions be empirically tested? And if they can, who has tested them, and what are the results? We have already mentioned the case of one set of such tests. Another case which springs to mind is the issue of the 'long-run' linearity of the saving and consumption functions. In this case, there was no real empirical test involved: the long-term linearity of these functions was in the first place established by *direct* historical generalisations carried out by Kuznets and others (incidentally, this is a case of pure historicism which should be wholly unacceptable to Positive Economists). It was only afterwards that economic theorists (Smithies, Duesenberry, Friedman, Modigliani and others) proposed rival theories in order to 'explain' this result. As a matter of interest there is an amusing implication in the theories of linear long-run saving (and consumption) function which is worth mentioning. These theories claim that the long-run saving (and consumption) rate would be constant. Yet, on the authority of Adam Smith, Ricardo, Marx, Arthur Lewis *and* W. W. Rostow, we teach our students of development economics that economic development is accompanied (if not preconditioned) by a significant *increase* in the community's aggregate saving rate. And, in our economic history, we learn that this is exactly what happened in the economic development of England, France, Germany, Japan, the Soviet Union, and elsewhere. It therefore turns out that an even *longer* period than 'the long run' would make the aggregate saving (and consumption) function *non*-linear, or 'shift upwards'. The only logical way out of this problem is to assert that the long-run linearity of these functions is true only of the capitalist – developed, industrial or whatever – societies. But this argument is not available to neo-classical theorists who, in general, recognise no boundaries to the scope of their generalisations in time and space. We shall discuss this issue in a wider context in Chapter 7 below.

THE METHODOLOGY OF POSITIVE ECONOMICS IN PRACTICE: II. THE CASE OF THE NEO-CLASSICAL CONSUMER THEORY

(i) A Historical Note on Utility Analysis

Early neo-classical economists proposed a micro-economic theory of consumer behaviour which was based on the theory of marginal utility. This theory stated that the (subjective) additional utility of consuming greater amounts of a given commodity diminishes and, in equilibrium, such marginal utilities will be equal to the corresponding (objective) market prices. The critics points out that utility, marginal or total, was unquantifiable. But the criticism was not taken seriously: the reaction ranged from quiet embarrassment to outspoken rejection. However, those who were quietly embarrassed finally managed to invent the method of 'indifference curve analysis' in order to meet the objection. Although the new approach ultimately rendered the same results as the old (except by a cumbersome and roundabout procedure) it was thought that it would avoid the use of the cardinal concept of utility. All that was now required was to state that a greater amount of consumption would give *more* utility to the consumer; it was no more necessary to specify the absolute quantity of utility enjoyed by consuming different quantities of the commodity. This is known as the ordinal concept of utility, and, as far as it goes, it does seem to solve the empirico-logical problem of the immeasurability of utility. However, almost concurrently with this development it was shown that in all choices involving uncertain expectations – that is, in nearly all choices made in the real, uncertain, world – the theory was indispensably dependent on actual *measurements* of (i.e. the assignment of *cardinal numbers* to) utility. Yet it was – and it still is – claimed that in the imaginary situation of perfect certainty (which is the basic assumption of many important neo-classical theories) the cardinal concept of utility was unnecessary: in this case, all that is required is a 'ranking of preferences' for *relative*, not absolute, valuation. Nevertheless, it was further claimed that utility *is* measurable, and a number of techniques and methods were proposed for such a measurement; but it was admitted that 'measurable' utility cannot be extended to the theory of social welfare (see Alchian, 1953).[9] Thus, the present general confusion (as opposed to consensus) in neo-classical theory – as observed in textbooks, lectures and past and present articles – is that (a) the *cardinal* concept of utility must be rejected since utility is not measurable; (b) it must be – and it has been – replaced by the *ordinal* concept of utility which does not require absolute valuation of utility or preference; (c) but the *cardinal* concept is unavoidable for a utility analysis of choice under uncertain conditions; (d) this poses no problem *because utility is measurable*; (e) even though utility *is* measurable, the ordinal approach (in conditions of certainty) is not dependent on it. In what follows we shall endeavour to show that (A) the 'ordinal' approach *is* – at least ultimately – *dependent* on the measurability of utility; (B) the methods and techniques suggested for 'the measurement of utility are useless in testing the neo-classical consumer theory; and (C) this theory is an axiomatic and untestable proposition.

(ii)   To Show that the Ordinal Approach Depends on the Measurement of Utility

Two highly respected and widely used textbooks (*Micro-economic Theory* by Ferguson and Gould, and the same title by Henderson and Quandt) expose the *ordinal* approach to the theory of consumer behaviour in the following terms. For a given income and taste the consumer has a utility function which expresses utility as a function of the amount of goods x_1 and x_2 consumed. If his income rises, so that he can now buy more of these goods, his utility would increase, although it is neither possible nor necessary to *quantify* this increase in utility. This utility function is normally non-linear, which means that the rate at which the consumer is willing to substitute x_1 for x_2 changes relatively to the amounts of x_1 and x_2 bought by the consumer, given his income: that is, 'the marginal rate of substitution' (or 'the rate of commodity substitution') is equal to the ratio of the marginal utility of x_1 to the marginal utility of x_2. It follows logically that the consumer would spend his income on the purchase of such amounts of x_1 and x_2 that would equate the ratio of their prices to the ratio of their marginal utilities – i.e. in equilibrium, the marginal rate of substitution of x_1 for x_2 equals the ratio of the price of x_1, to the price of x_2. But there are more than two commodities in the real world: the equilibrium condition for two goods thus obtained may be *generalised* to the case of *n* goods when the ratio of the marginal utility of each commodity to its price is equal everywhere.[10]

Now, let us consider the *general equilibrium* case first. It states that if there is to be equilibrium the consumer must purchase commodities X_1 to X_n in such amounts as:

$$\frac{MUx_1}{Px_1} = \frac{MUx_2}{Px_2} \cdot \cdot \cdot = \frac{MUx_n}{Px_n}.$$

But prices are measured in units of currency so that marginal utilities (divided by prices) must also be measured in units of currency. If so, then we are not only measuring utility, but we are counting it in pounds and pence. If not, the ratios would be absolutely meaningless. For example, if the ratios were all equal to 2/3rds in equilibrium, what would be the meaning of *number 2* divided by 3 units of currency? However, suppose it was argued that this generalisation is intended only for illustrative purposes (whatever that may mean) and that it is sufficient for the ordinal approach to be consistent in the two-commodity case – i.e. the case where:

$$\frac{MUx_1}{MUx_2} = \frac{Px_1}{Px_2}.$$

This would make the two ratios completely independent of the units in which they are expressed. Let us emphasise that the above condition would make equilibrium possible only for each pair of commodities at a time; it would *not* specify the *general* equilibrium condition. But, that apart, even this more limited result does not completely dispense with the problem of the measurement of utility. Suppose that in a given case the two ratios are both equal to ½. This would mean that both the price and the marginal utility of one commodity is *twice as much* as the other. Such a condition poses no problem for the relation of the prices, but what about the relation of the marginal utilities? Nothing can be twice (or *n* times) as much as something else *unless they are both measured in the same unit.* It is possible to talk about an increase or decrease in anger, love, utility or any other psychological mood; this indeed is the very ordinal concept of utility which the revised consumer theory claimed to use. But the claim is not true: when I say that my total or marginal utility from the consumption of something is *twice as much* as something else, then I am not merely expressing a change in the mood but *the amount* by which this change has occurred. Therefore, even the two-commodity case cannot ultimately avoid the *cardinal* concept of utility.

The above conclusions may be countered by the following arguments: it is not at all necessary to express the marginal rate of substitution as the ratio of the two marginal utilities. Indeed, consumer theory may be entirely presented without a single (explicit or implicit) reference to the term 'utility' or its derivatives. Consider the following statement of the two-comodity equilibrium condition: the rate at which a consumer is willing to substitute x_1 for x_2 is defined as the marginal rate of substitution. The reason why he is willing to substitute the one for the other at a certain rate is irrelevant. In particlar we need not specify that this is dependent on his utility, satisfaction or whatever. Given two or three basic axioms,[11] it would logically follow that he would buy such amounts of x_1 and x_2 as would equate the marginal rate of substitution with the price ratio. The shorthand ('mathematical') version of this condition would then become:

$$\frac{dx_1}{dx_2} = \frac{Px_1}{Px_2}.$$

This looks like a very persuasive argument: nevertheless it is not entirely satisfactory. First, our previous account of the 'ordinal' approach to consumer theory in terms of relative marginal utilities was not our own invention; more precisely, it was taken from two important textbooks of micro-economic theory which – at different levels – are used in teaching, perhaps more than any other textbook on this subject. In any case, to our knowledge, no other textbook avoids this method of presentation. These observations prompt two questions: one, why do these authors (some of whom have reached the peaks of achievement in neo-classical theorising) begin their textbooks by advocating the *'ordinal '* approach and then proceed to produce an ultimately *cardinal* theory? In general, why do we in fact teach consumer theory with reference to marginal utilities to our students at all levels? Second, our books, articles and specialised research are full of references to 'the utility function', 'marginal utility', etc., both within and outside the specific context of consumer theory. How can we then claim that such concepts are incorrect, irrelevant or redundant? It is clearly not acceptable to say one thing on occasional debates, and do the opposite for the rest (note, however, that our argument is not on the use of the term 'utility' or its substitutes. It concerns the description of the marginal rate of substitution as a ratio of two marginal 'entities' – whatever they may be called).

None the less, let us suppose that these objections are not strictly relevant to the argument, and directly examine the claim that the

equilibrium condition defined by $\dfrac{dx_1}{dx_2} = \dfrac{Px_1}{Px_2}$ avoids the measure-

ment of utility. This proposition may only be stated for the two-commodity situation: It is not possible to generalise it to a set of $n > 2$ commodities. Within this limit, it means that (given the three basic axioms) the consumer would value x_1 and x_2 in a ratio which would correspond to their relative prices. There are then two ways of interpreting this condition. One is that, in equilibrium, the rate at which the consumer *prefers* x_1 to x_2 must be equal to the ratio of Px_1 to Px_2. This would simply involve a terminological change and nothing else: it is as impossible to say that I prefer something *twice as much* to something else as it is to say my marginal utility of the one is twice as much as the other. The second interpretation of this condition is that, in equilibrium, the consumer is *willing to exchange* x_1 for x_2 in the same proportion as their prices. If these are apples and oranges then, in equilibrium, the consumer is willing to exchange one apple for two oranges when the price of apples is

twice as much as oranges. In this case $\dfrac{dx_1}{dx_2} = \dfrac{1}{2}$. But what is the

meaning of the ratio of one *apple* to two *oranges*? How can an elephant be divided by two donkeys? It may be retorted that, in spite of appearances, we are not dividing an apple by two oranges; we are simply measuring apples in terms of oranges. That is a reasonable argument; but *it could only mean that the (subjective) value of an apple to the consumer is twice as much as the (subjective) value of an orange.* We are back where we had begun. Let us look at the same problem in a different way. *Either* it is *observed* that the consumer buys apples and oranges in proportion to their prices, in which case we have no theory, and certainly no equilibrium theory. We have simply made an observation which may (or may not) be generally true – let alone it being the *equilibrium* condition. It is, in other words, trite. In any case, the theory as it exists has not (and could not have) been 'derived' from any number of such observations. *Or,* it is *theoretically believed* that, in equilibrium, the consumer would buy apples and oranges when the rate he is willing to exchange one for the other corresponds to the market rate (i.e. the relative prices). In this case we do have a theory but it involves the measurement of subjective preferences: if the rate at which the consumer is willing to give up apples for oranges is determined *independently of the market prices,* then in equilibrium his 'willingness' to have apples is (in our example) *twice as much as* having

oranges. All this is not to mention the fact that $\dfrac{dx_1}{dx_2}$ and the

indifference curve must come from a function, and unless this is a purely empirical function – which is not generally the case – then it must be a theoretical (utility, preference or whatever) function.

(iii)   To Show that the Proposed Methods of Measuring Utility are Irrelevant

Up to now we have argued that the so-called ordinal approach to consumer theory would not escape the problem of absolute valuation of utility, preference, willingness or whatever, no matter in what guise it is presented. So what, we may be told, for what they teach you in lectures, textbooks, etc., is nonsense; utility *is* measureable: we have proposed methods and techniques for measuring it; and we have even, occasionally, applied these techniques. Therefore, let us take up the case of these techniques and their applications. It would take too long to consider all the complexities and intricacies of the case, including all the niceties of 'monotonic' and 'linear' transformations, aggregation of 'certain' and 'uncertain' utilities, etc. Here we shall discuss such measurement techniques with reference to a simple example which is easily extendible to the more complex cases (and if this was met with disbelief, then perhaps we shall take up the challenge elsewhere).

The simplest (but sufficient) version of the argument could be as follows: suppose we present a consumer with three commodities, x, y and z, and we ask him to rank his preferences not by simply saying in what *order* he would rank them (such as 'I prefer x to y and y to z') but also by attaching a 'weight' – call it 'utility' if you will – to each of these. This can be achieved in either of two ways: (*a*) either we leave the consumer to attach his own 'weights' – i.e. numbers – to each commodity; (*b*) or we present him with a table of possible weights and ask him to select the column which comes nearest to his own weighting. For example, in Table 3.1 there are three columns all of which show the same *order* of preference, but the degree of intensity of preference is different from one to the other: in column 1 x is *twice* preferred to y and y *twice* preferred to z; in column 2, x is *three times* preferred to y and y *one and a half times* to z; and so on (clearly unless some kind of restriction is imposed, there could be a very large number of such alternative columns, but let us put that

Table 3.1

Commodities	*Weights*		
	1	*2*	*3*
x	8	9	6
y	4	3	4
z	2	2	1

aside). Therefore by choosing one column the consumer would clearly indicate not only his *order* of preference, but also his *intensity*; thus, we will have obtained *cardinal* 'weights'.

However, – whichever procedure, (*a*) or (*b*), is used – this is either circular or impossible. Suppose x is 'a house' and y is 'a motor-car'. Let us assume that the consumer owns neither of these two 'commodities'. Normally, a house is more expensive than a car, though not always. Now on this assumption the consumer may prefer a house to a motor-car. But how can he say *by how much* he would prefer the one to the other *unless he already knows the relative price of the two commodities in question*? Ask anyone whether or not he would just *prefer* (let alone by how much) a house to a car, and he would tell you 'it depends' – *on what: on their market values*? If he already knows the relative values of the two goods, then his 'weighting' is no more than a reproduction of the relative market prices – i.e. it is not *he* who is 'weighting'; they have already been weighted for him. Alternatively, if he is asked to choose one system of weighting out of many (such as those in Table 3.1), then either he chooses that system which he knows to be closest to the relative market valuation, or his 'choice' would be absolutely meaningless: he is being forced by the 'questionnaire' into a 'choice' which he cannot possibly make. That is (by virtue of the fact that he has been, willy nilly, subjected to such a 'test') he has no choice in dismissing the whole thing as impossible; and so he would inevitably 'tick' one of the columns. This type of 'investigation' may be worthy of advertising campaigns; it can hardly be regarded as 'empirical evidence'.

(iv)   To Show that the Neo-classical Consumer Theory is Untestable

It automatically follows from the above arguments that the neo-classical consumer theory is logically circular and empirically untestable. Nevertheless, let us give the devil one more chance, and see how he can protect the fruits of 'productive hands' against the 'idle hands' of the critics (for the reference to 'idle hands' see Chapter 2, note 11). Let us suppose that, for some superhuman reason, the consumers could attach absolute 'weights' to their choice of products: that is, let us give away the above argument against the so-called measurability of utility, and assume that such techniques produce meaningful results.

Given this assumption, we would now like to see whether or not the neo-classical consumer theory is empirically testable. The prediction of this theory is that a consumer spends his income in such a way as it would equate the ratio of the marginal 'weight' of each commodity purchased to its market price. It would still be impossible to produce a satisfactory (as opposed to *self*-satisfactory) test of this proposition, because of the problems associated with the number of tests required, the sampling procedures in each test, etc. But that may be a 'small practical problem'. Let us see if this theory is, on so many favourable assumptions, *in principle* testable. So we select a 'representative' sample of commodities and we ask 'representative' samples of consumers in different income-groups to attach different 'weights' to those commodities. We then calculate the marginal weights in each case and we discover that in the case of most of the consumers and most of the goods the ratio of the marginal weights to prices happens to be equal.

Would such a most favourable result on such most favourable assumptions corroborate the theory? Not for a second: for in a test of this kind we are no more asking the consumers to attach weights to hypothetical and otherwise nondescript commodities such as 'a house', 'a car' and 'a holiday' (which, for the sake of argument, we assume they can meaningfully do); on the contrary we are asking them to give weights to oranges, apples, fillet steaks, pork chops, etc. And, unless they are morons or they have just descended from outer space, *they themselves have a pretty good idea of the relative market valuation of these commodities. Therefore, they are going to reproduce these relative prices in their so-called independent weightings.* Thus, we have not 'verified' the prediction of this consumer theory by our 'successful' tests. We have merely measured relative prices by relative prices in an indirect fashion. The whole thing would collapse almost on *any* assumption.

(v)   A Special Application

An important case of the application of the marginal utility theory is the determination of the equilibrium supply of labour by an individual. The early – cardinalist – formulation of this problem was logically unambiguous. It stated that leisure entailed utility, and work *dis*utility. Therefore, in the most efficient allocation of his time the individual worked for as long as the marginal disutility of labour equalled its price (i.e. the market wage rate). Apart from the familiar objection to the cardinal concept of utility (and disutility), this theory may be criticised on another ground. The theory implies that at *all* levels of work, labour involves disutility. Psychologically, this is unlikely to be generally valid; it is more probable that up to a certain (arbitrary) level, working is pleasant – that is, it renders utility. Contrariwise, at a certain arbitrary level, leisure could become unpleasant and therefore render *dis*utility (boredom is a well-known psychological phenomenon). This is a testable proposition – either by survey methods or by controlled experiments. The latter assumption would pose some complications for the determination of a unique equilibrium level of labour supply for a given wage rate. In this case it is likely that 'the equilibrium' could be reached below or above the wage rate for different individuals; if so, it would involve a psychological rent by those who can *afford* to work less.

The 'ordinalist' presentation of the above theory explicitly poses a choice between income and leisure, and determines the equilibrium supply of labour as the residual time *not* spent on leisure. If *money* income is the alternative to leisure then (taking this as the *numéraire*), in equilibrium, the marginal rate of substitution of leisure for income would be equal to the *money* wage rate. If *real* income (or wage-goods) is the opportunity cost of leisure then, in equilibrium, the MRS would be equal to the *real* wage rate. In either case, if the MRS is defined as the ratio of the marginal utility of leisure to income (which is normally the case) then it follows that, in equilibrium, the latter ratio is equal to the (money or real) wage rate. This relationship implies cardinalism even more clearly than the general theory of consumer choice between two commodities, which we discussed above. Because, in this case, the ratio of the two marginal utilities is equal *not* to another (price) *ratio*, but to a certain *amount* of money (or goods) – i.e. the money (or the real) wage rate. On the other hand, if the MRS is defined merely as the rate at which the worker is 'willing' to substitute leisure for income (without an explicit reference to the marginal utilities) then the same criticisms as those for the general case (in Section (ii) above) would apply; but they would be more readily convincing. First, the rate at which the individual is 'willing' to exchange leisure for income (unlike the case of apples and oranges) cannot be observed in the market. All that can be observed is the number of hours worked for a certain wage rate. Second, the rate of 'willingness' to substitute leisure for income, if it is to be determined independently of the market wage rate, must ultimately depend on subjective preferences just as this was true of the general case above; except that in this case the MRS, *however defined,* would be equal to an *absolute* amount of goods or money. It is worth mentioning that, assuming leisure involves both utility and disutility, then the 'ordinalist' approach would encounter problems in determining a unique equilibrium solution in analogy with the traditional version of the theory. We conclude that there is no substantial or methodological difference between the traditional and the modern versions of the neo-classical theory of consumer behaviour, except that – to its credit – the former uses a much simpler approach in order to obtain the same results. It is also candidly cardinalist. *Yet neither of these theories is consistent with logical positivist (or Popperian) methodology.* Indeed, the application of the term 'theory' to either of them requires a good deal of stretching.

THE METHODOLOGY OF POSITIVE ECONOMICS IN PRACTICE: III. THE FATE OF TESTABLE HYPOTHESES

To be sure, there are a number of neo-classical theories which *are* testable, and which have been put to test. Take the example of the Heckscher–Ohlin theorem of international trade. It predicts that a country with a relatively greater endowment of one factor of production, say capital, would export the commodities which use more capital in their production, and import those which use more labour. Investigating the further theoretical implications of this hypothesis, Samuelson discovered that, in such a case, inputs prices (e.g. the wage rate) should equalise across the trading countries.[12] This conclusion was so patently absurd that it should normally have destroyed the original theory on purely theoretical grounds; but it did not. Some time later, Leontief carried out an empirical test of the Heckscher–Ohlin theorem for the United States' pattern of international trade. The test was unsuccessful: it looked as if the United States, being endowed with relatively more capital than labour (in comparison with her trade partners) *imported* capital-intensive commodities – a result which was contrary to the prediction of the model. The response to this unfavourable (and unexpected) result was to hypothesise that the American labour force may be (perhaps 'three times') more efficient than that of her trade partners. If so, then the American economy would be more endowed with labour (measured in 'efficiency units') than capital.[13] On this interpretation the result of the Leontief test would be consistent with the prediction of the Heckscher–Ohlin model. This would certainly be a reasonable interpretation had the greater efficiency of American labour been established independently of the test and its result. Unfortunately this was not the case so that the assumption of greater efficiency could only be seen as an after-thought. That is to say, it appeared to be a circular argument in order to defend the theory against the apparent refutation of the empirical test; a theory, moreover, which had already been effectively refuted on grounds of logical absurdity.[14] Needless to say such 'empirical' tests sometimes involve the use of impure data and unreasonable technical assumptions which would make their results – whatever they may be – automatically suspect. But one wonders if there would have been a similar reaction if *the same procedure* had appeared to confirm the theorem. In general, if the tools of empirical investigations are held to be unreliable, why is it so necessary to test anything at all? We may be right in thinking that the Leontief test has not refuted the Heckscher–Ohlin theorem; but we would not be Positive Economists in that case. The episode has been since known as the Leontief Paradox. They do well to call it a paradox for indeed it is a paradox when a system of thought preaches a certain methodology which it does not observe; it is even a greater paradox when the same system of thought ruthlessly insists that alternative theories, both old and new, should observe the methodological criteria which the orthodoxy preaches but refuses to practice!

The case of the Phillips Curve – relating the rate of inflation to the rate of unemployment – is too well known to merit a long discussion. We shall simply mention those features of this episode which have not been emphasised before and which directly relate to the subject of our discussion. The Phillips relationship was originally not much more than a statistical generalisation from history.[15] Therefore, methodologically, it was neither Popperian nor logical positivist. Once it was presented it was not difficult to 'discover' some kind of theoretical basis for it. Within a very short period of time the Phillips relationship caught the imagination of economists so much so that, in retrospect, one could even speak of a Phillips Curve Industry: national and regional Phillips Curves using data for different countries and time-periods filled the learned journals. One or two critical doubts about the basis of the relationship were cast, but they were simply ignored.[16] Then, towards the end of the last decade, massive *indirect* evidence – i.e. the concurrent increase in the rates of inflation and unemployment – began to shake up conviction in the Phillips relationship. None the less a theoretical 'solution' to 'explain' even this massive 'anomaly' was soon discovered (Kuhnians please note) though this 'solution' has not been generally accepted. It was 'discovered' that the Phillips Curve has been 'shifting outwards'. But the 'solution' is inherently untestable for it depends on a knowledge of the *expected* rate of inflation and the circular concept of 'the natural rate of unemployment'. It *may* be correct – anything *may* be correct – but it turns Positive Economics upside down. . .

The question which remains to be answered is, Why? Why do Positive Economists claim they do what they do not do? Why do they expect others to do what they themselves do not do? It would be hard to provide a *direct* answer to this question. But it can be answered indirectly, by answering a related question: *How* is it possible to sustain this considerable gap between the theoretical claim and the actual practice? In one word, the answer to this question is Power. The established 'majority' has the power of appointing and disappointing members of the economic profession, and controlling the content of the learned journals. There is no 'secret conspiracy'; it is a self-justificatory mode of behaviour; or, if we are to believe Thomas Kuhn, it is the 'normal' scientific attitude. The critic of the method or substance of the theory does not have to be met by rational argument unless he has already been established by a fluke; he can be simply dismissed with contempt; he would also have to face the covert but real threat of reprisals. This is a fate which few men would risk of inviting to themselves in *any* social context. Those who do, may take some comfort in the fact that they have been 'struck not by a sin but by a catastrophe' (see, further, Chapter 5).[17]

POPPER, POSITIVE ECONOMICS AND THE LOGIC OF SOCIAL-SCIENTIFIC DISCOVERY

Popper has been wrongly identified as a logical positivist by friend an foe alike. By the group of Positive Economists who claim to be his followers; and by a group of philosophers and social scientists who reject logical positivism. This myth has been so widely believed that even on occasions Popper himself has felt impelled to deny it with some indignation.[18] Indeed, the myth is so strong that even a learned and dispassionate author such as Leszek Kolakowski seems to have believed it, although with some important reservations. For example, in his excellent (though brief) treatise on *Positivist Philosophy* he makes the claim that Popper's position 'dismisses all metaphysical doctrines and religious beliefs as meaningless'.[19] Some of the confusions may be due to the record of past personal associations; especially the fact that Popper was a personal friend of some members of the Vienna Circle – for example, Rudolph Carnap – at the height of this Circle's activities in Vienna. But, whatever the circumstantial evidence, there is no objective truth to the assertion that Popper is a logical positivist.

First, let us try and present a case as strongly as possible for those who claim that Popper's views are not significantly different from those of logical positivists. Popper suggests the criterion of falsifiability as the line of demarcation between science and non-science. This is fundamentally no different from the logical positivist rule of verifiability: what is falsifiable must be in some sense verifiable. Popper's description of the process of scientific discovery may be a little more sophisticated than the logical positivists': the process of falsification avoids the embarrassing problem of deciding on the number of sufficient tests for verification; but this merely improves the logical status and the realism of the logical positivist theory of knowledge. Popper, like logical positivists, regards metaphysics and value judgements as meaningless and nonsensical, and he believes in the uniqueness of scientific method. To sum up, both Popper and logical positivists (with minor differences) describe empirical testability and testing as the unique method of science which is applicable to all problem-solving disciplines (including the social sciences). And they both reject history as a useless source for the development of any body of scientific knowledge. What then is this alleged difference between Popper and the logical positivists, even though Popper himself may claim it exists?

For the sake of brevity the major differences between logical positivists and Popper may be outlined in the following way.

1. Logical positivism expects primary hypotheses to be formed by 'immediate' sense-experience or 'direct' observation; Popper, on the contrary, regards an initial hypothesis as a *theoretical* 'hunch', a conjecture, perhaps a value judgement or even a myth, which may be rooted in past (personal or historical) experience. He further argues that it is logically impossible to arrive at any hypothesis by 'direct' observation; in his own words: 'all observation is theory impregnated'.

2. Logical positivism describes a statement as scientific if and only if it is verifiable; Popper regards a statement as scientific if and only if it is falsifiable. These two are not logically identical criteria: what is verifiable is also falsifiable; but what is falsifiable may not be verifiable.

3. According to logical positivism all unverifiable statements – whether metaphysical or normative – are meaningless noises. According to Popper, unfalsifiable statements of whatever variety can be meaningful and contain significant knowledge; but they cannot be described as scientific knowledge unless and until they become falsifiable.[20] His theory of the growth of scientific knowledge states that science develops through a process whereby initial metaphysical and normative hypotheses are tested against experience. It follows that, although not all metaphysical and normative ideas would evolve into scientific theories, all scientific theories would have their roots in metaphysical and normative beliefs. Furthermore, we saw earlier that the logical positivist rejection of value judgements as (at best) tautological boomerangs against logical positivist philosophy itself. Popper faces no such dilemma, first because he does not hold value judgements as tautological and, second, because he openly admits that his own criterion of falsifiability is normative.[21]

4. Logical positivists demand the *verification* of scientific theories by *empirical tests*. This demand involves many problems, two of which are very important. The first problem is that the number of successful tests which are required to determine the truth of a theory is not (and cannot be) specified. The second problem is that once a theory is regarded as 'verified', there is no clear procedure for rejecting it if future events tend to falsify it. Popper demands the *falsification* of scientific theories by *rational and/or empirical criticism*. As long as a theory has not been falsified it may be retained; but it cannot be regarded as established for all time. This makes it easier both to accept the existing theories and to reject and replace them by new and better theories. Furthermore, the process of falsification is not purely empirical; it can be rational. As long as a theory is inherently open to argument, criticism and rejection, it could be subjected to attempts at falsification.

5. Both Popper and logical positivists insist on the uniqueness of scientific method. But the implications of their respective positions are quite different – indeed worlds apart. For logical positivist

scientific method is unique within the narrow confines of their own criteria. Popper regards scientific method as unique within the broad framework of openness to criticism. He has emphatically insisted that there is no such thing as *the* scientific method. The logical positivist view of 'the scientific method' had divided the social scientists into two groups: those who regard the application of *the* scientific method to social sciences as impossible because of the difficulties of satisfactory empirical testing and 'controlled experiments'; and those who would nevertheless claim that 'the scientific method' is capable of application to social sciences without, however, demonstrating it in their own practice. It used to be fashionable in the past two centuries to claim that all science (including social science) could be reduced to physics. This view may be described as *substantial reductionism*. The positivist claim that *the method* of all sciences can be reduced to *the method* of physics is the methodological analogue to that discredited view; it may be described as *methodological reductionism*. Anybody who rejects the first view must reject the second, unless he holds that the methods and results, the means and ends, of an intellectual activity are entirely separable. There can be no *complete* (logical or socio-logical) separation of the method and the substance of an inquiry: if economics cannot be entirely reduced to physics, then economic method cannot be completely reduced to the method of physics.

The above argument is consistent with Popper's view that *there is no single method of scientific discovery, even though the general approach to scientific discovery must be unique.* This general approach includes the following features: (i) it must be rational; (ii) it must be – at least in the first instance – theoretical; (iii) it must be realistic – i.e. it must be directed towards the solution of real problems; (iv) it must permit and encourage the emergence of bold and new ideas. Popper himself summarises the position in these words (which are borrowed from Marx): 'revolution in perman-ence'. We conclude that, according to this interpretation, Popper's logic of discovery is fundamentally different from the logical positi-vist philosophy. And, whereas scientific method in the sense of the latter neither is nor can be unique; in the sense of Popper, it both can and should be.

Popper's views have evolved and matured. Indeed, the late Imre Lakatos has identified 'three Poppers'. 'Popper 0' is the youthful philosopher who, according to scattered autobiographical remarks, rejected almost everything which was empirically unfalsifiable. Lakatos, describes this attitude as 'dogmatic falsificationism'.[22] 'Popper I' is the author of *The Logic of Scientific Discovery* (original German edition 1933) who developed his youthful outlook into a coherent epistemological philosophy; Lakatos describes this attitude as 'naïve falsificationism'. 'Popper II' – 'the sophisticated falsificationist' – is the author of numerous books and articles in the sixth, seventh (and now eighth) decade of this century who – if we are to believe Lakatos – makes a shallow compromise with Thomas Kuhn, and – as the saying goes – throws the baby out with the bath water.[23] In fact this so-called sophisticated falsificationist is a figment of imagination. But there is another 'Popper II'; a sophisticated falsificationist who regards openness, criticism, realism and novelty as the most fundamental features of scientific method. This attitude brings the *specific* methods of natural science down to earth. It gets rid of the metaphysical aura of respect which has surrounded them; and it makes a superficial emulation of these methods in the social sciences unnecessary, irrelevant and even dangerous. Any theory which is open to criticism contributes to scientific progress; any theory which is closed to criticism retards it. That is all.[24]

An assessment of Popper's philosophy, and its relevance to social sciences, would be dangerously incomplete without a discussion of Popper's critique of historicism. We shall present a brief and critical analysis of Popper on historicism in an appendix to this chapter. Meanwhile, we must emphasise here that Popper does not – indeed he cannot – regard historical knowledge as useless and irrelevant. He places the root of all scientific knowledge in history; he regards scientific progress as the process whereby *past mistakes* are corrected; he makes extensive use of historical knowledge in elaborating and demonstrating his own ideas; he taught himself Greek in order to read the classics in the original, because he felt that a great deal can be learned from their ideas and methods.[25] Yet the tragedy is that he, perhaps more than anyone else, is *used* as the authority for rejecting all historical knowledge as useless to the social sciences. We have now reached a stage where an orthodox economist rarely mentions the words history, economic history, even the history of economic thought, without a contemptuous downturn of the lower lip. History happens to be one of those rare subjects a knowledge of which would be almost indispensable to the progress of the social sciences. A knowledge of the history of ideas would provoke new theories, prevent boring repetitiveness, contribute to the acquisition of the admirable trait of intellectual modesty and, in general, put scientific problems in a broader perspective. Above all, it could make us wonder about the many ways in which we could be mistaken. Likewise, a knowledge of the history of events – itself not entirely independent from the history of ideas – could make men more tolerant, prevent the repetition of past mistakes, indicate the dynamics of 'the human nature' (and the network of social relations) and expose the evolutionary nature of social and economic institutions. We shall discuss this subject more extensively in Chapters 5, 6 and 7. Here we conclude that whoever has rejected *historical knowledge* as valueless, it cannot have been Popper. Positive Economists, 'Behavioral' Sociologists and the practitioners of the Science of Politics seem to have got it wrong again.

INSTRUMENTALISM AND POSITIVE ECONOMICS

In the history of science and philosophy there has always been a certain tension between theory and practice; ideas and instruments; thoughts and actions. This is not quite the same tension as that which exists between the pure scientist and the applied scientist, although the two tensions are somewhat related. The tension between ideas and instruments has its counterpart in popular debates such as whether art should be pursued for 'art's sake' or for 'the public good'. Such a debate is obviously not ideological: for example, there are both Marxist and non-Marxists who advocate 'art for the social good', even though they differ among themselves on the definition of 'the social good'.

Nicolò Machiavelli was perhaps the first prominent thinker of modern times who assessed the relevance and usefulness of a social idea *purely* by its success; that is, by its desired practical consequences. Both in *The Prince* and *The Discourses* he argued that political success is contingent upon the right course of action, which is in turn determined by 'the art of the possible' (these are not his words). This attitude has been generally interpreted as the philosophy of 'might is right'. Whatever we might think of Machiavelli's advice to Cesare Borgia – the prince to whom these political precepts were addressed – it looks as if it has been well taken by generations of politicians until this day. In some sense Machiavelli's attitude may be reduced to a total separation of 'what there is' and 'what there ought to be'. Therefore, those who believe in such a total separation should have no complaints against him.

Francis Bacon and Bishop Berkeley were not directly concerned with *social* philosophy when they advocated similar ideas about the nature and significance of scientific knowledge. Nevertheless they were social beings. Bacon himself was – up to a point in his career – a very successful politician of doubtful moral virtues: he was tried and condemned for a criminal abuse of his office. Berkeley was a religious dignitary, and this may have influenced his theory of knowledge. Yet we need not consider these facts in a logical assessment of their philosophies. Bacon's famous motto 'knowledge is power' summarises his belief in the value and significance of the *social consequences* of knowledge. This motto is in one sense tautological, and in another sense normative. Knowledge obviously affords the power which it is supposed to afford; for example, literacy makes men literate, and nuclear physics makes it possible to annihilate the human race. This is a tautology. Knowledge can also be sought *exclusively* for the power it creates over nature, society and individuals. In this case it would be a norm. And if we ought to seek knowledge exclusively for the attainment of *specific* powers, that would be an ideology. In this sense it would be the epistemological counterpart to the Machiavellian 'might is right'; or the Arabic expressions 'right lies in the sword' and 'he is right who wins'. This philosophy is normally known as instrumentalism. Berkeley's instrumentalism was probably an attempt to reconcile religious doctrines with scientific knowledge such that neither was abandoned for the sake of the other. For, if the value of scientific knowledge is in its practical (or technological) consequences *and nothing else,* then we may accept and use such knowledge without worrying about its deeper implications for ontological truths. Once again scientific knowledge becomes an instrument and nothing else.

In fact the total separation of ideas from action is neither logically nor sociologically possible. A theory which is empty of a real social and physical problem is at best a flight of fancy; an exercise in pure logic. A practical scientific achievement without any roots in veritable theoretical knowledge is at best an accident and (in any case) it would be very difficult to improve without further theoretical investigation. 'Right' cannot be exercised by a mere assertion; an empty boast. 'Might' cannot be right without a subjective definition of the latter. Even Hegel, who asserted that 'what is real is reasonable' ('might is right') also added that 'what is reasonable is real' ('right is might').

Since the latter half of the nineteenth century pragmatism and instrumentalism have been most influential among American philosophers. In particular, William James and John Dewey were the greatest advocates of these philosophies in the United States. William James's pragmatism is best expressed by his statement: 'if the concept of God works satisfactorily in the widest possible sense then it is true';[26] in other words, truth is usefulness and nothing else. For John Dewey a scientific theory was valid as long as it was technologically *useful*. It is important to note that, in its modern form, this philosophy is the product of the most purposive and technological society. That is why Russell pointed out – to John Dewey's indignation – that the latter's instrumentalist philosophy cannot be isolated from its social context.[27] The well-known American expression 'nothing succeeds like success' sums up both the logic and the sociology of this philosophy. Therefore, it is not surprising that instrumentalism has been so influential both among the dissenting, unorthodox, American neo-institutionalists, and among the established, orthodox, American 'Positive Economists'.

The *explicit* assertion of instrumentalism by 'Positive Economists' was a reaction to an increasing amount of evidence and criticism against the assumptions of neo-classical theory. In Chapter 1 we briefly mentioned Robbins's classification of neo-classical assumptions into 'the fundamental' and 'the auxiliary' categories. The fundamental assumptions were described as self-evident; it followed that all logical deductions based on these assumptions would be universally true in time and space. But the auxiliary assumptions were given a lower status. This argument was explicitly designed to prove the universal – *a*historical and *a*societal – truth of the most important economic theories.[28] However, the argument can be criticised on purely logical grounds, irrespective of the motive(s) involved. First, the definition of these classes of assumptions involves circularity: what is 'self-evident' must be Fundamental, and vice versa. In this way it is also self-defeating. For example the very fundamental assumptions of profit-maximisation and 'perfect knowledge' are anything but self-evident; therefore, they do not qualify to be in the class of fundamental assumptions as described by Robbins. Second, there is, and there can be, no self-evident truth about anything. Truth, any truth, is a subject for *discovery* by whatever method. It does not manifest itself except in spiritual inspirations which are beyond the reach of rational inquiry. There is such a thing as common sense, but this refers to a social *consensus* about the truth of a given problem – and it may be mistaken. Nothing was more a matter of common sense than the manifest idea that the earth is flat and stationary, and that the sun rotates around it. It was nevertheless incorrect. Apart from that, this argument by its very nature cannot prove the universality of anything: if self-evidence is the criterion, then what is 'self-evident' now may have been 'manifestly' false in the past.

In fact, Robbins's argument created more problems than it had intended to solve. For it placed the truth of economic theories squarely on the truth of its assumption. But the empirical truth of some of these assumptions began to be questioned when, for example, empirical research by survey methods tended to indicate that businessmen were more conscious of their average rather than marginal costs. The 'full-cost' theories of the late 1930s were a reaction to such findings. After the war Positive Economists had to face a dilemma: how can a body of logical positivist knowledge be based on empirically invalid or unverifiable assumptions? The simple answer to this question is that it cannot. To be consistent with logical positivism, primary hypotheses must be derived from immediate sense-experience. In order to face up to this problem some 'Positive Economists' resorted to instrumentalism as a line of defence, while still describing themselves as Positive Economists. Fritz Machlup, who had even had personal contact with the Old Vienna Circle, argued that the truth of the assumptions did not matter at all.[29] And when T. W. Hutchison rightly objected to this 'double-speak', Machlup accused him of being 'a reluctant ultra-empiricist'.[30] Milton Friedman's social and institutional affiliations were probably more consistent with instrumentalism than Machlup's; but, in any case, his systematic statement of instrumentalism (which he does not so name) appears as the leading article in a collection of essays entitled *Essays in Positive Economics*.[31] Many participants in the ensuing debate, notably Ernest Nagel, Andreas Papandreou, Jack Melitz and T. C. Koopmans, criticised Friedman's position on various logical grounds.[32] None, however, brought out its instrumentalist affiliations and none demonstrated the falsehood of its arguments from 'the' methodology of natural sciences.

Friedman tries to prove his case mainly by means of examples, all but one of which are imaginary and need not detain us. The one historical example he cites – Galileo's Law of Inertia – is truly important, and it should be taken seriously. He argues that the Law of Inertia – stating that a body freely falling in a vacuum accelerates at the rate of 32 feet per second – is based on an empirically false assumption because there is no such thing as vacuum. Therefore, the truth of the Law is demonstrated by its result alone; that is, by the fact that freely falling bodies do accelerate at such a rate. This argument suffers from several confusions. First, the assumption of vacuum is not false; for, vacuum conditions may be artificially created. It may be retorted that *perfect* vacuum cannot be created. But this is no argument: *nothing* can be *perfectly* known or created, for perfection itself is a religious or metaphysical abstraction. Whoever produced a perfect circle? Would it mean that the assumption of a circle is false? The Law of Inertia can be tested in 'imperfect' vacuum conditions within an insignificant margin of error; no science can do better than this. Second, let us suppose for a moment that Friedman is right; that the assumption of vacuum is false and that the Law of Inertia may be tested only by its results. Since, by assumption, vacuum does not and cannot exist, we can only test the Law by measuring the rate of acceleration of a body falling freely *in the atmosphere*. If we do so, we shall find the Law of Inertia is falsified; that is, we shall discover that freely falling bodies do *not* accelerate at the rate of 32 feet per second; they accelerate at lower rates. Hence, by assuming that the assumption of vacuum is false we reach the conclusion that *the prediction of the Law is also false*. Therefore, on Friedman's own premises, we should discard the Law of Inertia because, to use Friedman's own terminology, 'it does not work'.

It is on such a basis that Friedman goes on to claim that all scientific knowledge is a 'false-description' of reality; only it is a 'false description' 'which works', and, therefore, by the logic of William James, it must be 'true'. Here Friedman confuses description with abstraction. If an abstraction has a counterpart in reality at all, then it is not a 'false-description' of reality; it is intended as a true descripton of reality in a set of well-defined circumstances which, like any other description, may turn out to be true or false. Let us discuss the status of Friedman's own 'monetarism' with regard to his methodological instrumentalism. His monetarism is based on a version of the old quantity theory of money whose very important policy implications – in which Friedman and his followers have the greatest interest – is indispensably dependent on *the assumption* that the velocity of circulation of money is stable. He himself, and some of his followers, have 'tested' this assumption and reached the conclusion that it is correct. As is well known, their procedures for such tests and, therefore, their self-confirming results, are open to a great deal of argument. However, the question is: if the truth of the assumptions of a model do not matter at all for its 'usefulness', why do they – Friedman and the disciples – bother to test the assumption in this case, and claim that it is *empirically* correct? Now *the prediction* of the model is that the growth of the money supply beyond the level justified by the aggregate flow of goods and services would lead to price inflation through an 'artificial' expansion of aggregate demand. There is no doubt that a price inflation is normally accompanied by increases in the money supply. But this would not prove that the latter is *the cause* of the former – it could be the other way round. Therefore, in order to know *the direction of causation empirically,* we would have to know whether or not the velocity of circulation is stable: that is, *we would have to test the basic assumption of the model.* Otherwise we would end up with two opposing 'as if' hypotheses: (i) the (arbitrary) expansion of the money supply would result in price inflation 'as if' the velocity of circulation were stable; (ii) price inflation results in the expansion of the money supply 'as if' the velocity of circulation were *un*stable. We could then choose whichever 'as-ifism' would be in line with our prejudices and declare that the model, or its rival 'works'. This may indeed be 'useful' in an ideological – but not scientific – sense. But here we are concerned with science, not ideology – and so, apparently, is Friedman.

The instrumentalist interpretation of 'Positive Economics' has now quietly spread among many 'Positive Economists' without argument or criticism. As we have seen, the Friedman position is summarised such that if the prediction of a theory turned out to be true, we may conclude that the theory was true as if its assumptions were true. That is to say, once it has been shown that a theory 'works' we may 'pluck up' whatever assumption 'from the air' as its analytical basis. But the disciples have gone further than the master himself. For example, in their influential textbook, Ferguson and Gould categorically state that:

> For the purpose of *explaining* business behaviour it is sufficient to assume that entrepreneurs act *as if* they tried to maximise profit. For the purpose of predicting business behaviour the *as if* assumption is the only justifiable one [emphasis in the original].[33]

It is likely that even Machiavelli, Bacon, Berkeley, James and Dewey would have repudiated the first sentence of this (unargued) statement. However, they further add that:

> *In any area of thought* a theoretician does not select his assumptions on the basis of their realism; the conclusions and not the assumptions are tested against reality [emphasis added].

Finally they issue the following statement which – for all those endowed with some critical faculty – we record here in silence:

> That is, perfect competition frequently *works* [emphasis in the original] as a theoretical model of economic processes. *The most persuasive evidence supporting this assertion is the fact that despite the proliferation of more 'sophisticated' models of economic behaviour, economists today probably use the model of perfect competition in their research more than ever before* [emphasis added].[34]

A learned journal's anonymous referee once wrote (apparently with approval) that economists are, generally, logical positivists in theory and instrumentalists in practice. That is an appropriate epitaph both for logical positivism and for Positive Economics. We have already seen how these practical instrumentalists react to the discovery that a cherished theory '*does not work*'. The examples of the Heckscher–Ohlin theory, the cost curves, the Phillips Curve and many more, are a salutary reminder for that. *They are therefore not even consistent instrumentalists.* If 'it works' then it must be true as if its assumptions were true. If it 'does not work' then there must be a fault in our vision, or the assumptions must be false. Come what may *it must be true* because 'we use it more than ever before'. Paul Douglas, the late distinguished American economist, reflecting on some personal experiences reminiscent of the above standards, once quoted the following Ruba'i from Omar Khayyam:[35]

> Myself, when young, did eagerly frequent,
> Doctor and Saint [or Sage] and heard great argument
> about it and about, but ever more,
> came out by the same door wherein I went!

CONCLUDING REMARKS

In this chapter we tried to fulfil a number of interrelated tasks. We argued that logical positivism is *logically* untenable: because it insists that initial hypotheses must be derived from immediate sense-experience; it regards metaphysics as nonsense and value judgements as inherently tautological; and it demands verification exclusively by direct empirical tests – in particular, the application of these criteria invalidate logical positivism itself.

Our discussion of Positive Economics showed that: in theory, there has been some confusion between Popper and logical positivists among Positive Economists; in practice, Positive Economists do not adhere to their own criteria of scientificity; some of them have shifted their methodological grounds to instrumentalism which is strictly inconsistent with the logical positivist – and in open conflict with Popperian – philosophy; and, finally, even the instrumentalists are not consistent with their own instrumentalism in practice.

Our interpretation of Popper's philosophy was intended to show the basic difference between him and logical positivists which is, nevertheless, much less than the difference between him and Positive Economists. In addition, it purported to indicate the way in which Popper's logic of scientific discovery may be relevant to the social sciences once its most fundamental elements – namely openness, receptivity and criticism – are emphasised. It included a critique of Popper on historicism – not on point of substance but on point of reference – and its unjustified consequence for the use of historical knowledge in scientific and social progress which he himself cannot have intended.

The entire discussion of this chapter was on the logic of the growth of scientific knowledge in general, and of economic knowledge in particular. But scientific activity – as a part of the pursuit of all knowledge – is not merely a *logical* but also a *social* and *psychological* process. Indeed we had occasions to allude to some sociopsychological factors even within the present logical context. Men, including men of science, are not logical automata but – to quote Aristotle – 'social animals', and psychological entities. Their past personal, cultural and social histories are likely to affect their systems of valuation, their modes of thinking and even their analytical methods. In one word, men are not God! Therefore, scientific research, as all things human, is influenced by categories which are not strictly logical. Personal interests, moral values and ideological outlooks – however these may be defined – make up a part of this influence. These concepts and issues will be discussed in Chapter 6. But the academic community as a distinct profession has certain attributes which, within the social context, may even transcend moral and ideological predilections; that is to say, attributes which, within given professional networks, may result in similar patterns of academic behaviour even when ideologies are different. Chapters 4 and 5 discuss some rival explanations of this specific problem and the light which it could shed on the growth of economic knowledge.

APPENDIX

A CRITICAL NOTE
ON POPPER'S CRITIQUE OF HISTORICISM

POPPER ON HISTORICISM

Popper's attack on historicism as a logically invalid and a sociologically unacceptable approach to scientific discovery has been clearly and forcefully stated in his *The Poverty of Historicism*. His other famous book – *The Open Society and its Enemies*, which also contains a (less) systematic attack on historicism – has a wider scope. He describes historicism as the pseudo-scientific approach to the discovery of objective knowledge which purports to formulate laws and theories on the basis of *direct generalisations* from history. This in fact is what the Comteans and the economists of the German Historical School had tried to do. Historicism has two important implications. First, that *the* scientific method – that is, *the* method of the natural sciences – is Empiricist: 'it begins with observation and it derives theories and laws from it'. Second, that the future course of history is accurately predictable: 'social phenomena, like natural phenomena, are preordained and predetermined'. We have had many occasions in this book to prove the falsehood of the first implication. As for the second implication all that can be logically said is that determinism – like indeterminism – is a metaphysical notion; therefore, it is scientifically indeterminate. For all we know it may be true; but we simply do not know. As Alexander Gerschenkron once brilliantly put it: 'how can we know what we would know if we knew?[36] Sociologically there can be little doubt that determinism – 'soft' or 'hard', historical or otherwise – would completely destroy all notions of morality, freedom and responsibility.[37] Therefore, the poverty of historicism is, in fact, the twin poverty of Empiricism and determinism. We concur entirely in this view of historicism.

Unfortunately, in attacking historicism Popper has made two eventful mistakes. The first mistake is that he has identified Marx's method – and his broader outlook – as being essentially historicist. The second mistake is his belief that orthodox economics pursues a scientific method along the lines which he himself has identified. These mistakes have had two unfortunate consequences. First, they have led a group of philosophers and social scientists (not exclusively Marxist) to reject Popper's ideas without learning more about them. Second, they have provided a good excuse for orthodox social scientists to reject *all historical knowledge* as irrelevant to the study of society. It is unfortunate that a full critical discussion of Popper on these issues is not possible within the limited compass of this book. All that can be done is to present some partial arguments and evidence in support of our claim that neither Marx was a historicist, nor orthodox economics is scientific in any sense which is acceptable by Popper.

MARX AND HISTORICISM

In this section we intend to show, by argument and evidence, that Marx was neither a historicist nor a historical determinist. In other words, the accent is on Marx's method, not his ideas, even though methods and ideas are not entirely separable. Let it be said at once that this brief (and necessarily incomplete) argument is not intended to defend the person of Karl Marx, whom, in any case, Popper has described as a serious scholar and a lover of real freedom.[38]. Nor is it meant as an apology or a defence of Marxist ideology if only because this has been done by many rational and irrational defenders of greater fame and fortune. Finally, we state categorically that Marx – unlike God, his prophets *and* all the upholders of intellectual bigotry – was fallible; therefore, in principle, he is not immune from rational criticism.

Popper's criticism of Marx is mainly based on the two interrelated charges that he was a methodological historicist, and a metaphysical determinist. Let us examine (some of) the evidence to determine the truth of these assertions. To begin with, it is important to note that Marx was a prolific writer on a variety of subjects over a period of some forty years. *The Paris Manuscripts* of 1844 betrays no historicist tendencies at all; it also rejects historical determinism. That is also true of *The Poverty of Philosophy* – the polemic against Proudhon – which was Marx's first full publication on political economy. In this book his total reliance on Ricardo for his economic arguments and his mockery of Proudhon's pseudo-Hegelian philosophising would leave little room for a charge of historicism. In *The German Ideology,* co-authored with Engels, he attacked both the Hegelian idealistic determinism, and Feuerbach's materialistic determinism. The Eleventh Thesis on Feuerbach emphasised the significance of human action in changing the world. *The Communist Manifesto* was what its title said. It was a political manifesto addressed to political activists engaged in a real struggle. As with all such manifestos it involved the use of an emotional language, exaggeration and over-optimism. It was published and distributed in the midst of a revolution. Yet, even this included a reformist programme, including full franchise, national health, etc., most of which, by now, have been taken for granted in many Western countries. Marx's evaluation of the Bonapartist coup of 1851, and the personal role of Louis Bonaparte – in his famous *The Eighteenth Brumaire of Louis Bonaparte* – is a brilliant and realistic analysis which should be a shining example for all the historicists, behaviourists and believers in 'conceptual truths' on how a conscientious piece of social analysis is conducted. Likewise, in his assessment of the rise and fall of the Paris Commune (1870–1) he was guided neither by emotionalism nor by inevitability. He recognised that the Commune was engineered by the (misconceived) actions of its promoters; and it failed also because of their mistakes. He wept bitterly over their indiscriminate massacre by the victors; but he did not overlook the errors of the victims. Marx's 'pure' economic theory, his attempt to produce a 'general equilibrium model' for the capitalist economy (which we believe to have been misdirected) used a method which was the very antithesis of historicism and Empiricism; in its technicalities it was Ricardian and nothing else. In fact the only possible issue (among so many) which may give the faintest impression of historicism in Marx's method, is his theory social dynamics of socio-economic development. Let us, then, investigate Marx's method at its 'weakest' point.

Marx's view of social development – like Popper's view of scientific progress – was evolutionist; that is, he believed in progressive change in economic technology and social institutions. It was for this reason that he embarrassed Darwin by offering to dedicate *Capital* to his name (nevertheless in a short passage he dismisses Darwin's own Malthusian interpretation of his theory which became a basis for the ideology of Social Darwinism[39]). All of the five most important socio-economic modes which he identified had been already recognised by other thinkers before him. The case of the primitive communal society somewhat corresponded to the earlier concepts of 'the state of nature' except that Marx's primitive society was not a wholly abstract 'model': it was a societal – not *pre*societal – state where ownership, production, distribution and specialisation were all carried out on a communal basis. Both then and later anthropological reports – from Maine and McLennan to Malinowsky and Evans-Pritchard – confirmed the reality of such social organisations even in some contemporary primitive societies. The classical slave-based political economy of Greece and Rome had been well known. So had the medieval feudal society of Europe – Adam Smith is as good a source on this as any other. So was the capitalist industrial society which had emerged almost before their bewildered eyes. The 'unfamiliar' features of Asiatic societies had been noticed and analysed since the Greeks. Montesquieu, Adam Smith, James Mill and Hegel had all had their say on that subject. Marx neither invented these types of society nor even discovered them. There was no inductive generalisation from history.

Marx in fact tried to discover a *theory* in order to explain such basic transformations. In doing so he made two important observations. One, that the most outstanding distinguishing feature of these social models was the dominant form of property (slaves, land and bondage, capital, etc.), the nature of property ownership (private or communal) and the available productive technology. Two, that if and when productive technology advances so much that it cannot be accommodated within the existing institutional framework, the society would be transformed through the intervention of those social classes which would benefit most from such a transformation. He then resorted to a detailed study of history in order to fill in his theory with factual evidence. Let us – for the sake of argument – suppose that his theory is wholly mistaken. But how can this method be regarded as *historicist*. Marx did not stop at this. He further investigated in detail the causes of the English industrial revolution. Turgot, Adam Smith and Ricardo, before him, had all identified capital accumulation as the most important cause of economic growth. Marx proposed the *theory* of primary capital accumulation – the accumulation of capital over a very long period as a *precondition* for industrialisation. This was a falsifiable hypothesis; and it has been falsified. The German industrialisation under Bismark, the industrialisation of north Italy after the Risorgimento, the industrialisation of Japan in the Meiji period, industrialisation in Russia and the Soviet Union – although in all cases they confirmed the indispensability of capital accumulation for industrialisation, they demonstrated that accumulation could be not only a *precondition* but also a *condition* for it: you could industrialise almost concurrently with accumulation.

However, it was on the basis of his *theory* of social change, described above, that Marx predicted the advent of the socialist society. This was neither prophetic nor Utopian. Like any piece of scientific prediction it was based on well-defined and rigorous conditions. It was on those conditions – such as the growth of unemployment due to overproduction, the decline of the rate of profit because of accumulation, the misery and disenfranchisement of workers around him who truly had little 'to lose but their chains' . . . – that he regarded the socialist revolution as inevitable. This is neither historicist nor deterministic. Some of those conditions were fulfilled; others were not, partly due to factors which he did not foresee (for example the role of imperialism in extending the market for industrial goods), and partly due to the direct and indirect ideas of men like himself. It was not he who was holistic and Utopian; it was the Utopian Socialists whom he criticised for hoping to bring about a *total* change under *any* circumstances.

Marx was a scientist not only because he combined analysis and fact, theory and practice in providing precise explanations and solutions for *real* problems – which may or may not have been mistaken. More importantly he was a scientist because more than anything else he was critical and anti-dogmatic; and he was also intellectually honest with himself and others. He once described the suppression of truth as 'the sin against science'. He neither wrote Engels's *Anti-Dühring* not Bukharin's *Historical Materialism*, nor Stalin's *Dialectical and Historical Materialism*. If 'by their fruit shall ye know them' – which Eric Roll cites as a summary judgement on Marx – is a valid criterion, then the great physicists of early twentieth century must be held responsible for the catastrophe of Hiroshima; Christ must take the blame for the Spanish Inquisition; and His phantom deserved to have been burned at the stake by the Grand Inquisitor of Dostoevsky's *Brothers Karamazov*, whose authority was 'based' on His teaching.

ORTHODOX ECONOMICS AND SCIENCE

Popper has asserted, more than once, that economics has demonstrated the applicability of scientific method to the social sciences. We have no quarrel with the view that scientific method – as it was outlined in our interpretation of Popper's philosophy – both can and should be used in the social sciences. But the claim that the actual practice of orthodox economics is scientific – coming from Popper – is truly astonishing. We have already discussed at some length the truth about the 'scientific method' of Positive Economics. Apart from that, this is a 'science' which is more 'holistic' than all the holists. A substantial portion of mathematical economic theory is not even directed to the explanation and solution of problems which exist in reality; let alone having a factual and empirical content. At the other extreme, there are economists who *begin* by looking at data and manipulating them either in order to 'discover' a problem or to set up an empirical model and 'derive conclusions' from it. Some of these issues will be discussed more extensively in the following chapters. The only explanation of this otherwise mysterious view of Popper's on orthodox economics is that he must have been misinformed by economists themselves. Hayek once complained that he had been misled by philosophers and scientists into accepting positivism (not logical positivism) as the true method of natural sciences. As he makes it abundantly clear, Popper could have had no share in this.[40] It is not unlikely that Popper has been misled on the methodology of orthodox economics by economists whose judgement he trusted. There simply can be no other explanation.

4

PARADIGMS, PROGRAMMES AND THE DEVELOPMENT OF ECONOMIC KNOWLEDGE

PIECEMEAL CHANGES AND TOTAL TRANSFORM-ATIONS

The growth of anything is gradual and continuous, and its development is periodic and discrete. This contrast between growth and development has been observed in organisms, individuals, social entities and bodies of knowledge. The foetus grows continuously in the womb, but it develops into a full human being shortly before birth. A child grows and changes gradually, but he goes through a major transformation over the period of puberty. Economies and societies are in constant evolution, but they undergo basic and radical reorganisations on few occasions. Clearly, growth is a necessary condition for development; just as clearly, it may not be a sufficient condition. Individuals may grow without developing into mature human beings, and ideas may evolve without succeeding to add significantly to the existing knowledge. Indeed, there is no reason or evidence why development itself should be necessary – i.e. inevitable – in all comparable cases. Even the Darwinian and other theories of biological evolution do not claim such an inevitability. The fact that a group of apes, bears or whatever, may have once evolved into human forms does not mean that the existing apes are likely to follow suit some time in the future. Unfortunately, this is a simple lesson which – in a wide variety of fields – seems to be readily forgotten: even if development itself is inevitable it does not follow that *all* development is inevitable. Indeed, it is likely that in the fields of human thought and action no development would be possible without a commensurate supply of effort.

The history of scientific progress seems to lend support to the hypothesis of the continuity of growth and the unevenness of development. We note and speak of the Copernican Revolution in astronomy, the Newtonian Revolution in mechanics, the Darwinian Revolution in biology, the Keynesian Revolution in economics . . . such references make it clear that certain developments in the history of various sciences have been so fundamental that they may be regarded as altogether rare and extraordinary. Clearly, knowledge has been growing in the past few centuries but there are only few instances of historic moment. Yet, these observations by themselves do not provide us with any *theory* of scientific process. The question is how these basic transformations occur and whether or not they share a common process.

Thomas Kuhn's theory of scientific revolutions is an attempt to supply an answer to the above, and related, questions. It must be stated at once that Kuhn's use of the concept of scientific revolution is much wider in scope than it was implied in our introductory note. Specifically, Kuhn seems to regard almost *any* scientific advance – any real increase in scientific knowledge – as a 'revolution'. In other words, revolutions in the sense of Kuhn do not necessarily have to be of a kind of earth-shaking significance which is associated, say, with the Darwinian Revolution. Many historical examples of 'scientific revolution' which he cites are no more than piecemeal and partial advances. This is an important observation because it shows that his theory is in fact concerned with describing the process of scientific *change,* be that growth or development. The question then arises: in what sense do we have to regard any real increase in the existing knowledge as a scientific *revolution?* Kuhn's answer to this question may be surmised to be the following: because all such real increases in knowledge – big and small – occur only on certain occasions and as a result of considerable struggle. Therefore, in Kuhn's usage of the term it is the *resistance* to a new theory which seems to define its revolutionary status. Nevertheless, many of his readers, especially among the social scientists, have tended to interpret his theory as a description of the process of *major scientific transformations*; that is, of revolutions in the much narrower sense. This (partial) misunderstanding of the scope and significance of Kuhn's theory may account for some of its all too sudden success, particularly among social scientists. Another reason for this popularity is the claim that Kuhn's model offers a 'sociological' analysis of scientific progress. This is a debatable claim which we shall put to critical examination later in this, and the following, chapter.

Whatever the reasons, Kuhn's theory of *The Structure of Scientific Revolutions* quickly captured – if not captivated – the imagination of many in different fields, and with diverse ideological outlooks. It claimed many converts not only among philosophers and natural scientists; but, perhaps, more widely among social scientists, including economists. And, among the latter group, it not only attracted radicals and other dissenting and critical tendencies; it also persuaded a good number of the orthodox and the conservatives. Yet, in general, the 'Kuhnian' economists, and other social scientists, tended to apply the theory to their own fields without adequate assessments of it within its own context, or sufficient rigour in its application to their own disciplines. At any rate, little was said or written about what this theory would make of Positive Economics which still survived (and survives) autonomously in the minds of some Kuhnian converts. In this chapter we shall discuss the theories of Kuhn – and following from this – Lakatos, together with their attempted applications to the history and methods of economics.

THE STRUCTURE OF SCIENTIFIC REVOLUTIONS

Kuhn defines 'normal science' as the proper realm of (normal) scientific activity. Normal science itself is based on some significant scientific achievement in the past. This historical achievement – described as a 'paradigm' – sets the boundaries for the 'research agenda' of (normal) scientific work. The research agenda will not include a critical investigation of the established paradigm; on the contrary, it is the ruling paradigm which defines the terms of reference of normal science, and the scope and limits of the research agenda. It follows that normal science is a dogged, routine and almost unexciting occupation whereby scientists concentrate their efforts on solving 'puzzles'. These puzzles may have been left unresolved on the original succession of the ruling paradigm, or encountered by its further cultivation. Hence, no scientist would waste his energies by challenging the foundations of the dominant paradigm: the discovery or occurrence of counter-instances would be simply regarded as new 'puzzles' requiring solution.

The paradigm begins to be threatened only upon a systematic emergence of serious 'anomalies' which cannot be ignored or accommodated for long – in particular a persistent and significant inconsistency between the paradigm and 'nature' (i.e. the empirical world). Indeed, so significant and stubborn these anomalies may be that they may lead to a scientific 'crisis'. Yet, even the mere advent of a crisis will not be sufficient to overthrow the ruling paradigm. In Kuhn's own words:

> Though [the scientists] may begin to lose faith and then to consider alternatives, they do not renounce the paradigm that has led them into crisis.[1]

Only the emergence of an alternative paradigm which can resolve or accommodate (at least) the more important anomalies, would provide the sufficient condition for the rejection of the existing, dominant, paradigm:

> To reject one paradigm without simultaneously substituting another is to reject science itself. That act reflects not on the paradigm but on the man. Inevitably, he will be seen by his colleagues as the carpenter who blames his own tools.[2]

A 'scientific revolution' occurs when both those conditions – the emergence of a crisis *and* an alternative paradigm – are fulfilled. It is at this point that resistance to change weakens and finally breaks down. The establishment of the new paradigm at one and the same time meets three important requirements: it provides a solution to the scientific crisis; it affords a new (scientific) 'world view' (which is perhaps what is normally called a 'conceptual framework'); and, finally, it supplies an alternative research agenda for the scientists to work on. Henceforth the revolution subsides and normal science resumes its puzzle-solving function within the new paradigm.

Kuhn's theory has a number of broadly attractive and novel features worth mentioning. It was presented at a time when most (empiricist) theories of knowledge tended to give a lopsided emphasis to the logic, as opposed to the sociology, of scientific research. It offers (at least to some extent) a descriptive rather than a normative theory of scientific progress. It provides some insight into the (normal) scientist's view of his role and function *vis-à-vis* his subject, his profession, and the human society. It even offers implicit advice on how to succeed (or fail) as a member of the scientific community: it appears that 'success' may be more due to conformism than originality; and 'failure' may often result from a combination of creativity and criticism. Yet, the theory can be criticised on some important grounds.

A critique of Kuhn's theory may be organised along the following lines. First, we must assess the theory in its own context, and in relation to the natural (or 'mature') sciences to which it refers. Second, we must apply the theory to the history and method of economics and determine its relevance to the 'structure of revolutions' in economic science.

An assessment of the theory in its own context raises issues regarding precision and clarity, logic, method, sociology and so forth. In relation to clarity, one of the earliest problems encountered by Kuhn's theory is the *exact* meaning and significance of the concept of paradigm. In the postscript to the second edition of his book, Kuhn himself acknowledges this problem; in fact, he cites a 'sympathetic reader' as saying that 'the term is used in at least twenty-two different ways'.[3] His own solution is that with some 'editorial work done, two very different usages of the term would remain'. He calls the first usage 'disciplinary matrix' and the second 'shared examples'. A disciplinary matrix is composed of 'paradigms, paradigm parts or paradigmatics' which 'form a whole and function together'. The most helpful interpretation of the disciplinary matrix (for someone brought up with *pre*-Kuhnian terminology) is to regard it as a set of basic ideas, a system of thought or conceptual framework (making up the paradigm) which encompasses a number of theories, hypotheses and concepts (corresponding to paradigm parts of paradigmatics). But it is unlikely that Kuhn would agree to this interpretation and, therefore the ambiguity still remains: his own emphasis is more on the *types* (rather than *categories*) which compose the matrix – e.g. 'symbolic generalisations', 'metaphysical paradigms', etc., which need not be pursued further in this essay. Kuhn's description of the second usage of paradigm – i.e. shared examples – is less ambiguous but little short of a full quotation could make its meaning clear. Perhaps the most important function of shared examples is their tacit but fundamental contribution to the development of a common scientific language and – more significantly – a common approach to similar problems not yet encountered by the individual scientist. Be that as it may, neither usage of the concept of paradigm helps clear an important, almost central, question. It is this: does the theory of scientific revolutions only apply to wider systems of thought, conceptual frameworks or whatever; or does it equally apply to all the models and theories based on such a system or framework? From the historical illustrations in the main text the reader gains the impression that they are *all* subject to the process described by Kuhn; but this is nowhere clearly stated.

The distinction is important on both historical and psychological grounds. On the one hand, since the theory tends to be a *historical generalisation* about scientific progress it would require many more examples of cases where even theories and hypotheses limited in scope are seen to have resisted change with the tenacity of broader paradigms. On the other hand, it would be easier to grasp the psychology of 'the scientific community' in sticking to its *total* framework of thinking and research until it reaches a dead end; but it is not clear why it should do so in the case of less important theories the rejection of which may neither threaten the basic framework, nor 'the scientific community' as a whole. Indeed, why not sacrifice a small part in order to strengthen the whole?

There is a fair amount of circularity in the Kuhnian theory. For example the concepts of normal science, crisis, scientific revolution, etc., are somewhat circular, though some circularity of this kind may be regarded as unavoidable. But the very process and structure of scientific revolutions itself is in danger of being no more than a tautology, and this is something which cannot be easily overlooked. The problem is this: the process of *scientific* revolutions as described by Kuhn is, to say the least, the most important line of distinction between 'mature' and 'immature' science; it is only *mature* sciences which are dominated by a single paradigm, while *immature* sciences – still being in the period of their scientific prehistory – are infested with competing paradigms or schools. This distinction is precisely what gives the theory its rigour and selectivity; or, in other words, makes it look like a theory rather than a tautology. Yet, both the theory and its wider factual content tend to be true of all times, all places, all disciplines, all science, all art and, indeed, the process of change in the entire sphere of human existence. Consider the following examples as evidence. The 'paradigm' of Judaism was replaced by the 'paradigm' of Christianity; the 'paradigms' of Zoro-astrianism and of the Eastern Christian Churches were replaced by the Islamic 'paradigm'. The 'paradigm' of romanticism gave way to the 'paradigm' of realism (in the nineteenth-century European literature) which in turn surrendered to the 'paradigms' of expressionism, surrealism, Socialist Realism and so forth. Impressionism swept aside the 'paradigms' of expressionism and Pre-Raphaelitism, while Cubism – in the teeth of stubborn opposition – overthrew Impressionism. The 'paradigm' of *Pax Romana* was defeated and replaced by the 'paradigm' of feudalism, itself finally destroyed by the paradigm of capitalism through the English Revolution ('Civil War'), the Glorious Revolution (1688), the French Revolution, the Industrial Revolution, etc. The competing 'paradigms' of the Persian and Byzantine Empires were overthrown by the single paradigm of the Islamic Empire. . . . It would take too long, but in all such cases it is possible to present a detailed description of related 'anomalies' and 'crises' no less 'convincing' than the examples cited by Kuhn from the history of *mature* sciences. Kuhn himself is aware of this fact, but — if anything — his response seems to reinforce the objection:

> Historians of literature, of music, of the arts, of political development, and of many other human activities have long described their subjects in the same way. . . . If I have been original with respect to concepts like these, it has mainly been by applying them to the sciences, fields which had been widely thought to develop in a different way.[4]

Here, an important point seems to have been overlooked. 'Historians of literature, etc.' do not *distinguish* their subject from all other fields by these universal, tautological, characteristics of the process of change. Nor could they do so precisely *because* they seem to be true of all times, all places, and all human activities. More significantly, they do not distinguish 'mature' literature (or art) from 'immature' literature on the grounds that the former would have the peculiarities of 'literary revolutions', and the latter would not. . . . There are even examples of the Kuhnian *immature sciences* – which incorporate competing paradigms – where each *one* paradigm would seem to display characteristics similar to those which Kuhn describes for the single, dominant, paradigm of *mature sciences.* This tautology has two separate, though related, aspects. The first aspect concerns a line of demarcation for 'mature' and 'immature' sciences (if not for science and non-science). Clearly Kuhn's theory of the process of scientific revolutions does not solve this problem, as it is shared by mature science, immature science, non-science and even non-intellectual fields. It is possible that Kuhn has tacitly assumed Popper's rule of *falsifiability* as the distinguishing feature of science from non-science. If so, the difference between Kuhn and Popper would reduce itself *not* to a disagreement on the normative criterion of *falsifiability,* but on the descriptive process of *falsification.* That is, where Popper argues that the process of scientific discovery consists of *continuous attempts* to falsify refutable hypotheses, Kuhn would maintain that scientific progress takes place *occasionally* when the same refutable hypotheses meet with a crisis, and change through a revolution – i.e. falsification is accepted by the scientific community only in *extraordinary* circumstances.

The assumption of falsifiability cannot be easily discerned from the original text of Kuhn's monograph, or its later postscript. However, in his later remarks Kuhn almost categorically admits to the implicit assumption of testability in his model.[5] This may resolve the *first,* normative, aspect of the problem, but its *second,* descriptive, aspect would still remain: if scientific progress shares the same general characteristics with all other developments, then what is the difference between the structure of *scientific* (let alone *mature-*scientific) revolutions, and all the rest? If there is none, then what we have is a statement of the structure of *revolutions* in general – a mere tautological claim that all ideas, systems, relations, etc., change when confronted by a crisis and a more 'acceptable' alternative. That is all!

So much for problems of clarity and logic which arise from Kuhn's theory. There are, however, further problems associated with his *method.* Kuhn's theory is supposed to be a historical (or empirical) law, a general theory formulated by 'inductive' generalisation from historical facts. If so, it would have to face the charge of pure Empiricism or (its equivalent) historicism. There are (at least) two problems associated with purely Empiricist (and historicist) generalisations. The first problem is that even if they describe a certain pattern in the past (or at present) accurately, they do not tell us anything about the future pattern. The second problem is that pure Empiricism, (or historicism) is logically impossible: the researcher must have an *a priori* impression of what he is looking for before he examines the 'facts'. It is not unlikely that Kuhn had already had this 'impression' from his casual observations of *contemporary* scientific behaviour, before he examined the history of science carefully in order to verify his hypothesis by corroborative evidence from history. Yet since his historical evidence is necessarily selective and limited, the danger remains that he may have generalised *the contemporary* scientific behaviour to all times past.,

There is yet another problem associated with Kuhn's *method*. His approach is (one way or the other) historical, implying that history in general is marked by periodic revolutionary changes. If this is the case, then how is it possible that *a part of that history*, the history of the process of scientific progress, has remained *unchanged* since the fall of Adam? How can the process of scientific discovery have remained the same as in Ancient Greece; in semi-feudal mercantile Europe of the seventeenth century; in the early capitalist period of the following two centuries. . . ? This observation turns the supposedly most distinctive ('historical' and 'sociological') features of Kuhn's theory on their heads; it reveals its essentially ahistorical character. We shall return to this point in Chapter 5.

One last point about Kuhn's *method*. It had been widely believed that Kuhn's theory is descriptive or positive, as opposed to prescriptive or normative. This belief was (partially) mistaken for it is fairly clear from the original text itself that Kuhn's theory has been intended to be both descriptive and prescriptive – that is, both describing how scientific progress takes place, and prescribing how it ought to take place. For example, his claim that a scientist who (even in a 'crisis') gives up the dominant paradigm (in the absence of an alternative) would be viewed as 'the carpenter who blames his own tools' is a hint at his own value judgement. In any case he has now explicitly confirmed that his theory is both positive and normative.[6] Therefore Kuhn's theory may be restated in the following manner: *as a matter of fact* sciences progress through the process described by Kuhn; besides, they *ought to* progress that way. More explicitly, normal science is what normal scientists do, and what normal scientists do is *right*. This position could be defended by the following argument. Science has progressed precisely through the process described by Kuhn; therefore if it is to progress further this should be the correct scientific attitude. This argument, however, confuses simple description with casual explanation. Suppose that Kuhn's description of the characteristics of scientific progress is logically consistent and historically incontrovertible; even then, there would be nothing in it which proves that these characteristics are the cause, or causes, of scientific progress (in fact there is *no* casual explanation in Kuhn's theory at all). For it would be equally plausible to argue that (for some other reasons) scientific advance has been possible *in spite of* the kind of resistance to change put forward by normal scientists. The least that can be claimed with equal plausibility is that scientific progress might have been even more rapid and impressive had scientists been more critical of the ruling paradigm at every stage. Let us nevertheless suppose, for the sake of argument, that the process described by Kuhn is an indubitable *fact* and the certain *cause* of scientific progress. Even on the basis of such a wild assumption the value judgement that 'normal scientists ought to do what they in fact do' would imply that *normal science is right because it is successful*. This is an ideological view of scientific as well as social progress, and it is a poor comment on life in the Great Technological Society. We shall look at this issue again when, in Chapter 5, we discuss the social context (or the sociology) of normal science, or, rather, normal academic profession.

OF PARADIGMS AND REVOLUTIONS IN THE HISTORY OF ECONOMICS

Kuhn's theory was greeted with an extraordinary enthusiasm by social scientists, including economists. New theories must be given a reasonable and respectable, but critical, reception even though that would be against the spirit of 'normal science'. But a merely positive response to a new *fashion* is neither critical, nor respectable. Yet it was not only the novelty and fashionableness of Kuhn's theory which accounted for its extraordinary success among social scientists; it was also its peculiar appeal both to conservatives and to radicals on the basis of their (widely differing) predilections. The conservatives (rightly) thought that the new theory would justify their habitual resistance to change; the radicals (wrongly) believed that it could be used to sound the bells of (scientific) revolutions. This interest was not confined to the historians and philosophers of economics; it extended widely into the conversations and publications of the 'non-specialists'. In economics the term 'neo-classical paradigm' became – and still remains – almost a household designation for neo-classical economic theory. To quote one example the authors of an article on 'Neo-classical *versus* Evolutionary Theories of Economic Growth', wrote, in its preamble:

> In economics [*as in physics*] what we refer to as theory is more a set of basic premises . . . *than a set of testable propositions* . . . inadequate or incomplete explanations of even contradictions with the data, generally are interpreted as *puzzles* . . . to be worked on . . . rather than grounds for their rejection.[7] [emphasis added]

This quotation is all the more remarkable because, first, it shows the *formalistic* preoccupation of many economists to describe their subject as scientific, and especially comparable with *physics*; second, it shows a confusion between the *testability* of a theory and the retainment of that theory when it is contradicted by *tests* (how can a set of *un*testable propositions be contradicted by 'the data'?); and, lastly, it overlooks the fact that Kuhn's theory concerns not so much the testability of propositions, as their survival even when they are falsified.

However, even the specialist applications of Kuhn's theory to economics were largely based on imprecise readings or simply wishful thinking. The *relativism* of his theory – the idea that truth is system-bound, culture-bound or merely time-bound – acted as a Pavlovian agent for the Radicals to expect the immediate onset of a revolution. The same relativism comforted the orthodox in thinking of themselves as 'normal scientists' just like those 'in physics'. Finally, the neglect of that relativism prompted some social scientists to toy with the fantastic notion that to convert their 'immature' into a 'mature' science they simply had to exert pressure on their academic subordinates to make them 'toe the line' of their 'dominant paradigm', and engage in solving its 'puzzle'.[8] No wonder that Kuhn himself received this news almost with indignation.[9]

In most of their 'applications' the Kuhnian' economists, and other social scientists, overlooked some (or all) of the following important elements in Kuhn's theory. First, that even if Kuhn had argued that scientific theories need not inherently be *testable* (which is not true) his theory is not an attack on *testability*. Second, that a mature normal science excludes the existence of competing paradigms. Third, that a scientific revolution is impersonal and unpredictable, certainly not one which would occur on an earnest appeal of a group of dissenting scientists: indeed, such dissenters would be 'carpenters who blame their own tools'. Fourth, that a crisis (as the *necessary* condition for a scientific revolution) must show a persistent incompatibility between the dominant paradigm and the world of empirical reality. Fifth, that a crisis is not a *sufficient* condition for a revolution: a new paradigm must emerge which would be acceptable to the scientific community as a superior theory or framework; and, lastly, that the victorious paradigm would be incompatible, nay, *incommensurable,* with its predecessor.

A knowledge of the history and method of economics makes it clear that the above list would automatically exclude *any* application of Kuhn's theory to this subject. Yet, on the basis of Kuhn's theory, some Radical economists advocated the confrontation of the Radical to the orthodox 'paradigms' by emphasising its greater adequacy in explaining problems of class conflict, racism, income distribution and so forth. Somehow the point was lost that the century-old Marxian 'paradigm' had already had similar claims of superiority over neo-classical theory without managing to replace it. Also, the fact was overlooked that the very existence of *competing paradigms* is a mark of 'immaturity' for a science and it would automatically preclude it from the terms of reference of Kuhn's model. Anyhow, it was rather optimistic to believe that the Radical 'paradigm' could replace neo-classical theory on account of such a campaign, though this has no bearing on the legitimacy of the effort itself. Alternatively, if the idea was to divide the profession between the two 'paradigms', then what would be the relevance of Kuhn's theory which would simply dismiss such a division as characteristic of immature science?[10]

Another approach to such an 'application' was to search for Kuhn-type 'revolutions' in the history of economics. 'Seekers are finders' – as the Persian saying has it – and, in particular, two turning-points in the history of economics were represented as Kuhn-type revolutions: the emergence of neo-classical theory, and the advent of Keynesian theory.[11] We need not repeat some of the above points which are relevant to such an enterprise. But there are others. A revolution requires a crisis precipitated by a persistent class of *empirical reality* with the predictions of the ruling paradigm. Yet it is difficult to think of any such situation in England, Austria (or elsewhere) at the time of the 'marginalist revolution': the only example of such an anomaly might have been the conflict between the rising standard of living *in England* and a crude interpretation of the classical subsistence wage theory. Yet even this is subject to two important qualifications: (i) the subsistence wage theories of Smith and Ricardo did not define the wage rate as a *biological* constant but a *sociological* minimum – that is, they regard subsistence as a (changeable) minimum level of consumption consistent with traditional patterns and social norms, in different societies and (therefore) also at different stages of economic development. Therefore their subsistence wage theories were not inconsistent with an absolute increase in the economic welfare of workers. The Malthusian concept of subsistence (and together with it his 'iron law of wages') was probably the only classical theory which regarded subsistence as the biological minimum required for mere survival. Unfortunately, however, it was this theoretically crude, ideologically biased and empirically nonsensical view which was (and, to a large extent, still is) regarded as the classical notion of 'the subsistence wage rate' by economists and laymen alike; (ii) the 'final' (later 'marginal') productivity theory of distribution, innovated by the early neo-classicals, itself had no real empirical content. It was the result of purely logical deduction; it was superior to *the Malthusian* iron law of wages to the extent that it did not blatantly contradict the fact of an average standard of living above a *biological* minimum.

That apart, if such a clash between theory and reality was to cause revolutionary changes in economics, is it not striking that neo-classical theory itself has been surviving such conflicts almost since the time of its inception? More significantly, is it not astonishing that the neo-classical 'paradigm' replaced the classical 'paradigm' even though it put equal emphasis on the concept of equilibrium – which is probably the most persistent and critical 'anomaly' between economic theory and empirico-historical reality. The 'Keynesian revolution' was certainly antedated by something resembling a Kuhnian crisis. Nevertheless, the Keynesian 'paradigm' was *not incompatible* (let alone *incommensurable*) with the neo-classical; and it did not totally replace orthodox economic theory – far from it; it was even reduced to less than what Keynes himself had probably intended, culminating in the so-called neo-classical synthesis.

A novel approach (briefly cited in Chapter 2) was Routh's argument that only one paradigm had dominated economic theory since the last quarter of the seventeenth century.[12] His book combines scholarship with an admirably critical approach and a rare clarity of expression. It is an intellectual and unpedantic exposition of the history of economic thought which could even serve as a model for the more 'scientific' pursuits in economic theory. In the application of Kuhn's theory he carefully avoids the claim that any Kuhn-type revolution has ever occurred in the history of economics. The argument is simply that a single paradigm has ruled economics since the dawn of classical political economy, and that the present crisis must indicate a radical departure from the existing framework. Nevertheless, Routh's case is open to disagreement on the following grounds. First, it would be inconsistent both with the letter and the spirit of Kuhn's theory to claim that a 'paradigm' had been established prior to Adam Smith. It is true that *The Wealth of Nations* was largely (though not entirely) a kind of synthesis. But it was precisely this synthesis which provided a comprehensive framework for further studies. Second, even the Smithian 'paradigm' did not rule exclusively in the sense of Kuhn. We have witnessed *competing* 'paradigms', emerging, disappearing and sometimes surviving since Ricardo, the most tenacious of which are the varieties of the Marxian and Institutionalist schools. Third, although neither the neo-classical nor the Keynesian theory may be regarded as revolutions in the sense of Kuhn, they were nevertheless major intellectual events in the history of economics which controvert the claim of total continuity. It will not be sufficient to say that nearly all neo-classical and Keynesian concepts and categories had been discovered earlier: Keynesian concepts may have been discovered haphazardly over two centuries of research; but *The General Theory* had a distinct theoretical integrity, intellectual impact and social relevance of its own. Fourth, by proposing an alternative paradigm (like the Radical writers before him) Routh seems to underemphasise the element of (mechanistic) determinism in Kuhn's theory which is bound up with its relativism – that is, a paradigm emerges an *totally* replaces the ruling paradigm when, in a crisis, 'the scientific community' feels it is acceptable as a superior framework. And, there is little sign of such a miracle *vis-à-vis* any new paradigm in economic theory. Finally, Routh seems to assume too readily that economics had become a 'mature' science, in the sense of Kuhn, in the same century as did physics, and nearly two centuries before the Darwinian Revolution in biology.

Some general remarks before concluding this section. Kuhn talks about paradigms, paradigm parts and paradigmatics. It appears that in a mature science paradigm parts and paradigmatics must also be unique; there must not be *competing* theories for the explanation of the same phenomena even within a single dominant paradigm or basic framework. It follows that each and every one of these paradigm parts is also subject to change only through the Kuhnian process of scientific revolution. Two observations may be made here with regard to the history of economics. First, that there have been many 'paradigm parts' which have risen and fallen (indeed quietly forgotten) without any serious 'anomalies', 'crises', 'revolutions', etc. For example, the purchasing-power-parity theory of the foreign exchanges, or the quantity theory of money. The second example is even more interesting because it has now risen once again like the phoenix from the ashes. This is totally anathema to Kuhn's theory according to which once a paradigm is discarded by a revolution it would be *incommensurable* with the superior paradigm replacing it, and it will never again be taken seriously. In the light of this fact, Bronfenbrenner's claim that the *return* of the quantity theory – 'the monetarist revolution' – is a Kuhnian episode is no less than puzzling.[13] Second, even assuming that the 'neo-classical synthesis' is the unique paradigm in economic theory, there exist so many *competing* 'paradigm parts' within its general framework. Consider the Keynesian and the monetarist controversy; the marginal productivity theory of wages versus the bargaining models; the two competing models of international trade theory both of which are used in teaching and research *even by the same economists*. The fact that at least five models of inflation are currently taught, and only some of which are subject to theoretical controversy; that in their research activities some development economists regard the real value of labour as determined by its shadow price in the rural sector, and some others as defined by its market price in the urban sector (many adopt a 'hybrid' position); that in the theory of macro-economic dynamics capital is sometimes regarded as finance, sometimes as machines and perhaps more often as 'putty–clay'. . . . So much for the Kuhnian credentials of economic theory as a 'mature science'.

THE LAKATOSIAN 'SYNTHESIS'

Philosophers of science, unlike social scientists, received Kuhn's theory with a critical attitude. Popper was (rightly) concerned about 'normal science and its danger'.[14] Feyerabend lost interest in the logic of science, and he was not impressed with its 'sociology'; therefore he went over to methodological anarchism: if the logic is a mere decoration, and the 'sociology' reveals an immutably orthodox and conservative pattern of behaviour by the scientists even *qua* scientists, then we can dispense with method and science altogether.[15] Lakatos, who had done no less than Feyerabend to promote Popperian ideas, proposed a 'new' theory which he described as 'sophisticated falsificationism'.

Lakatos's theory of 'scientific research programmes' is an attempted synthesis between Popper's logic and Kuhn's 'sociology' of science.[16] 'Naïve falsificationism' regards every scientific theory in isolation and demands its rejection when it does not accord with reality. Whereas a scientific research programme is the configuration of interrelated theories, no single one of which is viewed as being completely autonomous. Since a research programme is a collectivity of interdependent theories it follows that the rejection of each single theory will address itself to the entire programme. It becomes difficult to discard individual theories without reference to the programme as a whole. Yet, in contrast to Kuhn's description, this does not mean that *no* theory would be rejected by the process of falsification. It will all depend on the position and status of the theory within the programme. Here Lakatos divides a programme into two parts: the 'negative heuristic' and the 'positive heuristic'. A programme's negative heuristic is its 'hard core', or the very basic statements which hold the entire edifice. It is this *hard core* which is not normally subject to the Popperian process of falsification, and which displays paradigmic resistance to change (*almost*) à la Kuhn. By contrast the positive heuristic makes up the research content of the programme; it is more readily testable and it leads to the formulation of further concepts and theories described as the 'protective belt'. Hence, the hard core may survive piecemeal refutations, but the rest would be open to rejection and/or improvement. In Lakatos's own words:

> The negative heuristic specifies the hard core which is 'irre-futable' by the methodological discussion of the protagonists; the positive heuristic consists of a partially articulated set of sugges-tions or hints on how to change, develop the 'refutable variant' of the research programme, how to modify, sophisticate the 'refutable' protective belt.[17]

In a word the 'negative heuristic' is the Kuhnian, and the 'positive heuristic' is the Popperian element of this 'synthesis', except that even the hard core can change with less resistance than Kuhn has described for paradigms. In this connection Lakatos distinguishes between two types of research programme which he calls pro-gressive and degenerative. A progressive programme gives way to an alternative programme which has a greater (empirical) truth content or explanatory power. A degenerative programme resists change – even when it is legitimately challenged – by resorting to *ad hoc* procedures to defend itself. In any event the emergence of an alternative programme need not await a Kuhn-type crisis, since rival programmes could develop even when the ruling programme is not in doubt. Hence Lakatos's plea for tolerating 'budding research programmes' – which, incidentally, dispenses with the Kuhnian description of *mature* science, as the latter would normally exclude the existence of competing paradigms. Finally, Lakatos concludes his essay with the following – for some, not so reassuring – assess-ment of its contribution:

> Sophisticated falsificationism thus *combines the best elements* of voluntarism, pragmatism and of the realist theories of *empirical growth* . . . [it] does not side with Galileo . . . [nor] with Cardinal Bellarmino. . . .[18]

Lakatos's theory is made up of one (purportedly) *descriptive* and three *normative* elements. The descriptive part refers to the research programme and the features of its negative and positive heuristics. The first normative element is *falsifiability;* clearly no *falsification* ('naïve') or 'sophisticated') would be possible unless theories are *falsifiable.* The second is Lakatos's distinction between progressive and degenerative programmes; and the third is his plea of tolerance for 'budding research programmes'. The 'descriptive' part of Lakatos's theory is prone to a tautological interpretation reminiscent of Kuhn's account of scientific progress. Indeed Kuhn was quick to charge Lakatos with reading his personal philosophy into the history of science. We cannot claim competence to judge Kuhn's accusation; what is certain is that – like the case of Kuhn's own theory – similar concepts and processes (hard cores, positive heuristic, protective belt, etc.) can be 'read into' the history of almost every field of human creation: arts, literature, metaphysics, religion. The normative rule of falsifiability is precise, but the distinction between progressive and degenerative science is too vague: it can only be known *a posteriori*; even then what is an *ad hoc* procedure of defining a programme to one observer may be a standing procedure to another. What, in any case, if scientific research programmes were in fact characteristically degenerative, which – though not in these words – is exactly what Kuhn attributes to the paradigms of mature science? What, especially, if such degenerative programmes happened to be *successful* in some socially defined sense of this term? The same questions apply to the plea for the 'budding research programmes': what if, in practice, this plea was ignored and/or intolerance was justified on the grounds of 'success'? What would be the nature and degree of tolerance even if it existed: a *passive permission,* or a *critical reception,* of new ideas. What if it tended to be withdrawn the minute a budding programme began to bear fruits which appeared to endanger the existing programme?

It follows from the above argument that Lakatos's theory bypasses the social dimension of scientific research, even though there is some attempt at fusing the logic and the 'sociology' – the methodological norm and the social reality – of scientific progress. It is less of a synthesis than a compromise. That is probably the main reason why it was rejected by Kuhn and ignored by Popper.

Before concluding this section, let us discuss, as briefly as possible, a rather remarkable 'parallelism' between these theories of *scientific progress* and the various interpretations of the Marxian theory of *social development.* This theory, as it is well known, draws a distinction between the base (or infrastructure) of a social system – broadly characterised by the state and nature of its existing technological achievements – and the social edifice, or super-

structure – that is, the existing social relations which set the constitutions of social, political and legal conduct, and the institutions
of public and private morality. There are (at least) three interpretations of the Marxian theory of social change: one which makes
superstructural change a rigid function of basic, infrastructual transformations; another which allows for superstructural changes (and,
in particular, changes in socio-political constitutions and norms of
moral behaviour) even on the basis of the existing infrastructure;
and a third which regards social change (even including major
infrastructural changes) as a consequence of an interaction between
the basic and superstructural forces. The first interpretation is
rather remarkably 'parallel' to Kuhn's theory of scientific revolutions. The second interpretation is similarly in line with Lakatos's
theory where his 'negative heuristic', or 'hard core', corresponds to
the social base, the 'positive heuristic' to social relations and the
'protective belt' to the rules of social and moral conduct. Finally,
the third interpretation has a close affinity to our interpretation of
Popper's view which puts all change, big and small, permanently on
the agenda. It need hardly be stressed that this comparison does not
imply that any of the above philosophers are 'Marxists' according to
one or another interpretation. It is merely intended to expose
differences in scientific temper, and in attitude to human freedom,
among both Marxist and non-Marxist philosophers and scientists,
which seem to transcend apparent ideological commitments.

OF RESEARCH PROGRAMMES IN THE HISTORY AND METHOD OF ECONOMICS

Lakatos maintains the rule of *falsifiability*, but he argues that the
hard core of a scientific research programme is not subject to a
continuous process of *falsification*. Therefore, unless the rule of
falsifiability is observed by a discipline, then the Lakatosian description of the growth of scientific knowledge would not be relevant to
it. It would be possible to discover examples of a 'research programme' (including a base, an edifice and a 'protective belt') in any
field, even literature and ethics. However, the result of such an
enterprise, by itself, would not show the relevance of Lakatos's
theory of scientific research programmes to that field. In the
previous chapter enough was said to show that many elements in the

'hard core', the 'positive heuristic' and the 'protective belt' of the 'neo- classical research programme' are *not* falsifiable. In addition, the theory of scientific research programmes predicts that the positive heuristic of a programme would be subject to refutation and rejection at any time. Whereas we have shown that even that part of economic theory's 'positive heuristic' which *is refutable* and *has been refuted*, has been retained by the use of an *ad hoc* procedure. Let us recall that the use of such *ad hoc* procedures *even in defence of the 'hard core'* would show that the programme is 'degenerative' — let alone when they are used to protect the *'positive heuristic'*. What these simple observations would leave for economics from a Lakatosian point of view is best left to the reader to decide. But one thing is certain: rigour and consistency would preclude an explanation of the history and method of economics in Lakatosian terms, in spite of superficial resemblances. For, at its best, the result of such an effort would be no more than a methodological mimicry.

Lakatos himself had a few uncomplimentary words to spare about 'immature' sciences and their methods. Indeed, he advocated a greater stringency in the application of the rules to their case. His argument gives the impression that 'immature' sciences should be subjected to the strict rule of 'naïve falsificationism' – i.e. all of their theories must be falsifiable and all of them (hard or soft core) must be dispensed with when falsified. This position seems to be paradoxical on two grounds. First, if 'mature' sciences themselves cannot pass the test of 'naïve falsificationism', it is clearly impossible for 'immature' sciences to stand up to such a test. Second, Lakatos's 'sophisticated falsificationism' *describes how* 'mature' sciences develop, while his strictures about the method of 'immature' sciences seem to be more of an *edict:* why not issue the same edict for the 'mature' sciences too? Such problems may be characteristic of budding philosophical programmes, but they need not detain us. Lakatos's theory is *not* applicable to 'immature' sciences and its author knew it too.

Blaug's bold and rigorous attempt to explain significant changes in the history of economics in Lakatosian terms must be seen against his background.[19] For *on the assumption that since 1870 economic theory has fulfilled the Lakatosian criteria for a ('mature') scientific research programme* his argument would appear to be convincing. Yet this (implicit) assumption violates the facts, and for this reason alone, the explanation loses its logical (as opposed to tautological) validity. We are in perfect agreement with his view that a Kuhnian explanation of the Marginalist, Keynesian, monetarist (or whatever) 'revolutions' would face serious difficulties. Indeed, we have already argued this case much more strongly, and for many more reasons than he has mentioned. However, in an attempt to provide a reasonable explanation of these events, Blaug replaces Lakatos for Kuhn. He identifies a 'hard core' for classical political economy – the concepts of equilibrium, maximising behaviour, etc. – and he argues that the neo-classical 'research programme', while retaining this hard core, changed its 'positive heuristic' and directed attention to new research problems. The argument is persuasive, but it loses its force on the following considerations. First, 'the positive heuristic' of a programme unlike its 'hard core', is supposed to be open to *continuous* revision and rejection. In particular, the change of some or all elements in 'the positive heuristic' does not describe a turning-point – according to Lakatos it should be a *permanent* feature of a research programme. Yet, both in the 1870s and in retrospect, the advent of neo-classicism was a major turning-point in the history of economics. Second, a 'positive heuristic' – in part or as a whole – is supposed to be *refuted* by empirical facts and *replaced* by another which is more consistent with such facts. What empirical facts had refuted the 'positive heuristic' of classical political theory, and were consistent with that of neo-classical theory? Besides, in what sense was the (empirically) *untestable* marginal utility 'theory' more consistent with reality, than the tautologically self-evident full-cost theory of relative prices? Third according to Lakatos even when the *hard core* of a research programme is defended irrationally then that is a sign of the degeneracy of that programme. Yet the alleged neo-classical change of '*positive heuristic*' was established in the teeth of opposition. As a result, Jevons had anticipated this reaction so much so that he concluded *The Theory of Political Economy* with a long (and unexceptionable) eulogy on intellectual openness and honesty.[20] But to no avail. The resistance was not even mainly in the form of using *ad hoc* procedures to defend classical political economy (or the German Historical School) against the new theory: its adherents were in danger of losing their academic positions or forfeiting hopes of appointments and promotions.[21]

In contrast to the change from classical to neo-classical theory Blaug describes the Keynesian criticism as effecting a change in the *hard core* of economic theory. He identifies a new hard core, positive heuristic, protective belt, etc., with admirable precision. But if the *hard core* of a research programme is overthrown, then the new research programme should completely supersede the old. Is this true of post-Keynesian economic theory? One important example which Blaug cites for the Keynesian change in the *hard core* of economic theory is its emphasis on short-term disequilibrium, as opposed to long-term equilibrium. This would have been true had economic theory lost its preoccupation with the existence, properties and stability of equilibria in every conceivable problem, including the theory of economic growth. In fact, the Keynesian 'shift of emphasis' has done little more than forcing the theorists to recognise the fact that automatically self-adjusting short-term macro-economic equilibrium may not be possible. Otherwise, the post-Keynesian 'research programme' has been more concerned with *general equilibrium analysis* and *equilibrium growth theory* than any other problem.

CONCLUDING REMARKS

In this chapter we set ourselves the task of meeting the Kuhnian and Lakatosian *fashions* among social scientists. We conclude by remaining unfashionable. We have no doubt that these theories are serious propositions within the realm of philosophy of science. The fact that we have found them debatable even within their own terms of reference does not mean that they should not be taken seriously. No one would subject a theory to rigorous criticism unless he regarded it as a challenging and thought-provoking proposition. Our critique of Kuhn's and Lakatos's models must be seen in this light, although we would not retract a word of our criticisms unless they were shown to be mistaken. Indeed, it is the fashionable converts – those who rush into the adoption of an idea more or less *uncritically* – who do the least justice to its author. Such fashionable behaviour among social scientists is not merely confined to this subject; it is almost a permanent feature of our incurable attempts to redecorate the surface while leaving the structure intact.

One last word about the theories of Kuhn and Lakatos. A curious impression seems to have been gained by some critics that – especially in contrast to 'Popperism' – these theories are somehow liberating or 'permissive'. For example, Coddington has recently attacked Hutchison for criticising the models of Kuhn and Lakatos on these grounds.[22] It is certainly true that if the rule of falsifiability is put aside then – to paraphrase Lakatos – 'anything could go'. This could be the case whether or not we accept Kuhn's and Lakatos's specific models: if the rejection of the principle of falsifiability is a liberating policy, then such a liberation could have been achieved even before Kuhn and Lakatos proposed their theories. Conventionalists, pragmatists, instrumentalists, etc., never accepted the criterion of falsifiability without waiting for the theories of Kuhn and Lakatos to emerge. But, in any case, Kuhn does not reject the normative criterion of *falsifiability* (as opposed to the descriptive theory of *falsification*); and Lakatos accepts the first and adapts the second.

Kuhn's theory tells us that normal scientists both would and should defend the existing paradigm and reject novel alternatives except in occasional crises, etc. It would be interesting to know in what sense such a theory (and the related value judgement) is tolerant, let alone it being 'permissive'; *except, of course, for those in positions of authority.* The doctrine of Papal infallibility certainly affords a great deal of freedom in defending the Roman Catholic dogma and rejecting dangerous criticism. But this is hardly evidence of the Church's 'permissiveness' towards the Catholic community. It is in the latter sense that Hutchison seems to be (rightly) critical of Kuhn and – less justifiably – Lakatos's models which, with significantly different degrees of emphasis, tend to transfer all intellectual freedom to the guardians of paradigms and programmes. Let us suppose that Kuhn's theory is absolutely right – i.e. that science has invariably progressed in the manner which he has described; and that (therefore) it should continue to grow in that manner. Even so, the procedure would not be a tolerant (or 'permissive') framework for the scientist; if anything, it is more reminiscent of (Dostoevsky's) rule of Miracle, Mystery and Authority for the monk.

We shall now investigate some possible *sociological* sources of the rule of authority within the contemporary academic profession.

5

BIG SCIENCE VERSUS GREAT SCIENCE: A CONTRIBUTION TO THE SOCIOLOGY OF THE ACADEMIC PROFESSION

THE INFLUENCE OF EXTRA-LOGICAL FACTORS

Scientific discovery is both a logical *and* a social process. Therefore sociological, psychological and ideological factors also influence the growth of scientific knowledge. The concept of ideology, in its various meanings, implies that an (extra-rational) frame of mind, may set a limit to our purely logical efforts at understanding the world around us. Likewise, Freudian – and other psychoanalytical – categories are frequently used to show the impact of an individual's psyche on his mode of behaviour, system of beliefs and methods of evaluation. Thus ideological and psychological theories together emphasise that a man's *social* and *personal* history modify and constrain his 'purely' logical view of the problems which confront him. We shall discuss the concept of ideology, and its significance for the progress of economic ideas, in the next chapter. The role of psychological factors will be examined not as a separate category but in conjunction with the sociology of scientific discovery. For the psychological factors themselves may be subdivided into private or individual as opposed to public or social: it would be irrelevant, if not impossible, to generalise about the influence of *individual* psychology in relation to the growth of *public* knowledge; on the other hand, the influence of *social* psychology – i.e. the psychological characteristics shared by a community – cannot be isolated from the social environment on which it is based.

The reader may have been surprised by our implicit distinction between sociological and ideological influences, since – in the context of the present problem – it is customary to use these terms almost synonymously. For example, Mannheim's ideological theory of the growth of knowledge is often described as 'the sociology of knowledge'. The problem is resolved by distinguishing between two different concepts which are easily confused: the sociology of *science,* and the sociology of *the scientist.* The former concept refers to ideology which, as we have seen, describes the constraints to the growth of knowledge due to the prevailing mode of production. In its extreme form it asserts that the attainment of some truths, the discovery of certain kinds of knowledge, is simply beyond the capacity of a given social framework, whatever the attitude of the 'scientific community' which functions within that framework. It follows from this that science cannot progress *beyond a certain limit,* unless the mode of production (and the related social framework) changes first. By contrast, the sociology of the scientist, or the academic profession, is an attempt to explain why knowledge grows as it does – and academics behave as they do – even assuming that there are 'ultimate' boundaries to what can be learned at a certain stage of socio-economic development.

The confusion between these two concepts is largely due to the fact that the first has been discussed *ad nauseam,* while the second has received very little attention. In order to help clarify our distinction between these two concepts consider the following case. Suppose that in a given social framework there is a pool of *limited* potential knowledge (*and no more*) which *can* be discovered. But this would not provide us with any guarantee that it *will* be. The community which is concerned with the discovery of the limited amount of discoverable knowledge is the academic profession. Therefore, the latter's attitude and behaviour will largely influence by how much, and at what speed, this (limited) potential is realised. A theory of the sociology of the academic profession would seek to identify the social factors which mould its attitude and mode of behaviour. It may be retorted that ideological limits to scientific discovery also explain the limits to the efforts of (the majority) of scientists. For, by the extension of the concept of ideology, it may be argued that the scientists' class affiliations would influence their total vision of their subject. Yet this objection does not meet the hypothetical case cited above: let us suppose that class affiliations constrain – if not determine – the world view of the scientists; we would still want to know the factors which influence the amount of knowledge gained, and the rate of its discovery, *within that vision.*

Scientists are not merely constrained by their class affiliations, the stage of economic development or whatever. They are also subject to more immediate and more empirical pressures which would influence the direction of their thoughts and actions. We do not claim that these two groups of factors are entirely separable. However, we do claim that the second group must also be studied in its own right, especially as it has been ignored or effectively drowned in studies of the first.

LOGIC AND SOCIOLOGY

Any logical rule for the development of knowledge would be a value judgement. Yet, despite popular belief, this does not mean that it would have to be a purely subjective statement; a mere matter of opinion. Indeed, it is important to distinguish between two types of value judgement: statements of opinion, which *are* purely subjective, and statements of policy, which *are not*. To say that apples are better than oranges could be a value judgement of either type: if it means that apples *taste better*, then it is purely a matter of opinion or personal preference; but if it means that apples are *more nutritive*, then it is a statement of policy. It is clear that value judgements of the second type are testable even though they are normative statements.[1] Therefore, a logical rule for scientific discovery is not a matter of opinion if, for example, it claims to offer the most efficient method for the advancement of knowledge. This would make it open to rational and empirical criticism for, in principle, it could be shown to be mistaken.

A sociological theory of the growth of knowledge, by contrast, is a positive statement. It is an attempt to describe and explain the process of scientific discovery *as it takes place,* whether or not this is the best procedure with reference to the same set of normative objectives. 'The sociology' tells us what there is, and how it comes about; 'the logic' predicts what there could be and how it may be achieved. Ultimately the two cannot be completely separated: what I am influences what I will be; what I would like to become affects what I am. That does not mean that we should refrain from analysing each set of factors on its own; merely, that we should not lose sight of either set of factors in a comprehensive study of the subject. Here we wish to identify a number of social, historical and institutional phenomena which (we believe) influence the mode of conduct of the academic profession: *academic,* because it will be argued that all academic activities – 'scientific' or not – tend to share the same sociological features; *professional,* because it will be suggested that these sociological characteristics are largely a function of the professional framework within which modern academic activities are carried out.

To introduce the subject, let us briefly return to Kuhn's theory which is widely believed to be a sociological approach to scientific progress. Kuhn himself has lent credence to this – 'sociological' – interpretation of his model.[2] But the claim is not entirely correct. The theory states that, when a science becomes mature, only a single paradigm would dominate the field; thereafter normal scientific activity would be concentrated on solving the related puzzles until a crisis and the emergence of an (acceptable) alternative paradigm leads to a scientific revolution. But this is little more than a purely descriptive – as opposed to analytical and explanatory – generalisation. There is no casual explanation at all: *How* does a science become 'mature'? *What* makes 'normal scientists' behave as described? If this is the process of change in *mature* sciences, *why* are there strong similarities between it and *immature* sciences? *What* are the social factors which influence this uniform pattern of behaviour of normal scientists? *Why* do these social factors become significant only when a science becomes 'mature'? *Why* do they not change thereafter, for if they did then the process of scientific progress would presumably change with them? . . . Indeed, a sociology of science (or the scientists) which offers no answer to such questions is in danger of missing no less than the sociology of science itself. The only 'sociological' reference in Kuhn's theory is to the attitude of the 'scientific community' and, especially, 'the invisible college', whose consensus ultimately determines whether or not a dominant paradigm should give way to an emerging alternative. Yet, there is not much explanation about the nature and social significance of 'the scientific community' or its 'invisible' arbiters.

Kuhn's theory includes an important factual insight, although its analytical significance is not discussed or developed. It emphasises the fact that, within 'normal science', basic dissent and disagreement will not be tolerated by 'the scientific community'. The fact itself must have been known by almost every professional academic engaged in a 'mature' *or* 'immature' science. Nevertheless, Kuhn should be given the credit both for making it possible to mention this fact in 'polite' circles, and for giving it some kind of methodological function. He himself cites a number of better-known historical instances of this general rule of intolerance, of which the following is an interesting example:

> Lord Rayleigh, at a time when his reputation was established, submitted to the British Association a paper on some paradoxes of electrodynamics. His name was inadvertently omitted when the paper was first sent, and the paper was at first rejected as the work of some 'paradoxer'. Shortly afterwards, with the author's name in place, the paper was accepted with profuse apologies.[3]

This and similar examples serve to highlight a number of facts. First, that an apparently unusual idea would be likely to be rejected with contempt; second, that there would be a good chance of publishing such an idea if the author's reputation has been already established; third, that any nonsense by an 'established' author may have a better chance of being published than any reasonable contribution by an unknown author. There is a further possibility which the above example does not cover, but it is implicit in Kuhn's concept of normal science: when an 'established' author proposes an idea which threatens the existing 'paradigm' it may be published and even countered by rational arguments put forward by 'the invisible college'. But even when 'the invisible college' loses the case, 'the scientific community' would simply stick to 'the ruling paradigm' as if nothing had happened. Take the example of the controversy over the theory of capital in contemporary economic theory. For over two decades a number of distinguished economic theorists led by Joan Robinson have argued that neo-classical economic theory is based on a circularity which is ultimately due to the dichotomy between the concept of capital as *finance,* and as *physical products.* This argument was systematically countered by equally distinguished economic theorists led by Paul Samuelson until it became clear to all parties that it is an inescapable conclusion. Yet neo-classical theorists still continue in the old way as if nothing has happened. Let it be emphasised that we are not at all concerned about the *substantial* significance of this controversy and, in particular, whether or not the critics' arguments add a great deal to economic knowledge. We are simply concerned with the *methodological* significance of the debate. That is to say, as long as the neo-classical theorists regard this body of knowledge as a self-contained and logically consistent system, worthy of acceptance and further development, then they must be prepared to take its logical faults seriously. This example shows that logic on its own can be pretty powerless even in the best of circumstances – i.e. when the critics' reputations have been already established. As it happens the controversy over the theory of capital is *not* an example of anomaly in the sense of Kuhn. A Kuhnian anomaly occurs when evidence from the real world seems to contradict the implications or predictions of a theory. According to Kuhn when such a case arises normal scientists would not reject the theory unless the conflict leads to a crisis, etc. Whereas, the debate over the theory of capital concerns the *internal logical consistency* of the theory itself; there is no recourse to empirical evidence at all. It is very unlikely that even Kuhn's normal scientists would hold on to a theory which is *logically inconsistent.*

We have noted that Kuhn's description of the characteristics of normal science is in danger of being tautological and indiscriminate; that this description involves no *causal explanation,* and it implies that – once a science becomes 'mature' (for which maturity no independent definition is given) – those characteristics of normal science remain unchanged for all times. In the remaining part of this chapter we shall suggest a simple sociological model of the academic profession which might help clear up some of these questions. There is no pretence whatsoever that this is an entirely satisfactory or faultless model – merely that it is a model, and perhaps a pioneering one – of the sociology of the academic profession and the social psychology of the professional academic.

THE SOCIOLOGY OF THE ACADEMIC PROFESSION: THE BASIC STATEMENT OF A MODEL

For the sake of clarity we shall enumerate the basic elements of our model in this section, and discuss them in more detail in the following.

1. Many of the characteristics which Kuhn's theory attributes to mature normal science are a function of the emergence and growth

of professionalism in *all* scientific and intellectual pursuits.

2. Professionalism in scientific and intellectual activities is itself associated with industrialisation, the rise of the democratic and secular (though not necessarily liberal) state, and the growth of technology.

3. The greater the technological significance or the 'social' usefulness of a discipline, the higher the level and intensity of its professionalisation as an academic pursuit.

4. Such professionalisation makes it more and more difficult – in some cases almost impossible – to search for knowledge outside universities and similar institutions.

5. This turns the scientist and the scholar into academics; that is, full-time mental workers.

6. A *professional* academic regards his position and prospects *primarily* as a career. His *primary* aim is to attain a varying combination of material advancement and social recognition. He might well have entered a different profession or activity; that is, he might have pursued the same aims in a different career had it not been for accident and/or lack of alternative opportunity. It follows that the term 'professional' is here used not in contradistinction with the (pejorative) term 'amateur', but in contrast to the term 'vocational'.

7. Not every academic is a *professional* academic in the above sense, even though he is employed by an institution of advanced learning. But most are.

8. A typical professional academic is almost a complete layman outside his own discipline and a narrow specialist within it. The former makes it difficult for him to make a broader intellectual contribution to life in society; the latter reduces his chances of making *significant* contributions to the advancement of knowledge in his own discipline.

9. Academics are not merely subject to their wider professional framework. More immediately, they are members of a narrower group of disciplinarians (such as the British Association of the University Teachers of Economics and the American Economic Association) whose members communicate with one another through the learned (professional) journals. Something like this must be the more concrete counterpart to Kuhn's notion of 'the scientific community'. Let us call it the disciplinary profession.

10. It is the attitude of this disciplinary profession which largely determines the chances of appointment and promotion, and the

intellectual reputation of an academic. Therefore, the stronger and the more integrated the disciplinary profession the greater the constraint on the intellectual activities and views of the professional academic, given his primary objectives (see paragraph 7).

11. The disciplinary profession exercises some of the above functions by its control over the means of publication and propagation of disciplinary ideas. As a rule (*a*) the learned journals are less tolerant of ideas which threaten established views especially if such ideas are thought to be offensive to one or more senior members of the disciplinary profession; (*b*) they would prefer to publish shorter papers dealing with highly specialised and narrow points; (*c*) academic promotions and reputations are directly linked to publication. Therefore, publication for the sake of publication becomes an overriding objective for the professional academic, and this would automatically dictate intellectual cautiousness, a high degree of specialisation, and brevity for the sake of brevity.

12. The leadership of the disciplinary profession corresponds to Kuhn's concept of 'the invisible college'. The term 'college' is well-chosen, for, unlike the general membership of the disciplinary profession, members of its leadership compose a collectivity of peers. Only *they* are colleagues in the traditional sense of this term.

13. The above characteristics of the academic profession, and the professional academic, result in the following pattern:

(i)   There will be a tendency to concentrate on the solution of real or imaginary 'puzzles' instead of attacking substantial problems.

(ii) There will be a proliferation of printed material with comparatively little addition to knowledge. This makes the task of discrimination, both in reading and in assessment, difficult. In reading, the better works are drowned by the sheer quantity of the worse. In evaluation, the *number* of publications tends to assume an inordinate significance.

(iii) Originality in intellectual discovery acquires an inverted meaning. A piece of harmless nonsense could go if it has not been said before. A humble effort at reviving and enriching older but important ideas could be dismissed as 'old hat'. Any piece of work which does not display *cleverness* may be rejected as waffle. Any idea which is critically innovative and daring may (at best) be scorned for being 'too original'.

(iv) In the social sciences in particular, the 'research agenda' of academic work is set by the changing fashion which itself is mainly determined by the whims of 'the invisible college'. The ordinary *professional* academic becomes almost like a journalist who frequents the corridors of power for a 'newsworthy' item, or a professional speculator who is constantly watching out for the right assets in which to shift his investment. It is a game in which – to quote a famous *un*professional economist – 'he is victor who says *snap* neither too soon nor too late'.[4]

(v) The *un*professional academic (who is none the less a member of the academic profession) permanently faces three principal choices, none of which could be a great source of joy for him. The first is to give up resistance and join the professionals. The second is to stand by his principles and take the moral and material consequences. The third is to leave the profession altogether. He who takes the last choice resembles the scientist who, according to Kuhn's theory, 'rejects science itself' just like 'the poor carpenter who blames his tools'. According to our interpretation this would be a rejection not of 'science itself', but the unreasonable demands made by 'the invisible college', and an admission of defeat in defending those very intellectual ideals to which *ceremonious* homage is regularly paid by all. It would not be a rejection of the carpenter's *own* tools, but the malfunctioning tools which he is asked to use for producing a defective output.

(vi) All this can do nothing but retard the pace of scientific and intellectual progress. To claim the opposite is to stand the truth on its head. Occasional revolutions occur not because 'normal' professionalism – and its 'invisible' rulers – *positively* contribute to their occurrence; on the contrary, they succeed when extraordinary circumstances, crises or whatever, finally break the hegemony of the ruling 'invisibles', and – for a short but decisive period – throw them into disarray. There may be significant analogies between the modes of scientific and social development. But it would be hard to claim that (in 'mature' societies) tyranny or oppression is the 'normal' method of socio-political progress. Indeed, successful political revolutions commence at the weakest moment of an oppressive state precisely because its resistance to change *prevents* social progress for as long as it can.

Kuhn was quite right in being indignant at the curious charge brought against his theory that it advocates 'mob rule'.[5] For the theory describes the opposite: the iron rule of a few learned and respectable oligarchs over the disciplinary profession. In fact our own critique of Kuhn's theory runs a much greater risk of being mistaken for the advocacy of 'mob rule'. For a critic of our views may point to the obvious and perfectly valid fact that neither in science nor in society is it desirable or beneficial to engage in a perpetual replacement of existing ideas and norms without studious and careful assessments. We entirely agree with this principle while pointing to the equally obvious fact that there exist choices other than tyranny and mob rule – both in science and in society.

THE SCOPE AND LIMITS OF THE MODEL: ARGUMENTS AND EVIDENCE

Theoretical models invariably contain strong elements of simplicity and dogmatism. The statement of our model is no exception to this general rule; indeed, the elements of the model were deliberately so stated as to sharpen their significance and emphasise their interconnection in defining a certain mode of professional academic behaviour. That does not mean that the model is unique and universal either through *time* or *space*; a theory which 'explains' everything everywhere for all time is hardly a theory at all.

To begin with the limits to spatial generalisation, our model does not apply with equal force to all academic disciplines or – for that matter – all professional academics within a given discipline. Take the case of specialisation by individual academics. It is well known that there are – at times significant – differences between the intellectual calibre of various academics engaged in the same discipline. Therefore a high-calibred professional academic would be both a better specialist *and* more widely in command of his discipline as a whole than an academic with less intellectual endowments. In fact the former is likely to be a member of the leading élite of the disciplinary profession, 'the invisible college'. There are also differences in the applicability of our model to different academic disciplines as such. For example, the model is likely to be less applicable to disciplines which are less concerned with the solution of *specific* ('technical') problems – say literature, music, history and even philosophy. On the other hand, it is probable that *some aspects* of the model are observed more strongly in the *'mature'* sciences; while *some other aspects* are experienced with greater force in the *less mature* sciences. In particular, specialisation both in intellectual and in disciplinary knowledge seems to be more pronounced in the 'mature' sciences; so do professional hierarchical relationships and barriers to a change of existing ideas. Consequently the likelihood of a Kuhn-type crisis and revolution is stronger, and when they do come about, they tend to overthrow the existing 'paradigm(s)' irreversibly. Whereas, in the less mature sciences crises and *tendencies towards* revolutions seem to be more frequent, but they hardly ever result in a total triumph. Consequently resistance to change *through time* is greater, and the pace of scientific progress is slower, in the less mature sciences. That is one important reason why it is difficult to think of a strictly Kuhn-type revolution in the whole of the social sciences taken together.

The above observations provide a few hints about the scope and limits of our model *through space* – i.e. across the existing academic disciplines in the contemporary world. The more important questions concern its scope and limit *through time:* how does the academic profession develop in the manner described? What social and historical factors contribute to its emergence? What are the causes of its growth, and in what conditions is it likely to change?. . . It is sufficient to pose such questions to indicate that the proposed characteristics of the academic profession are neither accidental nor capable of generalisation to all intellectual activity from The Fall until Doomsday: they typify academic life, effort and relations within the broader confines of a given civilisation – that is, the modern industrial society. There are two major aspects to this problem which are directly interconnected: the emergence of democratic nation states and the revolution in the division of labour in society.

Let us discuss the first issue first. By the *democratic nation state* we refer to a certain type of social arrangement which, in some fundamental ways, differs both from the classical – and (occasionally) medieval – democratic city states on the one hand; and from the undemocratic plutocracies, or despotic states, on the other. It follows that liberalism is *not* a necessary condition for our conception of the democratic nation state. In popular parlance such states would be described as advanced – as opposed to under-developed – countries. Their mark of distinction is their *industrial and technological* mode of production – the *mass* production of *goods* (regardless of the relative degree of emphasis on capital and consumer goods); and the *mass* 'participation' in social and political processes (regardless of the relative degree of emphasis on individual liberty). Both the United states and the Soviet Union qualify for this broad definition of the democratic nation state *in spite of their admittedly significant differences in other respects.*[6] The democratic nation state is the heir to one form or another of the undemocratic, plutocratic or despotic, state. The most fundamental difference in the broader outlook of these two types of state is that the latter was backward-looking, reactionary or completely traditionalist. It regarded the very concept of deliberate change as being highly undesirable; even dangerous. It tried to suppress scientific or social theories which cast doubt on the existing official dogma: Galileo's, Locke's, Rousseau's or Voltaire's – it did not matter. Universities, where they existed, were by and large charged with the perpetuation and defence of such body of dogma. The typical 'scholar' was directly, or through the Church, or charitable endowments, an appendix to this oppressive, anti-progressive and dogmatic apparatus. The European Renaissance, whatever its origins, led to the emergence of a breed of men who were not content with the approved body of knowledge or its wider social framework. These were the men of Enlightenment. They had to take real political risks which could cost them their freedom or even their lives. They were not professionals in any sense of the term used above: their intellectual activity was not the primary means of their livelihood; they regarded it not as a profession but as a vocation; they did not consciously try to specialise in narrow fields although (inevitably) by accident or design they learned and wrote about some subjects more than others; they did not distinguish sharply between living and learning. That was the age of the dominance of undemocratic political authority and the faith in tradition. Both men of theory and men of action fought to destroy that authority and to break this faith: they fought for democracy, progress and (sometimes) freedom.

The modern democratic nation state is not exactly what they fought for – but it was, in part, the (sour) fruit of their struggles. It is one which, to a varying extent, replaced 'participation' for subjection, and the faith in progress for the faith in tradition. Some (radical romantic) critics of the modern society, such as Burke and Carlyle, anticipated the unexpected features of the emerging *faith* in progress; some like Nietzsche lived in its midst and pointed to its shortcomings. They were struggling against a rising tide and their own 'solutions' would not afford them a good swimming technique even at the best of times. Some (critical rationalists such as Marx) were caught between the moral and cultural damages, and the material benefits, caused by the new faith. Here, we are merely concerned with that aspect of the issue which has a direct bearing on the development of the academic profession. This development lagged behind the growth and consolidation of the democratic nation state itself. Traditional universities were slow to adjust themselves to the new atmosphere, and modern intellectuals and scientists were not too keen to join them. Neither Faraday nor John Stuart Mill nor Marx nor Darwin were university academics.

It is only by the turn of this century when universities begin to regain their former functions as the dominant, if not exclusive, institutions for the advancement of (modern) learning. The democratic nation state has its own (visible or invisible) constraints for the scope of human action, including the direction of intellectual development and the expression of (new or critical) ideas. This observation touches on the extent of *real,* as distinct from statutory, individual liberties permitted which, in any case, significantly differ from one democratic state to another. But, *other things being equal,* these constraints are largely a function of size – i.e. the larger and the more intricate the network of democratic interrelationships the more limited the extent of *real* (as opposed to statutory) freedom. Or, to put it in alternative terms, the larger 'the mass' in a 'mass society' the less freedom is enjoyed by each individual member of it. As a rule, such states do not enforce these constraints directly; rather, they rely on the distribution of power within the democratic apparatus for doing so. In the world of intellect this power is delegated to universities, and other professional academic institutions – in particular, the power to appoint and, if not dismiss, then *dis*appoint potential and actual members. In turn, the criteria for the exercise of such power is vested with the leading élite ('the invisible college') of each disciplinary profession. It does not follow that these academic authorities are necessarily 'stooges' of the state. They certainly do feel some degree of responsibility in keeping the academic order in line with the broader aims and objectives of the society; but outside this broader framework they enjoy a substantial degree of autonomy in exercising their power. This autonomous power enables the leading élite of each discipline to draw purely academic lines between proper and improper conduct. In practice, proper academic conduct is to operate within the established framework (or, as the popular expression has it, 'toe the line') and improper conduct is to search for new ones. Hence, the slowness of the pace of intellectual progress. This, too, is a function of size. The growth in the number and size of the institutions of the academic profession has made an important contribution to this process by increasing the anonymity and irrelevance of the individual academic. Such a rapid rate of expansion has been most markedly observed nearly everywhere since the Second World War. The contemporary professional academic is less free and more insecure than he has ever been in the entire history of the modern academic profession.[7]

Another aspect of the modern civilisation which has a direct bearing on the present problem is the revolution in the division of labour in society, its impact on the growth of technology and the consequences of the latter in its turn on personal and social existence. There is no need to elaborate on the significance of growing specialisation for economic growth and development. The facts are well known and indisputable. Nevertheless, Adam Smith – who did more than anyone before him to emphasise the beneficial effects of division of labour for the growth of material welfare – made two important observations on its nature and consequences which were almost universally ignored by the main stream of his intellectual descendants. First, that the division of labour arose from a tendency among men to co-operate with one another even without personal acquaintance. No man, he said, can gain more than a few friends during his lifetime; but the division of labour makes it possible for men – who would otherwise never meet – to co-operate in order to see to each other's needs, and improve their collective welfare, by specialisation and exchange. They do not so from a charitable motive but with regard to their own self-interest; yet it is the need for co-operation, not conflict or competition, which unites them in this attitude. There is no contradiction involved in this statement. Any co-operation arises from some notion of self-interest which happens to be in line with the interest of others. Charity is sacrifice not co-operation. In other words, division of labour emphasises individual differences (the 'other-ness' of each individual) as a basis for social and economic unity (the 'one-ness' of the society).

Second, Adam Smith made that seminal observation – mentioned in Chapter 2 – that the growth of specialisation was likely to subject *industrial* labour to growing boredom and 'stupidity'. The reference to modern manufacturing wage labour is rather obvious, though implicit, since Smith emphasises the repetitive nature of *such* division of labour and the long hours of work involved: 'The brewer', 'the baker', the artisans and craftsmen as a whole, are all examples of division of labour in general. But the nature of specialisation in *modern industrial society* is such that it confines the wage labourer to activities whose fruits are not clearly identifiable. The worker does not identify with the product of his effort and he is left with little motive for his work than a mere material survival. Furthermore, the criterion for success is to 'produce' the *maximum* amount of the *smallest* part of the final product. Charlie Chaplin tried to portray this situation in his famous film, *Modern Times*. There is little or no chance for creativity, a sense of genuine involvement in one's work, a feeling of relevance and social significance regardless of the nature of the work. There is a separation of work and living; of quantity and quality; of labour and its fruit; of the individual and the society; of the individual's 'self' and his 'soul'. No wonder that the richest but most technologically advanced societies experience the highest incidence of mental disorder, where anyone who has a travel agent is also likely to have a psychoanalyst.

This situation gave rise to the development of the concepts of alienation, social alienation and self-alienation in the nineteenth century. The concept of alienation in general is at least as old as the Old Testament. The striving of man to break down the door of 'this eternal prison cell' and reunite with his Origins – the mystic concept of self-purification in seeking eternal freedom – has been the highest aim of many known and unknown men, past and present.[8] The crucifixion of Christ and the Nirvana of the Lord Buddha are held out as supreme examples of such a reunion, or liberation, by their followers. Hegel adapted the concept to his own – no less metaphysical – scheme of the movement of history towards the kingdom of Reason and Freedom. Marx brought it down to earth and linked it directly to the ill-effects of modern division of labour and the growth of technology for the meaning and quality of life for the mass of the people. Recent experiences – and, especially, the manifest dangers of an uncontrolled technology for the very basic human existence – have led to a revival of social and intellectual interest in the concept of alienation and the problems which it represents. As usual, there has been a good deal of intellectual obfuscation and/or over-zealousness in presenting the problem and suggesting solutions to it. This itself is evidence for that *intellectual* alienation which is a part of the broader concept: new, or newly revived, theories and problems tend to become yet another channel for academic entrepreneurship and/or practical indulgence in the current fashion. Herbert Marcuse, who had displayed a greater interest and insight into this problem than most of his contemporaries, ended up by becoming the spiritual leader of what Alasdair McIntyre described as 'the children's revolution'.[9]

What was true of the *manual* worker first, became equally true of the *mental* worker later. The scientist and the intellectual had been the direct or indirect leaders of technology and society. They strove for the growth of human knowledge in the hope of improving the material and social welfare of humanity. In doing so they enjoyed self-fulfilment both from the means and from the ends of their activities. They did specialise; but their specialisation was comparable to that of the craftsman, not the mass-producing worker of the modern factory system. They tried to solve *problems* which were, and remain, indivisible. Therefore, they could envisage and identify the fruits of their personal efforts. The solution to a problem is similar to the production of a whole violin; the constant preoccupation with one tiny aspect of that problem is like a lifetime's participation in the mass production of violin strings. Yet there is one important difference between the modern division of labour in material and in intellectual production. In the case of material production the conveyor belt mediates between the activities of numerous specialists in giving rise to the final, integrated, product: the motor-car is certain to leave the factory in one piece for all the world to see. But there is no such mediating agent for the highly specialised efforts of intellectual workers. Each one digs further and further into a small corner of the problem apart from the other, without there being an automatic or impersonal or even institutional agency which would bring all the pieces together and integrate the solution in one piece. Thus the whole solution is not only difficult to envisage by each single contributor – it may never be realised. It follows that the one and only advantage of great specialisation in material production, which is the growth of productivity, is lost to intellectual production – a fact which stands in total contrast to an ever-growing amount of *individual* 'output': papers which are seldom read and which very rarely provide a solution to anything at all. They do contribute, of course, to the advancement of the author's academic career, and this is more and more likely to become their sole function. How much all this has to do with the advancement of knowledge and the promotion of social welfare one is at a loss to know. Yet the strongest (rational) line of defence put forward by the defenders of modern academic professionalism and specialisation is that it is 'useful'.

There is evidence for some kind of 'useful' purpose served by this mode of academic behaviour and conduct, apart from its obvious 'usefulness' to the individual academic by promoting his career: it serves the requirements of a growingly impersonal and autonomous technology and technocracy; the rule of the Machine and those 'experts' who can communicate with small portions of it. We do not wish to indulge in science-fictional speculations, even though they look like becoming more and more scientific and less and less fictional. More explicitly, we do not claim that technology has now completely taken over the fate of man, even though it can be easily used to seal his fate for ever. We simply observe that the modern socio-technological fabric has become so intricate and so powerful that it is almost impossible for a single individual, or even a group of men, to confront it successfully. There can be no doubt that, *in this limited sense,* the Machine *is* ruling over the lives of men, and that – if the overriding social objectives remain such as they are – it is likely for this rule to become fully comprehensive. Already individuals have become prisoners of the small technological devices which they themselves own, be they motor-cars or television sets.

The professional academic who himself is a tiny link in this gigantic socio-technological structure can hardly be expected to apprehend its full dimensions – to cope with it, let alone to criticise, direct and reconstruct it. Indeed he becomes a mere servant to it. If he is good he plays the role of a maintenance technician; if he is not so good he would try to pretend to that role. Only when there is a total break-down is he asked to diagnose and prescribe; to search for a real solution to a real problem – he is not even allowed to anticipate the problem and suggest ways of preventing it. In any case he is generally ill-equipped to do so, morally, intellectually and professionally. This is the unique – as opposed to universal – social and historical atmosphere in which Kuhn's 'normal science' becomes literally normal. It was not so in the eighteenth, or even the nineteenth, century; it is not as acutely so in some societies as is in others even in our contemporary world. It finds its clearest manifestations in the most technologically advanced societies of our time where men specialise in the narrowest of fields; where such specialisation (or any claim to knowledge) is recognised only upon the proof of certificates; where the highest academic degrees can be given in the least possible intellectual subjects; where professional academics must 'publish or perish'; where individuals go berserk and shoot aimlessly at crowds of people; where 'nothing succeeds like success'. Popper makes the following observations on this situation as it affects normal science which are worth a full quotation:

The growth of normal science, which is linked to the growth of Big Science is likely to prevent, or even destroy, the growth of knowledge, the growth of great science. I regard the situation as tragic if not desperate; and the present trend in the so-called empirical investigations into the sociology of the natural sciences is likely to contribute to the decay of science. Superimposed upon this danger is another danger, created by Big Science: its urgent need for scientific technicians. More and more Ph.D. candidates receive a merely technical training, a training in certain techniques of measurement; they are not initiated into the scientific tradition, the critical tradition of questioning, of being tempted and guided by great and apparently insoluble riddles rather than the solubility of little puzzles. True, these technicians, these specialists, are usually aware of their limita-tions. They call themselves specialists and reject any claim to authority outside their specialities. Yet they do so proudly and proclaim that specialisation is a necessity. But this means flying in the face of the facts which show that great advances still come from those with a wide range of interests. If the many, the specialists, gain the day, it will be the end of science as we know it – of great science. It will be a spiritual catastrophe comparable in its consequences to nuclear armament.[10]

We have tried to argue that this is not merely characteristic of 'normal science', but of 'normal academic profession' in general; that it is a case of Big Professionalism replacing great vocationalism in shaping intellectual attitudes and efforts. According to a brilliant piece of classical Greek wisdom – quoted by Isaiah Berlin – 'the fox may know many things but the hedgehog knows one big thing'. There is a growing danger for the modern professional academic to qualify for neither description: he may neither know *many* things, nor even one big (i.e. *great*) thing.

CONCLUSION

All logical theories of scientific progress involve prescriptive statements. However logically sound and morally desirable a logical theory of scientific discovery might be, it does not automatically follow that it is generally observed by scientists. On the other hand, if such a logical theory is not a purely idealistic statement, then it must be a true description of scientific method and approach in *certain circumstances*. For example, it looks quite likely that a critical and undogmatic approach to knowledge and science was a dominant feature of scientific attitude from the Renaissance until the twentieth century, perhaps even the Second World War. This would mean that the broader social characteristics of science and the scientists were such that encouraged, permitted or tolerated a vocational attitude to the acquisition and advancement of learning. But changes in social and economic organisation and attitude have influenced the position and purpose of scientific and intellectual activity; consequently, they have also changed the social, moral and logical basis of the pursuit of knowledge. This shows that in describing *actual* scientific behaviour it is impossible to dispense with the sociological features which contribute to its formation. On the other hand, a 'sociological' description of scientific change which offers no casual explanation, and does not discuss the links between changes in society and in scientific attitude and conduct, tends to miss the sociology of science altogether: if social factors influence the mode of scientific and intellectual behaviour, then the latter is likely to evolve with changes in the social environment.

The development of the modern academic profession has been mainly a function of the emergence of the national democratic state and the revolution in the division of labour, both of which have rendered the human individual an increasingly powerless, faceless and isolated social entity. The modern professional academic is expected to specialise within a narrow disciplinary framework; to publish large quantities of work with relatively little consequence for the solution of real problems; to refrain from a broadly critical approach to his discipline and its established ideas; to serve the needs of a growingly dominant and complicated technology in place of leading it. The academic institutions, the disciplinary professions, and their leading élites, are the main instruments for enforcing these unwritten – but well-known – rules of academic behaviour. In such a framework it would be idealistic to expect the majority of academics to ignore the rules, both because their narrower self-interest would be at stake, and because many of them simply lack the intellectual equipment for doing so, since they have been brought up by the same system. It follows that a radical and gene-ralised change in the existing situation will not be effected by sporadic dissent, moral suasion or whatever, including statements and analyses of a kind which are offered in this essay. It is only a combination of public consciousness and the growing proximity of the abyss to which the 'technological mass society' seems to be leading us which may finally provoke a considerable change in both the means and the ends of social – even human – existence. Neither such a change nor lack of it is inevitable. Each of us would have a role and responsibility in helping or hindering it. For obvious reasons the intellectual community bears a greater responsibility in this. What is certain is that 'normal academic profession' is a social and historical phenomenon; it is incapable of generalising to all times past by selecting a few examples from history; is does not distinguish *mature* from *immature* science, but the *professional* from the *vocational* pursuit of all (scientific and non-scientific) knowledge; it does not promote the interest of science and human society in the best possible way. If it becomes permanently estab-lished 'it will be the end of science as we know it – of great science. It will be a spiritual catastrophe comparable in its consequence to nuclear armament'. This would be tantamount to the total abdi-cation of scientists and intellectuals from the most important and most vital function which they have served in history. If official and institutional science and knowledge go the same way as official and institutional religion went in the past, then there would have to be another renaissance – another great intellectual revolution – to liberate mankind from a degenerated science and its patriarchs.

6

VALUE JUDGEMENTS AND IDEOLOGY: MORALITY AND PREJUDICE IN ECONOMIC SCIENCE

THE PROBLEM

Few issues in the social sciences arouse emotions and controversy as strongly as the application of the concepts of moral judgement and ideological prejudice to the methods and substance of social theory. Yet few concepts are as frequently confused and misconstrued as these two concepts, by a large number of social scientists. These two observations are consistent, not contradictory. For, in general, the greater the confusion about a controversial subject, the stronger the degree of friction, and the heat which this generates.

Two distinct types of confusion are frequently met with respect to the twin concepts of value judgements and ideology: one is the total reduction of value judgements to ideology and vice versa – that is, the (implicit) belief that these two concepts are completely synonymous; the other is the confusion of the various meanings and implications of each concept taken separately. In this chapter we hope to clear up such problems of obscurity and misunderstanding; and assess the relevance and significance of norms, ethics and prejudices for the formation of (scientific) knowledge in general, and economic knowledge in particular.

The distinction between the concepts of value judgements and ideology (we hope) will become clear by the end of the chapter. But perhaps a few words on this subject may be helpful at the outset. Value judgements refer to *conscious* and *piecemeal* objective norms or subjective (moral) predilections – for example, that to eradicate poverty there should be a more even distribution of income; or, that there should be more political freedom enjoyed by the public. On the other hand, ideology refers to an *unconscious*, or 'semi-conscious', and *total* 'world view'. Even if ideology were assumed (as it is by some) to be a wholly conscious but total vision, it could not be reduced – as a concept – to a mere value judgement. It may be argued that value judgements are partial manifestations of total ideological commitments. That may be so. Although men with different – alleged or professed – ideologies sometimes share the same value judgements. But, in any case, it does not follow that these concepts can be reduced to a single category either for analytical or for practical purposes.

OF VALUE JUDGEMENTS

A most remarkable consequence of some of the above confusions is the very widespread view that a scientist, *qua* scientist, should concern himself with what there *is* rather than what there *ought to be*. (Indeed, it is sometimes believed that this is a sufficient criterion for a distinction between science and non-science; in Chapter 3 we demonstrated the falsehood of the latter view, and shall say no more about it here.) In economic theory this has become the line of demarcation between Positive and Normative Economics. No one can deny that there are statements which *explicitly* pertain to matters of fact, and statements which *explicitly* refer to matters of value. But beyond this truism – which we shall investigate further below – the above distinction is either trite or irrelevant.

The view that the scientist, *as such,* should address himself to questions regarding what there is, and not what there ought to be, can have any of the following (possible) meanings. First, it could mean that a scientist, in his capacity as a scientist, should not issue statements of a *form* which tells us what there ought to be: a physicist should not state that the combination of forces X and Y *ought to* generate energy Z; the economist should not assert that the relative prices of products A and B ought to be C. . . . But this is trite. Whoever in his role as a scientist has issued such a statement in the whole history of science? Second, it could mean that a scientist should not present an absurd statement of the type that X is what there is, but that in his view (as a scientist) there ought to be Y instead. Such a 'possibility' would hardly invite any comment, except that the scientist in question would be in danger of being certified. Finally, it could mean that a scientist should not misrepresent the truth in order to satisfy his own prejudices. This, of course, is a wholly unexceptionable maxim of intellectual behaviour. But, in the context of the present problem it is irrelevant. *Either* it means that the scientist should not conceal or bend the truth consciously, in which case it says no more than that he should not be a liar. Would that mean that non-scientists (or scientists without their professional hats) should be, or are free to be, wanton liars? *Or*, it means that he should not do so unconsciously, which is absurd: how can I try to do what I do *unconsciously*? In any case, unconscious distortions of truths are ideological or psychological categories; they do not imply moral judgements as *any judgement* is, by definition, a *conscious decision*. Therefore, to say that scientists, as such, should state what there is, not what there ought to be, is either trite or irrelevant. This, however, does not preclude a serious discussion on the role of value judgements in scientific discourse and discovery. For the problem itself is of great methodological – indeed, social – import.

Before proceeding to a discussion of the main issues it is necessary to discard one (implicit or explicit) claim; namely, that a scientist, *as such,* does not bear any responsibility for his 'objective' statements; and that he would be free to judge their consequences only *as an ordinary member of the public.* To be conscious of 'positively' contributing to potential death and destruction, and to denounce 'normatively' its consequences is not a particularly noble or consistent position. To advise Hitler, 'as a technologist', how a lot of raw materials can be produced from human corpses, and to regret, 'as a layman', the implementation of such a policy is either the worst possible kind of self-delusion, or (as it is much more probable) the most monstrous type of hypocritical apology. Certainly, it is a more ignoble position than Pontius Pilate's, and his likes; for the Roman was truly 'neutral'; he made no 'positive' contribution to 'what there was to be'.

In a general appraisal of the subject two questions need to be discussed first: (i) is it *at all possible* for individuals to develop theories, or report on observations, which are entirely value-free? (ii) if so, would this be (*at least in principle*) possible in *all* sciences or only in some – more specifically, in all sciences or only in natural sciences? In answering these two basic questions, scientists – and especially social scientists – usually divide into two broad categories: one group answers both questions in the affirmative; another group does so only in reply to the first question – that is, they assert that value-free theory and observation is possible in natural sciences but impossible in social sciences. As we shall try to show in a moment the answer to both those questions must be negative; that is, we shall argue that in *no* science is value-free theory or observation possible. But, while the position of the first group is thus claimed to be mistaken, the position of the second is even logically untenable: if 'value-freedom' is, in principle, possible, why should this be exclusive to natural sciences? The familiar replies to this objection run along the following lines. First empirical observations and/or controlled experiments are easier, and substantially more conclusive, in natural sciences; and second, the subject-matter of natural sciences is such that there can be appreciably less ulterior motives among natural scientists in formulating theories. The first argument is correct but irrelevant. It simply means that it is easier to refute theories in natural sciences *whether or not they contain subjective elements*. It neither supports the claim that a value-free natural science is possible, nor that a value-free social science is impossible; merely, that if subjectivity intruded in scientific ideas it would be easier to expose it, or nullify its effects, in natural sciences. That is all. The second argument is not entirely correct; it is also irrelevant. Some problems of natural science – such as many in genetics – have a direct bearing on social life and policy. Apart from that, ulterior motives include matters of pure self-interest – such as defending one's own theory, or an established idea, for psychological and/or career reasons – which do not discriminate between natural and social scientists. But even if this argument were entirely correct, it would still be irrelevant. For it would only mean that there is a greater temptation among social scientists to bend the truth; it would *not* mean that social scientists were incapable of formulating value-free theories if they wished to do so. Therefore, if it is *at all possible* for individuals to present value-free theories and observations then it must be possible for all sciences.

We assert that it is impossible in *any* science to present ideas of whatever kind which are, in the first instance, completely free of subjectivity. We saw in previous chapters that there are two basic, and conflicting, views of the process of scientific discovery: the one is best summarised by the motto 'all science begins with observation'; the other, by contrast, regards the process of scientific discovery as (at least) primarily theoretical and *a priori*. It automatically follows from the latter view that any scientific theory would be impregnated by subjective elements, for the simple reason that it is (at least immediately) a product of the human mind. Note, however, that this fact bears no relation to the issue of intellectual honesty or dishonesty. An *a priori* hypothesis is subjective by definition; that does not mean that it is necessarily dishonest nor, indeed, that it is necessarily incorrect.

That leaves us with the implications of the view that 'science begins with observations'. We have had many occasions to demonstrate the falsehood of this view in the foregoing chapters. Yet, even assuming it was correct, it could not support the claim that scientific theories could be entirely value-free, for the following reasons. First, facts in general, and scientific facts in particular, are not randomly observed. The observer – especially the scientific observer – is *looking for* them even before he succeeds in locating them. In other words, he uses certain criteria for *selecting* the *relevant* facts; and these criteria are themselves subjective, *a priori*, prior to the observation. Second, once selected, such facts, on their own, normally reveal or prove nothing as they stand. They are *processed* by certain procedures which are no part of that, or any other, observation; that is, by analytical and/or empirical *methods* which are entirely products of the human mind. Third, the so-called observer would even have to *select* the *appropriate* analytical and empirical methods – including laboratory tests – from a wide range of possibilities. . . . Finally, it is impossible to be completely value-free even in an *honest* reportage of the *barest* and *most 'random'* of all observable facts. Two men may report an 'observed' fact absolutely honestly; yet their respective statements may have a significantly different impact on their public. Compare: (i) 'In Nolandia the revolutionary forces have intensified their struggle for greater justice and freedom; in the latest confrontation no less than five-hundred of them were massacred by government troops'; (ii) 'In Nolandia the rebel forces have intensified their military activities against the ruling constitutional government; in the latest confrontation government troops inflicted a loss of no less than five-hundred men on the rebels.' . . .

What these arguments make of the concept of 'scientific neutrality' will depend on the precise meaning of this concept. If it means that scientists can, and should, be consciously honest, then there can be no objection. If it means that it is possible for *any* idea to be entirely value-free then it is false. If it means that men can be *indifferent* towards a certain problem then it is true; *but this is no more than saying that a certain* **moral** *position is described as indifference*: if I am indifferent between the survival and annihilation of the human race, the greater prosperity of the rich and the poor, the truth and falehood of a scientific proposition . . . it does *not* follow that I am avoiding a moral judgement; simply that I have reached the definite judgement that it is not necessary (or profitable) to take side on these issues. To forestall any confusion over this issue it is necessary to elaborate the argument a little further. It is neither impossible nor necessarily undesirable to be consciously neutral – i.e. indifferent – with respect to certain problems. An *impartial* judge or referee, a *conscientious* policy-adviser, etc., are all neutral in the sense that they judge the merits of the case without conscious bias. Furthermore, their neutrality is *morally right* because it is consistent with the calls of their office. It follows from this very example that neutrality *is* a moral position, a value judgement; but it does not follow that neutrality – or impartiality – by itself, and regardless of its context, is either necessarily *right or superior* to a conscious commitment.

To summarise: it is impossible for any idea to be entirely value-free even though it may have been formed by 'direct observation'; there is no fundamental difference between natural and social sciences in this regard; it is both possible and desirable for scientists to be consciously honest; ethical neutrality is meaningless, for indifference is itself a moral position.

Does this mean that objective knowledge is *inherently* impossible? Not at all. For even though *all* scientific ideas are value-impregnated, it does not mean that they are, therefore, incorrect; or that any idea is as good as any other. There are two basic methods which, *together*, test the objective truth of a theory *irrespective of its subjective elements*. First, criticism, for it is unlikely that the subjectivity of all the critics would be identical with that of the author – I may propose an incorrect idea, but my critics and/or nature can prove me wrong. This is a dialectical process in the literal sense of that phrase. Second, by the extent to which the predictions of a theory may be consistent or inconsistent with actual events. These two methods must be used jointly and – in particular – the *mere* consistency of a theory's predictions with actual events would not guarantee its truth: nothing can be true 'as if it were true' (for a demonstration of this point see 'Instrumentalism and Positive Economics' in Chapter 3). It follows that objective knowledge is possible when theories are inherently open to criticism *and* their predictions are not such that they would be inevitably consistent with all possible events. If a theory precludes the possibility of using these methods for an objective assessment of its claims, it may still be true; but there is no objective way of establishing its truth.

Up to now we have been discussing the status of descriptive or 'positive' statements – i.e. statements which *explicitly* pertain to matters of fact; we have said nothing about value judgements or 'normative' statements – i.e. statements which *explicitly* pertain to matters of value. It is commonly believed that *all* value judgements refer to matters of personal taste of opinion. Indeed, there is an almost universal consensus on this belief among social scientists. It is, nevertheless, incorrect. In Chapter 5 it was argued briefly that there are two distinct classes of normative statements, *only one of which explicitly contains matters of personal opinion*: when I say that a more even distribution of income is morally superior then I may be expressing my personal opinion and nothing else; but when I say that a more even distribution of income increases economic efficiency, or reduces social conflict, or mitigates hazards to public health . . . then (*whatever my real motives*) my statement is open to criticism and – at least in principle – can be proven wrong by actual events. We propose to call the first group of statements *moral judgements* or *ethical statements*; and the second group, *policy judgements* or *prescriptive statements*. The confusion of moral judgements with prescriptive statements is methodologically incorrect; besides, it can be socially dangerous. As an example of such a confusion, consider the following statement by a distinguished modern political economist – Milton Friedman:

> We do not regard it as 'discrimination' . . . if an individual is willing to pay a higher price to listen to one singer than another, although we do if he is willing to pay a higher price for services rendered by a person of one colour than by a person of another. *The difference between the two cases is that in one case we share the taste, and in the other we do not.* Is there any difference in principle between *the taste* that leads a householder to prefer an attractive servant to an ugly one and *the taste* that leads another to prefer a Negro to a white or a white to a Negro, except that we

sympathise and agree with the one *taste* and may not with the other?[1] [emphasis added]

But this is at best a half-truth: within its own terms of reference *it can be only true if all arguments against racial discrimination were moral judgements and nothing else.* Yet an argument such as 'racial discrimination is wrong because it results in civil strife, economic inefficiency, political instability or whatever' is not a matter of opinion. It is inherently a statement of fact, and can be shown to be incorrect. Compare the following prescriptive statements, none of which is a matter of personal *taste or opinion:* (i) 'If it is socially desirable to increase the geographical mobility of goods and economic resources, then it is necessary to construct an efficient network of transport and communications'; (ii) 'If it is beneficial to the community to prevent a smallpox epidemic, then members of the public must be innoculated against smallpox'; (iii) 'If a reduction of racial conflicts and the eradication of poverty are two important social objectives, then discrimination on grounds of race and colour must be prohibited.' Clearly there is no basic difference among these three prescriptive statements, all of which are open to refutation – either by pointing out that they have defined the social objectives incorrectly, or that the proposed policies would not attain those ends.

As it happens, the propositions of some scientific disciplines are typically prescriptive – *not* descriptive – in nature. Medicine is one; economics is another.

OF VALUE JUDGEMENTS IN ECONOMIC SCIENCE

The general case has been stated and economic science is no exception to it: all economic ideas, like all scientific ideas, are value-impregnated; individual economists can, and should, be consciously honest in proposing or assessing given theories (but they may not be); no economist can be *morally* neutral *vis-à-vis* any economic issue, for indifference is itself a moral judgement; economic theories may be objectively correct, but that can be ascertained only if they are inherently open to criticism *and* their predictions are not inevitably consistent with all possible outcomes. We showed in Chapter 3 that many basic neo-classical theories do not possess these two essential features for assessing their objective truths; and that those which do are usually defended and retained even when they are refuted. Our model of the foregoing chapter was meant to explain this pattern of behaviour.

The distinction between positive and normative statements – which some Positive Economists, together with some of their critics, even believe to be the sufficient criterion for scientificity – is meaningful only in as much as it states the obvious; that is, there is a distinction between explicitly descriptive statements and explicitly normative statements. We have shown that explicitly descriptive statements are value-impregnated, even though they may be objectively correct; and explicitly normative statements are not necessarily *moral* judgements, whether or not they are acceptable. The multiplicity of confusion about these concepts and their significance has led to the formal consensus among economists that *economic theory* is, or can be, value-free, whereas *economic policy* (necessarily) involves *moral* judgements.[2] Neither of these propositions is correct. But even if they were they would involve a logical contradiction. For they would mean that, in their scientific roles, economists may discover objective truths; but as soon as they use these objective truths in offering advice to policy-makers they would necessarily become involved in moral judgements. Suppose I discovered, 'objectively', that in a set of well-defined circumstances the devaluation of a national currency would have inflationary consequences. Suppose further, that – in such circumstances – I advised the policy-makers that if they wished to avoid inflation they should not devalue the currency. In what sense would this involve me in a *moral* judgement? What else could I possibly say which would be more honest and 'objective', and less dispassionate than this? Policy prescriptions *could* be dishonest; that is, they could be moral judgements disguised as dispassionate advice – but so could 'positive' statements. Policy prescriptions could also contain explicit moral judgements; in which case they would be openly known as such. But they *could* be neither. Therefore to maintain that economic policy categorically involves moral judgements is both incorrect and self-contradictory. Our distinction between statements of opinion (or moral judgements) and statements of policy (or prescriptive statements) is relevant to this argument. An honest policy adviser who, to the best of his knowledge, informs his client, or writes in his book, that in order to achieve objective X, method *Y* should be used is certainly making a prescriptive recommendation – but not a moral judgement.

We assert that *not only statements of economic policy, but nearly all the fundamental statements of economic science are, one way or another, prescriptive; that is to say, economics is characteristically not a 'positive' – i.e. descriptive – but a 'normative' – i.e. prescriptive – science.* When Adam Smith sang in praise of the division of labour he (explicitly) meant that if a rise in material welfare was a desirable public goal then the division of labour would contribute to it. When he argued that 'every frugal man is a public benefactor', he meant that if economic growth was an important social objective then thriftiness would help promote that objective through the accumulation of capital. Ricardo's theory of comparative advantage means that free trade would, or could, increase the material welfare of two trading partners: i.e. if this is the goal, then that is the method. John Stuart Mill defined the subject-matter of economics as 'Wealth . . . the nature of Wealth . . . including the operation of all causes by which the condition of mankind . . . is made prosperous or reverse. . .'[3] The neo-classical economists, past and present, have been largely preoccupied with the determination of conditions which would, or could, ensure the efficient allocation of resources; that is, conditions which would, or could, render the greatest aggregate material welfare from limited resources, *assuming that this is a desirable social objective.*

Correct or incorrect, these are all *prescriptive theories:* they purport to offer the best methods of achieving private or public objectives which are presumed to be desirable. Even theories concerning micro- and macro-economic equilibrium conditions, and their stability, are of this *prescriptive* nature. Because, assuming that such goals are desirable, they seek to investigate the conditions in which markets are cleared, and the full-employment aggregate output is produced. Economic growth is obviously a normative objective; theories of steady-state growth attempt to discover the conditions which fulfil this goal without a growing under-utilisation of resources, or price inflation and external deficits – which are held to be other important social desiderata . . . von Mises, who somewhere is his book, makes the trite or irrelevant remark that 'Economics has to explain . . . how prices are really arrived at, not how they ought to be arrived at',[4] displays awareness, somewhere else, that economics is indeed a normative science: he proudly admits that economic theory investigates the conditions of (perhaps maximum) prosperity, and he challenges whoever seeks the opposite to promote a science of poverty and dissatisfaction for himself.[5] 'Positive' economics does not exist. It is a product of misunderstanding. Economics is a normative, prescriptive, science.

This is clear enough. But it is a pretty unfamiliar argument and, for this reason, if none other, it may be prone to misunderstanding and misinterpretation. Therefore, let us explain the same point from a different angle. There is a totally absurd, but rather 'convenient', view according to which all theories regardless of their subject-matter – and the methods used in obtaining them – are simply *matters of opinion*. There is nothing, repeat nothing, in the foregoing arguments which would condone such a perfectly ridiculous position. On the contrary, we have emphasised that not only descriptive statements (though inevitably value-impregnated) are not matters of 'opinion'; but even prescriptive statements do not have to be matters of personal 'taste or preference'. Both types of statement can be incorrect; both can be dishonestly stated: *but neither statement has to be.* There is only one category of statement which necessarily pertain to matters of opinion – that is, the class of ethical judgements, such as 'red is *better* than blue' or 'racial discrimination is *unfair*'. The division of economics into 'positive' and 'normative' involves two basic mistakes: (i) that there is a substantial (indeed, the main, the 'scientific') body of economic knowledge which is purely '*descriptive*'. This is simply untrue, and we have already referred to a number of very important examples from past and present to prove the point; (ii) that the remaining body of economic knowledge – concerning matters of economic policy – is '*normative*', i.e. pertaining to matters of opinion on moral judgement. This is also incorrect: (*a*) because nearly all the so-called 'positive' statements and theories are themselves prescriptive; (*b*) because prescriptive statements are not necessarily matters of opinion; (*c*) because, in any case, an honest prescription based on a correct description is *not* a matter of opinion. There is no doubt that *policy decisions by parties and governments* are matters of ethical choice. There is no doubt either that a *policy adviser* may be biased in his advice. But these obvious truths have nothing to do with the case in hand. The point simply is that prescriptive statements are not necessarily matters of opinion; and, as a matter of fact, economics is a prescriptive science.

Economics is essentially a prescriptive science. But this fact neither means that economics is an inherently unscientific discipline, nor that economic theories are inherently 'matters of opinion'. We do not believe in a metaphysical superiority of any intellectual discipline which is – rightly or wrongly – described as 'scientific', over one which is not. Those who do – and they include many economists – need not infer from the above arguments that economics is not, or cannot be, a scientific discipline. Or – to expose another psychological weakness of many economists – that, *for this reason,* economics is less scientific than 'physics'. As a prescriptive science, economics can provide scientific solutions to real economic problems which happen to be normative in nature. Whether or not it *does* so has no bearing on the nature of the problems; it is basically determined by the attitude and methods of economists themselves. Scientificity is essentially a question of method and outlook, not the descriptiveness or prescriptiveness of theories: a prescriptive theory may be methodologically scientific; a descriptive theory may not be. To say that the chemical compound commonly known as aspirin is helpful in relieving headaches, though prescriptive, is not unscientific; but to say that the universe is finite (or infinite), though descriptive, can be unscientific. Either statement may or may not be correct. What distinguishes them is that the first statement *can* be proven false, whereas the second statement may not be. If economic theories are not scientific it is not because they generally concern prescriptive problems; it is because many of them are immune to criticism; because those which are not tend to be defended at all costs; because professional academic economics, and its leading élite, prefer intellectual conformity to intellectual criticism; because the emphasis in research is more on irrelevant or minor puzzles than on relevant and important problems; because the inordinate weight given to publication, and the resulting publication explosion, threaten to leave little time or incentive for broader reading, greater reflection and eventful discoveries; because even when the small minority tries to do the opposite, then – apart from incurring other costs – it is inhibited from making a commensurate impact if only for the reason that the great scientific majority often fails to understand their purpose and method.

Is there an ethical bias in orthodox economic theory? Yes, there is. Orthodox economic theory is ethically biased because, as a prescriptive science, it is lopsided and selective: in all its basic theories it addresses itself to one set of social objectives only; that is, the static (and, recently, dynamic) problems of the efficient allocation of national – and international – resources. And it ignores other important social objectives by arbitrarily relegating them to the realm of 'moral judgements'. For example, it pretends that the improvement of *aggregate welfare* is somehow a 'scientific', 'neutral', 'positive' or whatever social objective; whereas the promotion of *scientific welfare* is a matter for 'moral judgement', for 'personal taste'. Thus, orthodox economic theory makes the (implicit) ethical judgement that the society ought to value the former objective more than the latter (even if it was true that those two social goals were necessarily competitive). Great social objectives include an efficient and full utilisation of economic resources; a decent (yes, *decent*) minimum standard of living; a fair (yes, *fair*) distribution of income; an agreeable (yes, *agreeable*) condition for daily labour; a healthy (yes, *healthy*) environment for living. . . . These are not this author's own value judgements. *They are all important objectives sought by the human society.* No doubt, there are social groups which – for reasons of self-interest – value some of these objectives above others. But, as scientists charged with providing the best methods of solving all such problems we simply have no right to select a few for 'scientific' investigation, and demote the rest by throwing them into the dustbin of 'personal opinion'. Witness the fact that the most elegant, the most rigorous, the most popular *and* the most partial definition of the 'research agenda' of neo-classical economic theory defines economics 'as a relationship between ends and scarce means which have alternative uses'.[6] Yet, when, in 1933, this definition appeared for the first time, up to a third of the economic resources of western societies were out of work: there was no scarcity of economic means; only economic wisdom.

OF IDEOLOGY

Ideology is a tricky, at least slippery, concept. It could mean all things to all men. We have already noted that it is often confused as a moral judgement and nothing else. Sometimes it is used to describe nothing but conscious lies; sometimes lies in the soul. Sometimes it is intended to refer to conspiracies by interest groups;

sometimes to victimisations of men by blind forces over which they have no control. . . . It is, indeed, a jungle of a concept, capable of accommodating all sorts of species – especially in intellectual gang warfares. Yet, the concept of ideology is important in helping us to understand why men think and act as they do; or, at least, this is what it claims to do. Therefore, it cannot be laughed out of court; it qualifies for a critical evaluation.

First, let us dispense with irrelevancies. Described as a *moral vision* which defines the boundaries of our thoughts and actions, ideology would mean nothing but pure *faith*. Why, then, should we use a less familiar term and concept for something which is otherwise unambiguously apprehended by everyone? Defined merely as an *entirely conscious* framework within which men defend their personal and/or class interests, the concept of ideology would become indistinguishable from ordinary and empirical, even though systematic, selfishness, lies and conspiracies. For, it is obvious that – puttng aside pathological cases – when individuals and groups lie, or conspire against others, they do so solely in order to promote their own interests: what is the difference between a capitalist lying to his workers in order to increase his own profit, and lying to another capitalist in order to do the same? What is the difference between a capitalist conspiracy in one country so as to cheat another capitalist country, or a socialist country? What is the difference between a conspiracy by a socialist country to invade another socialist country, or a capitalist country? . . . No doubt there are different political and moral implications in all such cases; and, precisely because of the judgement involved, some would think that – in each case – one type of conspiracy is better than another. We simply wish to make it clear that such usages of the term and concept of ideology are redundant: pure faiths, lies and conspiracies – whatever the motives behind them – are known for what they are; the application of 'ideology' in such cases can serve little purpose but to cause an unnecessary conceptual and terminological burden. Finally, let us dispense with the most widespread, and the most nauseating, usage of the term and concept of ideology: when a man, *without further argument,* contemptuously dismisses another man's ideas and actions as being 'obviously ideological' – 'bourgeois', 'Marxist' or whatever – then *all* that he is saying is that he disagrees with the other man. It is the most insidious, the most arrogant, the most selfish and the most unjust abuse of the concept of ideology. It proves nothing but the manifest ignorance and the dialectical poverty of the 'debater'.

The concept of ideology has had a long and varied history. Its very basic elements go, at least, as far back as Plato, who insisted on a clear distinction between the world of cognition, or *appearance,* and the world of essences, or *reality.* Men could only perceive of appearances; of what their senses enabled them to perceive. It did not follow that what was accessible by their sensory perception was identical with the essence or reality of the phenomena which they observed. Had I grown up in total isolation in a confined space, my perception of the world would have been limited to my observations and experiences within that space; yet I would be mistaken in thinking that those were the ultimate boundaries of human and physical existence. Therefore, empirical knowledge can at best enable us to scratch the surface of reality, or true knowledge. It could also be misleading and dangerous. The conception of reality could only come (if at all) from within, not without, the human soul: 'the kingdom of God is within you'. This is a long, complicated and open-ended problem in the realm of Metaphysics which, beyond the above simple references, we cannot take up here. Throughout history saints and mystics of all denominations have been seeking the hidden truth, the essential reality of existence; many have reported experiences beside which those of the great prophets compare with the achievements of a theatrical magician.

Paradoxically, the term 'ideology' was invented at the turn of the nineteenth century, to denote *the science of ideas,* just as cosmology referred to the scientific study of the cosmos, or pathology refers to the science of organic decay. Its inventor was Destutt de Tracy, the director of the Institut de France, a high-calibred institute of scientific research whose neo-classical building still attracts visitors to the great city of Paris. Not unlike our own age, this was the period of the misconceived but undiluted and uncritical *faith* in reason, science and 'the scientific method'. Marquis de Condorcet wrote, in the last decade of the eighteenth century:

> The sole foundation of belief in the natural sciences is . . . that the general laws directing the phenomena of the universe . . . are necessary and constant. Why should this principle be any less true of the intellectual and moral faculties of man than for other operations of nature?[7]

Henri de Saint-Simon and his disciple Auguste Comte soon after set about to apply, in detail, Condorcet's extension of the 'belief in natural sciences' to 'the intellectual and moral faculties of man'. A brief summary of this intellectual atmosphere, and its consequences, has already appeared in Chapter 2. Laplace – whose Machine, when invented, would tell the whole history of the universe and predict its total future destiny – was a distinguished member of the Institut de France. Its director believed that a science of ideas could be founded which would rewrite the history of ideas – and assess ideas in general – scientifically; that is, by means of unbiased historico-empirical generalisation. We would then have 'scientific laws' for evaluating ideas and predicting the course of their future developments. Clearly, this was a declaration of war on Metaphysics, and religious beliefs. Yet its misconception of science, and 'the scientific method', quickly turned it (upside down) into a metaphysical concept.

Hegel, like Plato, was a master metaphysician, with the difference that the classical master had expressed his (difficult) ideas, on the whole, with reasonable clarity, whereas the modern master did so with considerable (some would say deliberate) obscurity. Whatever the causes of Hegel's formal obscurity, it has helped the growth of an unfortunate tradition (both in philosophy and in sociology) of a cult of grandiloquence, and obscure, if not obscurantist, expression. Indeed, the reader sometimes wonders whether a practitioner of this tradition has something valuable to say, or merely uses it as a cloak to hide the simplicity or emptiness of his ideas. At any rate, at the hands of Hegel the concept of ideology recaptured its Platonic elements. For the distinction between appearance and reality was also fundamental to Hegelian thought. History was a progressive but dilectical movement of Spirit or Mind towards Perfection, the Absolute Idea, or the total ascendancy of Freedom and Reason. What *exactly* Hegel meant by the Absolute Idea is still unclear to some lesser mortals. Bertrand Russell once deciphered the following sense from a highly complex definition given by Hegel himself: 'The Absolute Idea is pure thought thinking about pure thought.'[8] We have none better to offer. In his radical youth Hegel had been highly impressed by the power of ideas (as he thought) in effecting great social changes – by the French Revolution.[9] He emphasised that 'being and becoming', facts and aspirations – what there is, what there ought to be and what there will be – are not separable. At each stage of history ideas, and the reasons upon which they were based, were by definition imperfect; they conceived of reality only as far as the (spiritual) progress of history would permit them; not beyond that. Ideology was, therefore, our false – or, at least, partial and imperfect – consciousness, or conception of truth, at each stage of history; the truth, or the whole truth, would be known only in the final, perfect and eternal stage. Indeed, all the stages but the last one made up not the *history* but the *pre*history of man; for human life and its history would meaningfully begin when men could know the truth, the whole truth. It is important to emphasise one point which, in our view, is to Hegel's credit: Hegel was not a historical relativist; that is, he did not believe that truth is different at each stage of history – there was only one truth; it was our ideological (mis-)understanding of it which varied from one stage to another.

Marx stood Hegel on his head – almost. He attacked the view that ideas alone determined the course of events, and he stressed the role of natural environment, technology and institutions in influencing individual and social existence; and their changes. The scope of scientific discovery at each stage of history was limited because, at every stage, man set himself such problems as he could possibly solve. Or, what is the same thing, problems which demanded solutions bore a definite relationship to the (changing) needs and requirements of human life. Social and material constraints did not prevent speculation into the nature of any conceivable problem. But when a problem was too abstract, too irrelevant to the contemporary environment, it would be very difficult to resolve satisfactorily; and if somehow (by accident or ultra-genius) it was resolved, it would languish for want of application – it would be generally ignored until later, when socio-environmental relevance would force its being uncovered, or rediscovered.

Further, Marx argued that, in their conception of social reality, men were strongly influenced not only by their personal history and self-interest, but notably by their social history and class interest. They were neither conscious conspirators nor victims of T. S. Eliot's 'vast impersonal forces' – they were liars in the soul. Their knowledge of truth was such that it was consistent with their personal and class interest, but they were not wanton liars because of this; they genuinely believed in their own bent, or partial, truths: a man brought up in a certain environment, a certain socio-economic class, its material standard of living, its cultural and moral values, etc., would tend to view the world against that background. Yet this was (implicitly) intended as an abstract model: a general theory based – as they all are – on some simplified assumptions in order to focus attention on a single factor, or set of factors. Certainly, it did not claim to fit all cases at all times perfectly; or, that it was impossible for some individuals to break out of those constraints. This is a simple fact which, nevertheless, many Marxists, and most critics of Marx, have yet to realise.

There are, therefore, two concepts of ideology in Marx's thoughts which are at once distinct and interrelated: one, which explains the potential boundaries of all intellectual discovery at different stages of history (or within given social frameworks); another which explains differences in the conception of the same phenomena when these relate to matters of self- or class-interest. Put together: that which is possible to know within a given environment is generally limited to the needs, and by the achievements, of that environment; men's personal and social histories influence their knowledge of even that which can be possibly known. There is still one truth only; our limited means and aspirations prevent us from discovering it all at once; and our personal and social histories influence us in twisting those aspects of truth which have bearings on our self- or class-interest. For example, both Marx and Nassau Senior argued that profit (over and above the cost of capital and workers' subsistence) was a surplus, or residual, income. This was a 'unique truth'. The difference was that Senior defined it as a reward for the 'abstinence' of capitalists (from immediate consumption), while Marx described it as exploitation. Senior's view carried the implicit assumption that capitalists were legitimately entitled to what they initially owned; Marx's view carried the explicit assumption that they were not – indeed, he located the origin of capitalist properly in expropriation.

Marx – like Hegel before him – was not a historical relativist. Many Marxists were, and still are. But Marx was not a Marxist.

Lukács – the late distinguished Marxist philosopher and literary critic – developed and enhanced Marx's concept of ideology on the basis of an indeterministic and unrelativistic interpretation similar to the rudimentary sketch presented above. A discussion of his important contribution is, however, beyond the scope of this essay. Karl Mannheim, a qualified and critical follower of Lukács on this subject, presented a more academic – i.e. less *engagé* – analysis of the concept of ideology which is sometimes described as 'the socio-

logy of knowledge'. Yet, in spite of its inordinate fame and influence, Mannheim's contribution was both limited and misleading.
His descriptive classification of ideology (into 'general', 'particular', etc.) added little to the existing knowledge of the subject.
His argument that, at each stage of history, an undefined and
arbitrary group of free, floating intellectuals could rise above
ideological constraints was tautological; it also missed the point: it
misunderstood the concept of ideology as a statement of unexceptionable fact, rather than an abstract theory with a claim to
general, *not total,* applicability. It made an eventful mistake by
implying that, in their work, natural scientists were immune to
ideological intrusions, and that natural sciences alone could be
value-free. We have already demonstrated the falsehood of this
view. All science is value-impregnated; but it does not follow that,
for this reason, it is incorrect.[10]

OF IDEOLOGY IN ECONOMIC SCIENCE

We have seen that all scientific (including economic) knowledge is
value impregnated; that scientific objectivity is not impossible; that
ethical neutrality is not possible because indifference is itself a
moral position; that normative statements may express either
matters of taste, or testable prescriptions; that propositions of
economic theory generally are (or can be) of the latter kind; that,
therefore, economics is a prescriptive science; that there is an
ethical bias in orthodox economic theory in so far as it arbitrarily
discriminates between different socio-economic objectives. The
question now is: what is the relevance of the concept of ideology to
economic science and its development?

First, let us consider the relevance of the concept of ideology not
as *false,* but as *limited* consciousness. That is, the argument that
nature, the level of technology, and the socio-institutional framework (which include the existing stock of knowledge) both direct
and constrain the scope of discovery at each stage of history. This is
a reasonable argument. Expressed more rigorously, it states that,
given our needs and requirements, the means at our disposal, the
existing social organisation and the stock of knowledge on which to
build (most, if not all, of which are finite), the stock of discoverable
knowledge is neither infinite nor random: they yield a limited, and
socio-environmentally relevant, advance in knowledge; and when

those limits are extended, and needs altered, so will be the limits and directions of advancement in knowledge. Broadly speaking, it is rather clear why a workable flying machine could not be designed – among other things – before the invention of the internal-combustion engine, even though man's aspiration for (and attempts at) flying date back to times immemorial; why nuclear physics had to emerge, say, after Newton and Faraday, although the atomistic theory of matter has been with us since the Greeks; why Papin's 'steam boat' did not attract much attention, whereas (a century later) Watt's steam engine revolutionised production and life itself. . . .

By analogy, the Mercantilists defined profit as a monetary surplus – the difference between the buying and the selling price – because, in their socio-economic environment and organisation, profit was predominantly a return on merchant capital. They often identified the national income with the stock of money in circulation because the aggregate velocity of circulation of money was relatively low, perhaps even insignificantly higher than unity;[11] they sought a trade surplus for their respective countries, because no country exercised free trade. . . . Their theories and observations were simple; so were the economic frameworks whose problems they tackled. On the whole they were not too far wrong; certainly not as much as later economists gave them *dis*credit for. Classical economists faced the problems of a developing economy, a society in the process of industrialisation. So they investigated the determination of relative prices, the distribution of income, the causes of population growth, the conditions of economic progress, etc. Early neo-classicals flourished in mature industrial societies, dominated by small-scale production, limited public intervention and slow growth. Therefore, they concentrated on a detailed study of static micro-economic problems; there can be no doubt that some of the success of the Marginalist method was due to this general socio-economic environment. Contemporary neo-classical and Keynesian economists pay a great attention to macro-economic and dynamic problems for similar socio-environmental reasons. How well or badly these economists (past and present) have done in choosing appropriate methods, and solving the relevant problems, is another matter. None of this implies that truth is divisible; that each set of conditions gives rise to 'its own truth': it simply means that the questions we ask bear a relation to our living conditions;

and that different questions have different answers to them.

There remains the relevance of ideology as false consciousness, or total *class* bias or vision, and its relevance to economic theory, past and present. This is the subject on which feelings run particularly high, and accusations and counter-accusations are frequently made. This concept is certainly helpful in a *general* analysis of why we think and do as we do. But it is extremely difficult to apply *in particular*. For unless a person's ideological commitment is self-professed, it would be almost impossible to prove. It is usually a waste of time to criticise a theory mainly along ideological lines – in any case, there are more effective and less arbitrary methods of criticism available if we choose to employ them. As Schumpeter has put it, let us assume that an economist's ideas – say those of Adam Smith – are entirely ideological; given that assumption, what is worth criticising is how he argued his case and what analytical methods he used. [12] In other words: damn his (conscious or unconscious) motives; to what extent, and in what context, does he make sense, if at all? Sa'adi, the Persian classic, tells us about a young man who dismissed the preachers' prescriptions on the grounds that they themselves did not practise them. His father reminded him that he should assess what they *say*, not what they *are* or *do:* 'a good lesson should be learned, even if it is written on the wall'. A bad one does not have to be learned; it can be criticised and rejected.

This, in general, has been our line of approach throughout this book. We have examined economic theories, methods, value judgements, etc., and we have tried to show their weaknesses wherever we have found them. What real gain could there be if we now claimed that these are 'obviously due to ideological bias' (especially as we do not feel able to *prove* this)? In any case, a simple accusation of capitalist class-bias against orthodox economic theory would fly in the face of the fact that many neo-classical theories are unhelpful in solving the problems of the contemporary capitalist economy. And that is not because (or mainly because) of the limited capacity and potential of economic knowledge. It is because the theories answer either highly abstract or wholly imaginary 'problems'. The community at large does not take the theories and views of academic economists very seriously – and the *business* community least of all. Whatever the ideological basis or origin of the contemporary (professional) academic economics, at present it looks as if the method and substance of the 'research agenda' set by its leading élite (or 'invisible college') indicates a considerable amount of autonomy. We shall discuss this subject in some detail in the following chapters. As for the individual academic economists, many of them are more concerned about securing their posts and improving their prospects than defending Big Business. Perhaps the two are not entirely separable. But still it is *their own interest* which they are trying to defend. When, in Russia, the Bolsheviks were firmly saddled in power, they very soon attracted multitudes of 'converts' – not least from the professional and intellectual communities. It has happened elsewhere, and it could – it *would* – happen anywhere. That, indeed, is the tragedy. That, if anything, is the 'treason' of the modern intellectual community: their lack of commitment to any serious principle for its own sake; their readiness to submit to power regardless of its source, nature or moral foundation. . . . We have discussed the features of academic professionalism in the previous chapter.

It would be unduly repetitive to summarise the main arguments and conclusions of this chapter, as this has been already done at several stages. Economic theory is a prescriptive science; its ethical bias lies in its selectivity with respect to great, and equally important, social objectives.

7

ECONOMIC THEORY AND MATHEMATICAL ECONOMICS: ABSTRACTION AND GENERALISATION IN ECONOMIC SCIENCE

THE SIGNIFICANCE OF ECONOMIC THEORY

Any body of scientific knowledge must contain a hard core of fundamental theories. These theories – at least in the first instance – must be products of the process of isolation, abstraction and generalisation. That is, they must be based on simple – and *general* – hypothetical models of the world of reality which may turn out to be more *or* less true in their application to concrete, complex – and *specific* – situations. A scientific theory cannot be the result of a generalisation from 'direct' observation: there is no such thing as 'direct observation'; all observations presuppose hypotheses; empirical generalisations (or 'laws') can at best describe, not explain, the phenomena, because, by definition, they cannot establish casual relationships; they are, therefore, of little predictive value because they describe what has been 'observed', not what will be. This is true both of direct generalisations from contemporary, and from past 'observations'; both of empiricism and of historicism. Yet historicism has at least one advantage over empiricism: it cannot claim to be based on 'direct observation', and therefore it is more obviously impregnated with interpretive valuations.

Scientific theories are characteristically abstract and general. Indeed, this very fact has misled many into the erroneous belief that scientific theories must have *universal validity*. The simple point is somehow lost that *precisely because scientific theories are abstract and general, they must be incapable of universal application*. Moreover, the more abstract and general a theory the *narrower* its field of application. Abstraction enables a theory to specify the conditions in which it claims to hold – or, what is the same thing, to exclude all of the many more situations to which the theory would *not* apply. The resulting theory is nevertheless general *in the sense of explaining the relevant phenomena in all the circumstances which correspond to those specified conditions.* If the theory is borne out in those circumstances then it may be correct; if not then it is false. If it is successful in conditions other than those which are specified then it is not necessarily false; but the fact that it apparently 'works' is no guarantee for its truth.[1] If it holds in any and all circumstances then it is not a scientific theory: it is no more than a truism, a tautology or whatever.

The above argument applies to *all* scientific theories – including (in case anyone is worried) physics! More explicitly, it is a mistake to believe, as many do, that in the social sciences alone theories are incapable of universal application: it is often argued that, because of the 'constancy' of nature, theories of the natural sciences can be universally valid; but the dynamic characteristics of socio-economic phenomena make *universal* socio-economic theories unattainable. On the other hand, the opponents of this view usually retort by claiming that there are no such basic differences between natural and social phenomena. That is, they argue that theories of the natural sciences are universally valid but they insist that (at least in principle) this is equally true of social theories. A decisively confusing aspect of such debates is that they quickly transform into arguments on historical relativism.[2] They, therefore, end in a statement of metaphysical and ideological differences. We do not believe that philosophical visions and ideological commitments are of no relevance to this issue. We merely emphasise the fact that ideological arguments are unnecessary for the claim that not only social theory but *all* scientific theory is incapable of *universal application* in time and space: that is, we contend that, to show the truth of this proposition, purely logical and methodological arguments will be sufficient.

For example, compare the following statements, neither of which is universally valid: (i) *given a certain force of gravity,* freely falling bodies will accelerate at the rate of 32 feet per second *in a state of vacuum*; (ii) *given an industrial market society,* the equilibrium wage rate will be equal to the value of the marginal product of labour *in a state of perfect competition.* It follows from the first proposition that (*a*) the theory is *inapplicable* to situations where there is no gravitational force; and (*b*) even where there is a certain force of gravity the rate of acceleration of a freely falling body would be *32 feet per second* only in a state of vacuum. It follows from the second proposition that (*a*) the theory is *inapplicable* to situations where there is no industrial market economy; and (*b*) even in such an economy the equilibrium wage rate will be equal to *the value of the marginal product of labour* only in a state of perfect competition. In the two propositions taken together the existence of a gravitational force and an industrial market economy define the general scope of application; and the assumptions of vacuum and perfect competition specify the conditions in which the predicted events will be precisely obtained: in the absence of gravity nothing will fall; and outside the industrial market economy the *marginal* product of labour will not be the basis for the labourer's share of output. Likewise, when there is no vacuum the rate of acceleration will not be 32 feet per second ever in the presence of a certain gravitational force; and when there is no perfect competition workers will not receive the *value* of their marginal product even in an industrial market society.[3] Clearly, neither of the two propositions is *universally* valid, although both of them are abstract and general hypotheses. And this is true of *all* scientific theory. Which scientific theory was ever held to be more universally valid than Newton's Laws of Mechanics before Einstein demonstrated their limited applicability?

The hypothetical model of Robinson Crusoe – a parody of the neo-classical concept of homo-economicus extensively used by Cannan, Wicksteed and Robbins – has now been flogged to death both by its proponents and by its critics.[4] In general, the critics have tended to dismiss this model for its atomistic hedonism – that is, for the indispensable assumption of the liberal theory of political economy according to which each man maximises his own welfare apart from others. This issue is not unimportant; but it is unnecessary for proving the irrelevance of the model of Robinson Crusoe for the analysis of the economic problems of an organised society: to give but a few simple examples, the Crusoe model tells us nothing about aggregate unemployment, income distribution, the role of money, the causes of inflation and the conditions of economic development. In short, if the Crusoe model is correct then it may apply to all such cases when a 'modern' man is completely isolated from his own social environment. That is, if the model is correct then we should not expect a man in those conditions to commit suicide, go crazy or become a mystic; rather, we should expect him to proceed to allocate his material resources efficiently by considering (for example) the opportunity cost of talking to his parrot.[5] And that is all: even if the model is correct it tells us precious little about economic problems in an organised society, including a society in which individuals maximise their personal welfare with no regard to those of others.

To summarise, *all* scientific theory is abstract and general and, therefore, *no* scientific theory is universally valid either in time or in space. To claim otherwise is to confuse theory with tautology, science with sorcery or prediction with prophecy. There has been a long and largely inconclusive debate on what is known as 'historical relativism'. According to this doctrine knowledge of phenomena and events is relative only to the stage of material *or* spiritual development of man and society. Its critics reject this view for a variety of reasons such as its implication that, in the words of Popper, 'truth reveals itself by stages'. This is an important and ultimately metaphysical problem which we cannot take up here. But, unfortunately, it has tended to confuse the issues regarding the scope of application of scientific theories. For it would follow from the logic of historical relativism that scientific theories cannot be universally valid either in time or in space. Thus, the rejection of historical relativism is sometimes associated with the belief in the universal validity of scientific theories.[6] We hope to have solved this problem in the foregoing discussion. *We hope to have demonstrated that* **no** *scientific theory is capable of universal application, regardless of what we think of historical relativism.*

Let us illustrate the point with a brief discussion of the career of the theory of overproduction, underconsumption or 'demand-deficiency unemployment' in the history of economic theory. Mandeville had used the parable of *The Fable of the Bees* in order to prove to the ultra-Kalvinists of his time that *individual* thriftiness could lead to a decline in *aggregate* demand and, therefore, result in unemployment and economic poverty. In *The Theory of Moral Sentiments* (1759) Adam Smith attacked Mandeville's argument *not* (as it is often misunderstood) in substance, but in form. That is, *he accepted the substance of Mandeville's argument*, but he attacked him for having identified expenditure on 'luxuries' with *vice*: Mandeville, he wrote, had had no right to 'bestow such opprobrious names' on a legitimate and useful activity even on the part of those who could afford it 'without any inconveniency'. It was in *The Wealth of Nations* (1776) that Smith disagreed with the substance of Mandeville's view, although in this book he did not mention Mandeville's name at all. Here Smith argued that unproductive consumption – that is, the consumption of services which were not capable of reproduction – was anti-social because it diminished saving (which he correctly identified with investment in the developing economy which England then was). The link between saving, accumulation and development had been already discussed by Turgot in his *Reflexions* (1766).[7]

Malthus attacked this position. He argued that, without unproductive expenditure, there would be a real danger of overproduction (or underconsumption) in a capitalist economy. There were three ways in which Ricardo, James Mill and J. B. Say could combat Malthus on this issue: (i) to point out that *general* overproduction – as opposed to occasional gluts in *specific* markets – had not been experienced since the Industrial Revolution. However, although this point was sometimes implicit in their arguments, they did not give much prominence to it; (ii) they could attack Malthus's own line of reasoning; that is, they could reject his conclusion by criticising the analysis which had led to it. This they did with great vigour, though not with total success; (iii) they could try to show *independently* that there could be no danger of *general* overproduction in a capitalist economy. It was this line of argument which they chose to emphasise most, and which they handed down to generations of orthodox economists with the unfortunate consequences which are now only too well known. Their specific formulation is known as Say's Law.

Say's Law was based on the model of a barter economy. In such an economy every seller is at the same time a purchaser: if I exchange four apples for six oranges offered by Monsieur Say, then I am *supplying* four apples at the same time as I am *demanding* six oranges; likewise, Monsieur Say is *supplying* six oranges at the same time as he is *demanding* four apples. It follows that each of these acts of supply 'creates' its own demand. But aggregate supply is simply the sum of all individual supplies. If each individual supply creates its own demand then the sum of all supplies must also create the sum of all demands. That is, aggregate supply *must* be equal to aggregate demand, and there can be no possibility of general overproduction. It was true that England and France of the early nine-teenth century were not barter economies; rather they were econo-mies in which goods exchanged for money. But, money was just a 'veil', a medium of exchange, which had no active role in deter-mining the supply and demand for commodities.

Many modern macro-economists partially misinterpret Ricardo's use of the above model to deny the possibility of general over-production. For, as far as it goes, the above argument is much simpler than Ricardo's own application of it. More explicitly, the above argument not only negates the possibility of *general* (macro-economic) but also *specific* (micro-economic) disequilibria. *Indeed, it denies macro-economic disequilibrium by virtue of negating micro-economic disequilibria.* Ricardo was too clever to advocate such a ridiculous position which, at any rate, would have been refuted by everyday experience. On the contrary, he openly admitted the possibility, indeed reality, of temporary shortages and gluts in speci-fic markets. But, he argued, that to every specific glut there was a corresponding specific shortage so that in the short run specific gluts and shortages would cancel out and aggregate demand and supply would balance; and, in the long run, resources would shift from markets with excess supply to markets with excess demand and there would then be both micro-economic equilibria and macro-economic equilibrium in the economy. Yet his argument indis-pensably depended on the assumption that money functioned only as a unit of account and a medium of exchange; and that (at least with regard to the point at issue) this was the only difference between a barter economy and an industrial capitalist society.

The whole nonsense was due to a methodological misconception (so particularly, though not exclusively, characteristic of Ricardo) from which a lot of economic theory still suffers: the misconception that an abstract and general model must have *universal* validity. In the present example the misconception arose from the universal application of a model which was uniquely applicable to barter (and, perhaps, other non-capitalist) economies alone. It is now commonplace to argue that Say's Law is irrelevant since it claims that money is merely a veil, etc. Yet, even this belated discovery – now proudly paraded in every macro-economics textbook – under-emphasises *the methodological folly of Say's Law from which a much wider lesson can be learned:* Say's Law was *not* incorrect; it was correct for a barter economy; it was (and still is) reasonably applicable to a partially monetised but rural/commercial type of economy in which money primarily functions as a unit of account and medium of exchange. The fundamental theoretical mistake of Ricardo and his intellectual descendants was to apply Say's Law to an industrial capitalist economy.

No one better than Marx – that infamous ogre who perennially haunts the intellectual consciences of institutional Marxists and anti-Marxists alike – *ever* exposed the significant link between the methodological and the substantial error in the application of Say's Law to a capitalist economy. Here is a very brief excerpt from *The Theories of Surplus Value* on this subject:

> In order to prove that capitalist production cannot lead to general crises, all its conditions and distinct forms . . . – in short *capitalist production* itself – are denied. . . . Crises are thus reasoned out of existence . . . by forgetting the first elements of capitalist production: the existence of the product as a commodity, the duplication of the commodity in money. . . . Now even the social division of labour is forgotten. In a situation in which men produce for themselves, there are indeed no crises, but neither is there capitalist production. . . . Ricardo even forgets that a person may *sell* in order to *pay*, and that these forced sales play a very significant role in the crises. The capitalist's immediate object in selling, is to turn his commodity, or rather his commodity capital, back into *money capital*, and thereby *realise* his profit. . . . Money is not only 'the medium by which the exchange is effected'. . . but, at the same time, the medium by which the exchange of product with product is divided into two acts which are independent of each other. . . . Ricardo's and similar types of reasoning are moreover based not only on the relation of *purchase and sale*, but also on that of *demand and supply*. . . . At a given moment, the supply of all commodities can be greater than the demand for all commodities, since the demand for the *general commodity*, money . . . is greater than the demand for all particular commodities; in other words the motive to turn the commodity into money . . . prevails over the motive to transform the commodity again into use value. . . . [emphasis in the original][8]

In reading this passage alone an honest man's heart may cry out for a little intellectual justice for a thoroughly 'unsuccessful' scholar who has thus crammed most of the essentials of 'the Keynesian Revolution' in four pages even before Keynes was born.[9] Yet he has done much more: he has demonstrated the wider methodological lesson that general theoretical models are applicable to the specific conditions to which they refer. After having been 'thoroughly refuted' (or completely ignored) from Böhm-Bawerk through Hayek and von Mises to Positive Economists, Dr Marx is now in danger of being co-opted by neo-classical economists as a 'high-powered' (even though a little misguided) forerunner of general equilibrium theories. But, perhaps instead of converting his theories into mathematical formulae – or, at least, in addition to that – it may be of more value to pay a little attention to some of his most important methodological achievements and insights, such as the essential unity of social and economic problems, the limits to the scope of application of general economic models, and the great – almost indispensable – value of historical knowledge for socio-economic analysis. Indeed, without a profound understanding of history he is unlikely to have discovered the most basic flaw in Say's Law: that it denied capitalist production itself.

ECONOMIC THEORY AND MATHEMATICAL ECONOMICS   I: THE BACKGROUND

Abstraction and generalisation is a *logical* process. For this reason it is not unnatural for geometrical and/or mathematical techniques to be used, where appropriate, for the exposition of a theoretical model. The *explicit* use of such techniques in economic analysis has a long but discontinuous history. The examples of Cournot, Jevons and, especially, Walrus are too well known to demand emphasis. Walras was the first mathematical economist *par excellence*. Yet he himself did not succeed in founding a school of mathematical economics either in Europe, or in Britain and North America. In Europe the influence of the German Historical School was still in evidence until the First World War and, apart from that, the traditional European regard for history and social institutions was inhibitive of too formal an approach to the problems of political economy. In Britain and North America the influence of Marshall and Clark, though not anti-mathematical, was not too encouraging to grand mathematical model-building. Marshall and Keynes were both trained mathematicians. Yet neither the text of Marshall's *Principles* nor Keynes's *General Theory* demonstrated their expertise in mathematics. In his classic *Value and Capital* even Hicks banished his mathematical analyses to the appendixes. Other important contributions to economic theory before the Second World War – from Böhm-Bawerk and Wicksell through Pigou, Fisher, Hayek and Knight to Joan Robinson and Chamberlin – did not use a systematically mathematical approach, though they did occasionally resort to geometrical analysis and partial algebraic formulations.

The emergence and spread of mathematical economics as a distinct 'approach' to economic analysis dates back to the end of the Second World War. Briefly, this has been due to: (*a*) a shift of emphasis from a partial (Smithian–Marshallian) to a general (Ricardian–Walrasian) equilibrium analysis; (*b*) an upsurge of interest in the theories of growth, technical progress and other economic dynamics; (*c*) a revolution in the techniques of applied economics – i.e. economic statistics, econometrics, input–output analysis, economic planning, etc. – which (though the subjects themselves do not belong to the realm of mathematical economic theory) has made an indirect contribution to this by raising the mathematical requirement for a general knowledge of economics.

This so-called 'mathematical revolution' has had some very important and far-reaching consequences both for economic theory and for the economic professon. It has divided the profession into (at least) four distinct groups: the mathematical economists; the non-mathematical economists who regard the former with envious approval and admiration, and do their best to emulate them; the applied economists who, though they may use mathematical techniques with different levels of sophistication, are critical of the theory-orientation of mathematical economists; and, finally, other economic theorists, political economists, inter-disciplinarians, and so forth, who (sometimes for different reasons) believe that the 'mathematical revolution' has served to misdirect the development of economic science. In practice, however, many economists tend to hold their mathematical colleagues either in awe or in admiration, simply on account of their mathematical skills. The main reason for this is sociological: the 'invisible college' of the economic profession has become more and more dominated by mathematical economists; and, therefore, for a *professional* economist mathematical economics has tended to become the safest route to 'success' (see Chapter 5). It is worth emphasising that there is no *formal* ideological division over this issue. In particular, there are both neo-classical and Marxist mathematical economists, just as there are both neo-classical and Marxist critics of the 'mathematical revolution'.

ECONOMIC THEORY AND MATHEMATICAL ECONOMICS   II: A RATIONAL APPRAISAL

The following discussion contains a *rational* assessment of the 'mathematical revolution' in so far as it abstracts from the psychological and sociological factors which influence some economists in favour or against it. There are mathematical economists whose primary commitment to this approach is due to considerations pertaining to self-advancement. There are admirers of mathematical economists who are impressed by their professional 'success', and wish to swim with the current. There are applied economists who feel downgraded by the 'theoretical' excellence of mathematicians. There are critics who might secretly wish to have known more mathematics themselves. It is not unlikely that much of the controversy surrounding this subject is rooted in such social and psychological motivations. Yet is is perfectly possible to brush all this aside and examine the subject by means of rational arguments. We therefore begin our appraisal by making the following prefatory assertions: (i) the use of any technique, including mathematics, in any scientific pursuit, including economics, is legitimate, when it helps the analysis, its exposition and/or its precision; (ii) mathematics is one such technique, or medium of exposition. It is not *inherently* superior to any other; it does not, by itself, add to the substance of the theory; and it does not bestow any special honour on its user. Would anyone *now* believe that a skilful exposition of a theory in poetical metres would, as such, confer a higher status to its author? (iii) mathematical formulations of economic theories are at times helpful to clarity and economy of expression which – especially in view of 'the publication explosion' – are desirable; (iv) mathematical formulations of economic theories are at times unhelpful, obscurantist or mystifying when they tend to hide simple and clear ideas behind complicated and tedious techniques.

Issues concerning the growth of mathematical economics are, nevertheless, much wider in scope than a mere controversy over the use of mathematical techniques in economic theory. In fact the controversy itself has acquired much broader dimensions, with important implications for the purpose and methods of economic science in general. In a word, what is at stake is no less than the nature and significance of economics itself. These issues may be summarised as follows:

(i) The 'mathematical revolution' is a *comprehensive* application of the tools of mathematical analysis to the existing body of economic theory and its future developments. It is not simply a question of piecemeal use of mathematical techniques, where appropriate, in economic theory.

(ii) This may encourage the exclusion of important problems, categories or variables which are not easily susceptible to mathematical manipulation from theoretical investigation.

(iii) By contrast, it may lead to a growing concentration of theoretical analysis on remote problems and imaginary puzzles which happen to be readily manipulable by mathematical techniques.

(iv) The adoption of an irrational attitude by the economics profession in regarding mathematical formulations as *inherently* superior to those which use other methods, could lead to a situation where otherwise clear and intelligible ideas are artificially presented in the mathematical form, purely in order to demonstrate that the author is 'high-powered', and, thus, facilitate the publication of his works and the promotion of his career. Popper has aptly described such an attitude as 'the cult of unintelligibility, the cult of high-sounding language':

> This was intensified by the (for laymen) impenetrable and impressive formalism of mathematics. I suggest that in some of the more ambitious social sciences . . . the traditional game . . . is to state the utmost trivialities in high-sounding language. . . . Even among mathematicians a tendency to impress people may sometimes be discerned, although the incitement to do so is least in mathematics; *for it is partly the wish to ape the mathematicians and the mathematical physicists in technicality and in difficulty*

that inspires the use of verbiage in other sciences. [emphasis added][10]

Thus the Professor Emeritus of Mathematical Logic and Scientific Method at the London School of Economics. In developing this line of attack against 'the cult of unintelligibility' Popper agrees with Marx that 'in its mystifying form dialectic became the accepted German fashion'.[11] There is a growing tendency for mathematics – *in its mystifying form* – to become the accepted fashion in economic science.

(v) The greatest potential threat to economic science posed by the above tendencies is the real possibility for mathematical *forms* and *techniques* to determine the *substance* and *content* of economic knowledge. Mathematics is a simple, yet very powerful technique. There is virtually no limit to the application of the techniques and concepts of pure mathematics to *certain limited* problems and puzzles in economic theory. That is to say, while mathematics is relatively impotent in application to such real economic problems as the role of the state in the economy, the significance of political power in international economic relations, etc., etc., it is extremely adaptable to such puzzles as the life-cycle maximisation of utility by an individual, the stability of general equilibrium in the steady state, or (perhaps) the rate of return on capital on the day before Doomsday. Humour aside, these are pretty mild examples. A casual glance at some leading journals of economic 'literature' (or 'mathature'!) – especially those which give priority to mathematical economics – would be quite sufficient to demonstrate the point (for some examples see Chapter 8.) Mathematical economics began by the application of the concepts of *terrestrial* mechanics to economic problems. There is now a tendency to use concepts and methods of *celestial* mechanics – of astronomy and space-engineering – to economic science: a science which is essentially prescriptive; which, in spite of many genuine achievements, is still far from ready to offer substantial solutions to some important problems; which, together with other social sciences, is least intelligible in *mechanistic* terms.

(vi) An almost inevitable consequence of wholesale mathematicalism is the tacit or explicit belief that economic theories – especially when presented in the mathematical form – are *universally* valid. We have already argued that this is untrue of *any* science – that total knowledge of anything, though it may exist (or be claimed to exist) in some form, is outside the realm of science altogether. Yet the temptation to identify internal logical consistency – i.e. logical or tautological truths – with objective reality is very strong, especially (but not exclusively) when mathematical techniques are involved. In fact, from this point of view, the issue is quite old: the *a priorism* and pseudo-universalism of mathematical economics has a direct ancestry in Ricardo's method which we briefly discussed in Chapter 2. But even *purely a priori* knowledge – if it can be shown to exist – is not necessarily universal for it would normally depend on a set of assumptions which limit its terms of reference. Let us emphasise the distinction between these two issues: *purely a priori* knowledge may exist, although – in spite of many a brave attempt – no one has yet offered a rational proof for its existence. But even were such a proof available, it would, by itself, not guarantee the spatio-temporal universality of all *purely a priori* knowledge.

(vii) We saw in Chapter 3 that Positive Economics requires economic theories to be testable and subject to tests. We further saw in Chapter 4 that even a strict Kuhnian or Lakatosian interpretation of the history and method of economics (although partially incompatible with the methodology of Positive Economics) would have to accept the criterion of *testability* as its premise. This is what the establishment, the profession, the 'invisible college' themselves claim to insist on. Yet a growing number of mathematical economic theories are simply untestable. What then are we to believe?

Such blatant self-contradictions are – unfortunately – by no means confined only to the guardians of orthodox economic theory. Take the critique of orthodox economic philosophy by Hollis and Nell, which has many commendable features. Yet, in one extreme, the authors try to demonstrate the superiority of the techniques of linear-programming – that is, a highly empirical, down-to-earth approach to economic engineering (though this description does not necessarily make it invalid or unuseful) – and, in another extreme, they try to prove the existence of *purely a priori knowledge,* because they regard this as being superior to – or more certain than – empirical knowledge.[12] Which, then, is the 'correct' method: piecemeal empirical economic engineering, or wholesale and pure *a priori* speculation?

Throughout this essay we have rejected the division of scientific methods into purely *a priori* and purely empirical, as false and artificial. We have emphasised the value, indeed the primacy, of theoretical analysis; we have equally emphasised the significance of the world of empirical reality as it is, *or as it may be*, conceived. We have insisted on the essential unity of these two 'elements' for an intelligent and synthetic perception of objective phenomena, and scientific strivings for the solution of problems with which they present mankind. This attitude is best made clear by a distinction between *a priori theory* and *a priori knowledge*. An *a priori theory* which is no more than a logically or mathematically consistent model does not, *by itself*, bestow any *knowledge* of real phenomena. For the latter would further depend on the assumptions which the theory makes and the events which it predicts: in short, it would depend on whether or not it is open to rational and empirical criticism.

Abstraction is necessary for all scientific pursuits. This does not mean that every individual scientist does or ought to, resort to abstract analysis – that is, to be a theorist himself. But he would inevitably use concepts and theories developed by others. Yet there are limits to abstraction which may be divided into two categories: descriptive and prescriptive. We have already discussed the descriptive limit to abstraction. That is, we have argued that, *precisely because scientific theories are abstract and general, they cannot be universally valid*. The prescriptive limit to abstraction is, by contrast, not a matter of logic or fact, but a maxim of scientific policy. That is, if the primary aim of all science is to solve the important and outstanding problems of this world – which to quote Hayek – 'give rise to profound dissatisfaction' – then, to put it mildly, we must observe an order of priorities. In this sense it is quite meaningful to speak of useful and useless, relevant and irrelevant, abstractions: every useful and relevant abstract model should *correspond* to a real problem. Abstract analysis should be a genuine response to the questions which we face, if need be by the use of mathematical techniques – not the other way around. And, moreover, the questions which we try to resolve must be mainly concerned with real problems facing human societies, and mankind in general. Is it surprising that, in view of the abdication of professional academics and *ex officio* intellectuals – the 'puzzle-solving' 'normal scientists' or, as we prefer to call them, 'normal professionals'; Big Scientists, or, as we rather describe them, Big Professionals – some of the most intelligent, passionate and dedicated young men and women of this world – many of them nurtured, or more accurately, fed up in our professional institutions – have wrongly concluded that 'all knowledge is a matter of opinion'; and naïvely, but desperately, believe that they can change the world without knowing it, by thinking that they do already? There may be some occasional justification for our mockery of their intellectual innocence. There are certainly some good reasons for our indignation at their periodic resort to senseless violence (for not all violence is senseless). But in our mockeries and indignations we ourselves could have the moral courage to see our own share in the responsibility for their conduct. We ourselves may have the modesty to be a little self-critical; to laugh at our own intellectual gymnastics, and be angered with our own intellectual cynicism. We may all be guilty of what Popper describes as 'the perennial revolt against freedom and reason'. But, at least on the moral plane the difference between some of us and some of them, in this general revolt, is that we get paid for our subtle and inconspicuous rejection of freedom and reason, whereas they pay for their open, and sometimes violent, revolt with everything they possess, including their lives. . . .

(viii) Yet none of this is sufficient argument against a mathematical approach to economic analysis, let alone a piecemeal application of mathematical techniques to economic theory. It is what we produce with our techniques – what problems we solve or do not solve – which ultimately matter. Even apart from that, an individual university academic should have the freedom of choosing – without fear or favour – his own methods of investigation and topics of research. This ideal of academic freedom – the ceremonial lip-service paid to which is probably no less than the actual violation to which it is continuously subjected – must certainly be held firmly in the case of all intellectual pursuits. But an irrational claim for the inherent superiority of whatever set of techniques of analysis, and the use of the professional tactic of carrots and sticks for its elevation, propagation, etc., is quite unacceptable. It would certainly violate that ideal according to which we firmly believe that mathematical economists have every right to present their case as well as they wish. But that aside, the irrational, uncritical and authoritarian elevation of mathematical economics is prone to the very serious dangers which we have discussed. Economic science can afford mathematical economics in a 'peaceful coexistence' or even 'détente' with other approaches. What it cannot afford is the professional hegemony of mathematical economics especially if this is effected by a combination of chauvinism and professional power-politics.

(ix) The kind of methodological misconceptions which – though not necessarily inherent – are frequently observed in the attitude of pure *a priorists* and mathematicists may be further examined with reference to one particular example, presented to us by Arun Bose. His book entitled *Marxian and Post-Marxian Political Economy* characteristically employs mathematical model-building for a restatement of the general equilibrium model of competitive capitalist economies. However, before developing his 'post-Marxian' model he offers some arguments for the necessity of general equilibrium theories. And he further claims that any such model would be incomplete without the use of simultaneous equations. Here, we are only concerned with these aspects of Bose's study.

Bose begins his justification of general equilibrium theories by taking issue with Korni. It would be unthinkable to try and do justice to Korni's important contribution (in his book *Anti-equilibrium*) within the limited compass of this book. Put simply and briefly, Korni claims that economics cannot be a theoretical science; it is a 'real science' which should be based on 'systems theory'. It follows from this argument that all general equilibrium models – including its Marxian (and Marxological) variations – are irrelevant. [13] We generally concur with the spirit of Bose's disagreement with Korni *on these issues*, although not exactly for the reasons which Bose himself offers: Korni's rejection of the possibility or relevance of theoretical economics, if it is so intended, is mistaken, because – together with the *a priorists* – he seems to regard a theoretical science as a *purely* 'logical-mathematical' body of knowledge. If this were so, we would go even further and assert that *no* theoretical science is possible. We have already discussed the nature of theoretical science, and we have shown that *no* theoretical science is a purely 'logical-mathematical' body of thought. His identification of economics as a 'real' (or, better, realistic) science is indisputable, but this would not make it untheoretical. His advocacy of a 'systems theory' smacks of operationism and economic engineering (i.e. the practical counterpart to Empiricism) the theoretical basis of which we have already, criticised, and the practical consequences of which would aggravate the state of uncritical professionalism and specialism in science, and the rule of Machine technocracy in society. Yet – in spite of Bose's implicit claim – a disagreement with Korni on these points (or on the grounds suggested by Bose himself) would not automatically invalidate Korni's critique of general equilibrium models. *And it is especially this aspect of Korni's views which Bose wishes to refute.*

In his defence of general equilibrium models Bose makes the claim that:

A general equilibrium (or general interdependence) theory to demonstrate the *workability* of the capitalist market-mechanism, guided by the 'invisible hand', is needed by different writers for different (even diametrically opposite) reasons. Adam Smith needed it, because he wanted to argue that it works *ideally* (or at any rate better than feudalism). It was also needed by Ricardo, who thought that he had found a proof that it worked *badly*, though he saw no alternative to it. It was needed *no less* by Marx, who wanted to prove that a capitalist market-mechanism is comparable, as a *workable* system of *exploitation* of one class by another, to feudalism, or to ancient (European) labour slavery, neither of which are ruled by the market's 'invisible hand'. [emphasis in the original][14]

Let us examine the fact and logic in the above statement. If we are allowed to attribute motives (especially since we do not believe that motives necessarily invalidate theories) Smith may have wished to demonstrate the 'workability' *as well as the stability* of the capitalist system. Hence his use of the twin concepts of 'self-interest' and 'sympathy' which, according to Smith, would result in *harmonious progress.* This case has been strongly argued in *The Theory of Moral Sentiments* and, much less strongly, in *The Wealth of Nations.* Indeed, there is no complete and consistent logical proof in *Wealth* that a system of general equilibrium – with its well-known characteristics – would obtain; and there is ample empirical statements which show that the system, left to itself, is not harmonious or stable (see, further, Chapter 2). Yet, this is the time when the competitive capitalist system of political economy is only emerging – it is a phenomenon not yet sufficiently tried, and it is facing considerable obstacles and oppositions against its total establishment.

Ricardo did not have to prove – least of all theoretically – 'the workability' of the capitalist system. Who would need a theoretical proof for an elephant which is coming through the door? If we are allowed to attribute motives then his preoccupation with the formulation of a general equilibrium model may have been prompted by the desire to demonstrate what Smith had failed (or more likely had, by then, thought it to be silly) to prove logically. That is, to show by pure speculation that the capitalist system worked *perfectly*: that it was a stable, harmonious fault-proof order *if it was left to itself*. In any event it is least likely that Ricardo needed a general equilibrium model because 'he thought he had found a proof that it [the competitive capitalist system] worked *badly*'. How can you have a 'proof' prior to the theory which is supposed to give you that proof? On the contrary, in the *partial* model of his earlier *Essay on Profit* he thought he had discovered the proof of the *perfect workability* of the capitalist system. His later failure, and consequent depression, was precisely because he did not succeed in generalising that 'proof' for the whole of the capitalist economy. Besides, it is rather remarkable to claim that the author of the theory of comparative advantage, and the ardent defender of the *logical* ('therefore' *universal*) impossibility of general gluts in a competitive capitalist economy – for the latter of which Marx accused him of being an apologise – had found 'a proof that it [the capitalist system] worked *badly*'!

This brings us to Marx who – according to Bose – 'recognised . . . that the workability of the capitalist market-mechanism had first to be proved'[15] so as to prove its exploitative nature. Here, even more than in the former examples, Bose is confusing 'workability' with perfection, stability, harmony or whatever. It is a confusion between *existence* and *permanent or ultimate excellence*; between an ontological *proof of a reality*, and a metaphysical *proof of the perfection and the finality of that reality*. For his rather ambiguous choice of the word 'workability' renders itself to either, or both, of these interpretations. If by this word he means the mere *existence* of the competitive capitalist system, or even 'the capitalist market-mechanism', then it is astonishing to claim that – after a century of the rise and development of the capitalist system, its technological establishment, its political supremacy (since 1846) and the sociological revolution which these events entailed – Karl Marx, the author of *The Paris Manuscripts, The Poverty of Philo-*

sophy, Value, Price and Capital, Grundrisse and *Contributions to the Critique of Political Economy,* needed a theoretical proof of the existence of the capitalist system, and/or its market-mechanism in order to show that it involved the exploitation of labour by capital; and that this need could be fulfilled only by a theory of general equilibrium!

On the other hand, if by 'workability' Bose is referring to the proof of the permanency and perfection of the system – which might have been Ricardo's secret wish – then it is all the more astonishing that Marx, who regarded this system as a passing stage in history, imbued with exploitation, alienation and contradiction – that which he repeatedly described as a system of 'market anarchy' – intended to prove its perfection and/or permanence, by means of a general equilibrium theory. If we are to attribute motives (which, fortunately, because of Marx's honesty and openness is easier to do) it is likely that his interest in 'the transformation problem' was merely to show that even when there is a stable and perfectly functioning general equilibrium, in the system of 'competition capitalism' (his words), the exploitation of labour by capital, derived from theoretical labour values, would correspond to empirical market prices. That is, the general equilibrium problem as the so-called theoretical framework of 'research agenda' *had been given to him,* and he felt obliged to state his case even within that framework. This may be an acceptable, but by no means unique, interpretation of Marx's *motive* in this connection; but Arun Bose's interpretation is unacceptable. Besides, we should remember that the second and third volumes of *Capital* came out of a heap of unfinished manuscripts left by Marx which are, moreover, advisable to read jointly with the remaining manuscripts which now constitute the three volumes of *The Theories of Surplus Value.*

Yet, let us put all that aside. Let us assume that Adam Smith, Ricardo and Marx needed proofs of the 'workability' (whichever way we interpret this word) of the capitalist market-mechanism and they therefore formulated models of general equilibrium for exactly the motives which Bose attributes to them. What is the relevance of these claims for the defence of contemporary (Marxian or non-Marxian) models of competitive general equilibrium *for a monopolistic or imperfectly competitive* capitalist system? If the justification for these contemporary models is to provide a *theoretical* proof for the 'workability' (existence and/or perfection) of the *competitive* capitalist system, then what is the point of proving the existence of that which does not, at present, exist; let alone its perfection and permanence? Marx offered many theoretical proofs that the system of 'competition capitalism' would not last because of its *un*workability – that is, its tendencies to market concentration, monopoly, demand-deficiency crises, etc. – nearly all of which have been historically observed. They now constitute – at least outside economics textbooks – some of the most obvious facts of life. If, on the other hand, the aim is to provide a *theoretical* proof for the existence of *monopolistic* or *imperfect* market mechanism then this is not true of the existing general equilibrium models; nor, in any case, would it be necessary, just as we need no *theoretical proof* of the existence of the Sun. Finally, if it is a question of exploitation of labour by capital, then according to the established theories of imperfect and monopolistic competition – currently taught in the economics courses – labour is exploited because it does not receive the value of its marginal product in an *imperfectly competitive* capitalist economy. [16]

This leaves us with no *rational* argument in Bose's defence of the relevance, much less the necessity, of a general equilibrium model. At any rate one is left wondering why we badly need a Marxian or post-Marxian general equilibrium model which refers to 'political-economic models of *competitive* capitalism'. Would it not be more relevant for post-Marxian or post-whatever political economy to analyse the features of monopolistic and imperfectly competitive capitalist economies, and those of the poor countries of this world which are, strictly speaking, neither capitalist nor competitive? However, Bose's reference to 'one "Walrasian" property which every theory of "general interdependence" under competitive capitalism must have' may give us a hint on some other reasons for his defence of the necessity of a general equilibrium model:

This is the insight which made Walras cast the problem of general interdependence and long-run values in a competitive-capitalist market system in the form of the equilibrium values *derived from a system of simultaneous equations* [emphasis added] . . . the Marxian theory of value, capital and exploitation suffered much . . . from the *lack* [emphasis in the original] of this insight. . . . [17]

Or, in other words, the Marxian theory of value, etc., suffered from the fact that it was more realistic but less mathematical. For the recognition of sectoral economic interdependence itself does not require much insight; and even if it had done so at a time that must certainly have been before the French Physiocrats. Whereas the concept of *simultaneous* adjustments and equilibria is hardly a matter for *insight*; it is not even just an abstraction from reality, but almost a figment of imagination. Now perhaps a case can be made for the use of such an abstraction in theoretical analysis. But to call it an *insight* is clearly not a correct use of language. In any case this looks like an example of the case where a preference for the form, for the mathematical techniques, would tend to determine the content, 'the research agenda', of an approach to economic theory.

Finally, in case the reader may regard this interpretation as being unfair or far-fetched, we should refer him to Bose's later criticism of the assumption – described by Bose as 'Marxian', 'Ricardian Socialist' and 'Austrian' – that, under capitalism, 'labour is the only source of wealth or (exchange) value'. Because his reason for rejecting this assumption is that it is *factually untrue*:

> The proposition cannot be accepted as a 'socialist' value-judgement pure and simple, because it clearly *has* to do with *facts*. . . .[18] [emphasis in the original]

And this proposition – he goes on to add – is '*excluded*' by '*observable reality*'.[19] For our present purpose, we are not concerned with a debate on the truth or falsehood of this argument. Here we are simply concerned with consistency in approach and method. For, on the one hand, Bose has argued that theories of general equilibrium are necessary for a *theoretical proof* of the 'workability' of competitive capitalism – which, in the nineteenth century, was a palpable '*observable reality*'; and, at present, a clearly *non-existing*, let alone 'observable', *abstraction*. And, on the other hand, he has rejected a *certain theoretical assumption* on the grounds that *it is contrary to 'observable reality'*!

To summarise, *a priori* analysis – abstraction and generalisation – is indispensable to any science, including economics. The *logical/descriptive* limit to such analysis is that it automatically excludes universal validity in time and space. The *prescriptive* limit to such analysis is that it must correspond to a problem in the world of reality, and observe an order of priorities. Theorists are free to choose any set of techniques, including mathematics, when these are helpful to clarity, precision or economy of exposition. The dangers posed by the 'mathematical revolution' include tendencies to concentrate on remote problems and imaginary puzzles which happen to be more suitable for the application of mathematical techniques; to neglect some important problems and oversimplify some others beyond recognition; to let the form dominate the content of economic theory. In an academic environment even such tendencies should be tolerated when they are the result of an unconstrained preference by some individual economists. But if they are generally forced and encouraged by an extra-rational preference of professional economists, and their 'invisible college', for mathematical formalism, then we should perhaps begin to write a lament for economic science in poetical metres or mathematical symbols.

Finally, the re-emergence of the term 'political economy' in some economic writings, and the vagueness with which its content and method are associated, is relevant to the arguments of this essay in general, and the discussion of the present chapter in particular. Therefore, we have supplied a separate note on this topic in the appendix to this chapter.

APPENDIX

A NOTE ON THE FORM AND CONTENT OF THE TERM POLITICAL ECONOMY'.

INTRODUCTION

A satisfactory discussion of this subject would (without exaggeration) require a separate volume in its own right. Yet for reasons outlined below, such a volume would not even be a textbook or treatise on political economy – merely an inquiry into its history, nature and significance. This indeed is what we intend to present – though very briefly – in the following note.

ORIGINS OF THE TERM

As far back as this author is aware, the term 'political economy' – as a general description of economic theories and problems – has been first mentioned in the title of *Traité de l'Économie politique* (1616) written by Antoyne de Montchrétien, a French Mercantilist. It is therefore likely to have been used, though less prominenetly, even before this date. It was, however, not until 1767 when this term was put to the same use in England, in the title of Sir James Steuart's *Principles of Political Economy*. Yet, as a description of the subject-matter of economics it began to enjoy general currency only since Ricardo, Say, James Mill and other classics; that is, since the early nineteenth century. It would be a historical mistake to associate the term solely with *classical* political economy. It was not adopted by the Physiocrats, Smith and Marx as the title of their *magna opera*. By contrast, it was used as such by some early non-classicals including Jevons and Walras. Marshall, perhaps more than anyone else, popularised the modern term 'economics'. Yet the term 'économie politique' continued to be used, ot not to dominate, in French-speaking countries well into the present century.

ETYMOLOGICAL IMPLICATIONS OF THE TERM

Economus was the ancient classical (Greek) term used to describe principles of housekeeping (no doubt, initially, for ladies). When, in the Renaissance, interest grew in the issues and problems of managing 'national' economies, it must have led the authors to the invention of the term '*political* economy' for describing principles of *social* 'housekeeping'. Perhaps, to have been entirely consistent, they ought to have coined the term 'politiconomy' – i.e. principles of managing the society. But, as is well known, languages do not develop according to precise linguistic 'rules'. What we wish to emphasise by these references is that there is nothing in the term itself, nor its history, which signifies a very specific and exclusive approach or method. It may give the impression of a greater concern with 'macro-economic' problems; but this was partly due to the nature of the questions posed and, in any case, it effectively disappeared with the equal interest of the classics in 'micro-economic' issues.

METHODOLOGICAL AND IDEOLOGICAL IMPLICATIONS OF THE TERM

It must be clear from the above that, *historically*, the term 'political economy' has had *no* ideological implications whatsoever. Neither has it had any *special* methodological connotations; and, in particular, it does not distinguish a generally *unscientific* approach to economic problems from a generally *scientific* one. Ever since the early Mercantilists, economists have *explicitly* engaged in analysing economic problems and relations, and supplying specific solutions to the related questions. We have already argued at some length that most of these questions (both then and now) are – at least ultimately – of a *prescriptive* nature. We have further argued, with equal force, that this fact alone does not make economics either unscientific or 'subjective': science is not a *subject*; it is an *attitude*, an approach in dealing with whatever question, distinguished from other approaches and attitudes by *the specific methods* which it employs and results which it obtains. There are dangers, indeed real possibilities, of the intrusion of moral preference and ideological prejudice in *any* scientific activity. What is certain is that such tendencies are not inherent in the nature of the problem itself – there can be **scientific prescriptions** and **unscientific description**. There may be, indeed there usually are, personal motives of various kinds in the construction of scientific ideas. Yet Smith's advocacy of thriftiness for the sake of progress, Ricardo's theory of comparative advantage to promote increasing general welfare and Marx's theory of exploitation for defending the workers' interests were not unscientific. Because, even if they had appeared on the wall in the Feast of Belshazzar, they could – in principle – have been shown to be mistaken. They may have been – nay, they *were* and they are – used for ideological purposes. But this does not make *the theories* unscientific: Eddington's enthusiasm for Einstein's theory is likely to have been partially prompted by purely religious sentiments; yet this would neither make Einstein's theory unscientific, nor (we believe) Eddington a 'non-scientist'.

Economic theories *can* be unscientific. A good many of them *are*.
But this is not due to the *type* of question asked; much less the
appellations – 'economics', 'political economy' or whatever –
attached to the subject.

THE CONTEMPORARY IMPLICATIONS OF THE TERM

Nevertheless, there is (or there may be) a sense in which, the
contemporary usage of this term, could supply a methodological
and/or ideological demarcation line between different approaches
to economic problems. Indeed there are more such senses than one;
but as we shall shortly argue there is only one among them which
can act as any demarcation line at all.

First, the issue of ideology – *as an explicit frame of reference* – is
not relevant to this question: one can speak of Marxian economics *or*
political economy; of liberal economics *or* political economy. . . . It
goes without saying that, although both Marx and the original
liberal economists studied the same phenomenon of the competitive capitalist economy, they were considerably different in their
sentiments towards it; they viewed its causes and consequences
differently; and in their vision of its prospects they (sometimes)
posed different questions. But these facts have no bearing on our
specific problem. It would be quite legitimate – as a matter of
semantic convenience – if we now chose to refer to a *liberal*
economist by using the term 'economist'; and to a *critic* of liberal
economics – a Marxian, conservative or radical economist – by
applying the term 'political economist'. But, by itself, this would
add nothing to the distinction: one could still speak of liberal,
Marxian, etc., economists (or, for that matter, political economists)
with sufficient clarity. And, as we have shown already, it would
certainly not mean that the liberal economist, as such, is a
'scientist'; and the non-liberal political economist, as such, is a
'non-scientist'.

Second, the realm of economic policy need not be identified with
the term 'political economy' though – once again – as a mere question of semantics it should not matter. For, economic policy –
defined as the conclusions of a set of economic theories – is *not
inherently* a field for moral judgement any more (or less) than the
theories on which it is based: in principle, both economic theorists

and economic advisers may or may not be prejudiced. If a theory is correct then its conclusions must be correct. If a correct theory predicts that, in certain conditions, public investment would reduce unemployment then this becomes a policy prescription; if the same, or another, theory correctly predicts that, in the same conditions, pubic investment would be inflationary then this becomes another policy 'prescription' or, rather, conclusion. These policy conclusions are, in principle, the results of those theories; they could be as correct or incorrect, as prejudiced or honest, as scientific or unscientific, as the theories themselves. Let us emphasise: *there could be, and there sometimes are, moral judgements involved in such matters; but these are not – they cannot be – because something is an economic theory and another thing is a policy prescription* (see further 'Of Value Judgements in Economic Science' in Chapter 6.

There remains one sense – *methodological* – in which the term 'political economy' *could* be used to indicate a real distinction. This is *not*, as we have repeatedly said, a distinction between a broadly scientific and non-scientific approach. Rather, it is a distinction in method *within* any (let us say, a scientific) approach to economics. Political economy could be used to refer to all approaches to economic science which:

(i) place a high priority on the understanding and solution of important and real economic problems in contrast to minute puzzles, etc.

(ii) recognise the importance of other, 'non-economic', social facts, categories and theories, in their analysis of specific economic problems; and make an ernest effort to allow for such 'variables' in their analyses and solutions.

(iii) use *any* set of techniques (including mathematics) which are appropriate for the problem in hand; but never allow *any* set of techniques to dominate, much less determine, the choice of problem.

(iv) always maintain the history of (the relevant) ideas and events as a background to their study – even though they may not necessarily spell this out on all occasions. Such a regard for history is not due to any extra-disciplinary interest or prejudice: a knowlege of the history of ideas can afford an overview of the science; it will certainly cut down repetitive waste; it will supply a full range of methods, approaches, etc.; it will contribute to an intellectually modest and self-critical outlook (at least) by demonstrating past follies. A knowledge of the history of events will provide examples of divergences between theory and experience, prediction and facts; it will show the connections between ideas and objective reality; it will demonstrate the ways in which various constraints intermingle with individual or collective action in shaping social and economic change.

In this sense we can speak of political economy without any of its previously discarded connotations. Thus, we may refer to Marxian, liberal, radical, scientific, non-scientific, theoretical, applied . . . political economy which would unambiguously imply the above *approach* to economic problems, notwithstanding other differences among them. Indeed, it is probably in this very sense, and none other, that classical economics has been exclusively identified with the term 'political economy'. For, although not all and not always, the classics tended to observe the above (general) methodological maxims. This of course has no bearing on the truth or falsehood of their theories, or their different moral and ideological predilections.

8

UNTO THIS LAST [1]
SOME EVIDENCE FROM CURRENT RESEARCH

Throughout the previous chapters we cited a number of basic economic theories and methods in order to illustrate our arguments, and support our appraisal. In this chapter we shall present some more evidence from the mass of current publications in the learned journals. This is neither a simple nor a pleasant task, since it would inevitably involve a relatively small sample of theoretical articles written by a few contemporary economists. However, these articles have been selected for their contents and methods, which represent the dominant trends in theoretical research and publications. In choosing them there was no prior list of authors or subjects, for we have no quarrel with thinkers, merely with thoughts. The sample consists of two groups of articles. The first group contains some – generally, though not entirely – more substantial articles in terms of length and/or subject-matter than those in the second group; consequently, they have been discussed in greater detail.

SOME SUBSTANTIAL ARTICLES BY REPUTABLE THEORISTS ON IMPORTANT SUBJECTS

1. Share-cropping and the Modern Corporation
An article entitled 'Incentives and Risk Sharing in Share-cropping' (J. E. Stiglitz, *Review of Economic Studies*, vol. 41 (1974) pp. 219–55), opens with the following words:

> At least from the time of Ricardo, economists have begun their investigation of how competitive markets work . . . by a

detailed examination of agriculture. Even today, agriculture is taken as the paradigm . . . of a truly competitive market (or at least this was the case until the widespread government intervention in this market). . . . Risks in agriculture are clearly tremendously important, yet remarkably the traditional theoretical structure has avoided explicit treatment of risk sharing in agricultural environments [with the consequence that] it makes suspect the traditional conclusions regarding share-cropping. [p. 219]

Since the root of most of our later comments on this article is in these prefatory remarks, it will be helpful to make the following points.

1. The claim that, since Ricardo, 'economists have begun their investigation of how competitive markets work . . . by a detailed examination of agriculture' is *generally* incorrect. In fact, *from Ricardo until the Second World War* very few economists have made such a 'beginning'.

2. Ricardo's own choice of 'the corn model', in his *Essay on Profit* (1815), must have been *least* prompted by the imaginary 'fact' that agriculture was 'a truly competitive market': 1815 was the year of the (new) Corn Laws against which Ricardo fought through parable and parliament. They were abolished decades after his death when the Irish potato famine of 1846 finally led to the triumph of the Anti-Corn-Law League – an influential pressure group for free trade in agriculture, led by 'Ricardian' intellectuals and businessmen ('for the sake of those rotten potatoes', said the Duke of Wellington).

3. On the contrary, Ricardo's choice of 'the corn model' (in search of a theory of distribution for a capitalist economy) is likely to have been determined by the ease of analysis which this model afforded: one homogeneous product, etc. They are well known.

4. At any rate that is the reason why contemporary one-sector growth-modellists tacitly or explicitly use the same 'paradigm'.

5. In most periods and places 'widespread government intervention' in agriculture has been the rule, rather than the exception: in Britain, with the major exception of the period of High Farming (1850–75); in France, Italy, Germany, Japan, with brief and minor exceptions; everywhere in the developing countries. Indeed, *the author may have been generalising from the recent history of Ameri-*

can agriculture, although – until a few decades ago – even America was hardly a general model of freedom in *international* trade.

6. These points acquire analytical significance when the author begns to refer to 'share-cropping'. Thus, he continues:

> Is it really true that share-cropping results in too low a supply of labour because workers equate their share of output times the (value of the) marginal productivity of labour to the marginal disutility of work, whereas Pareto optimality requires the (value of the) marginal productivity of labour be equal to the marginal disutility of work? . . . [p. 219]

7. Share-cropping is not an example of competitive (or even, *within a capitalistic framework, un*competitive agriculture, distinguishable from others merely by its 'distribution system'. It is a *traditional mode* of production; a system of land *tenure*; a sociocultural framework and a way of life whose only significant similarity with capitalistic homestead farming in the United States is that human beings mix their labour with nature in order to produce fruits of the earth. Share-croppers are not *workers* employed on wage contracts; they are *peasants*; they enjoy certain *traditional rights of cultivation* though not necessarily tenure; their unit of labour is neither an hour nor a soul – it is an *entire household*. . . . Marx criticised Ricardo for using an explicitly hypothetical model of a capitalistic agriculture because he thought that Ricardo was applying the institutional/technological framework of capitalist production where (at the time) they did not dominate.[2] In the present case all basic distinction between *traditional agriculture* and *modern capitalistic farming* is assumed away. . . .

8. We have already exposed the (dubious) foundations of utility analysis, in general, and the 'marginal-disutility-of-work' theory of labour supply, in particular (in Chapter 3). Yet this was based on the (implicit) assumption of the existence of a capitalist economy operating on wage contracts. Here, though, the question is whether or not traditional peasants 'equate their share of output times the (value of) the marginal productivity of labour to the marginal disutility of work, whereas Pareto optimality requires. . .'.

9. There follows a statement of purpose:

> Our object is to formulate a simple general equilibrium model of

a competitive agricultural economy. . . . The model is of interest not only for extending our misunderstanding of these simple economies but also in gaining some insight into the far more complex phenomena of share holding in modern corporations. Our focus is on the risk sharing and incentive properties of alternative distribution systems. [p. 219]

10. The 'general equilibrium model' is familiar from our arguments in previous chapters. As for 'a competitive agricultural economy' – i.e. *traditional peasant agriculture* – and the 'insight' gained from its analysis 'into . . . *shareholding in modern corporations*' our preceding comments may suffice. This is an example of the kind of incredible 'universalism' on which Say's Law was based (see Chapter 7).

11. On page 223 we read: 'all individuals are assumed to be expected utility maximizers'. We have already discussed the analytical and empirical bases (or their absence) for 'utility and all that' (see Chapter 3). Here a further (historico-sociological) note on its *maximisation* is relevant: the assumption of 'utility maximisations' has its roots in the historical phenomenon of the early British (and perhaps other) capitalists who seemed to strive for the highest rate of profit, a large proportion of which they then accumulated. Whether or not any or *'all individuals'* in a capitalist economy *now* maximise or wish to maximise 'expected utility', it is hard to know. But one thing is more certain: *a traditional peasant* is more likely to be preoccupied with the physical survival of himself and his family; the avoidance of potential 'trouble' (which may include periodic robbery, rape, requisitioning, expropriation, etc., by many agents, even including rural policemen); and salvation in the next world as (perhaps a partial) compensation for damnation in this.

12. The mathematical general equilibrium model (in two parts) is then extensively developed on the basis of the above, and other, assumptions. We believe that the technical arguments are faultless, if only because we ourselves are not well-equipped to criticise some of them without further consultation.

13. This model gives rise to some hypotheses *about the historical transformation of traditional into modern agriculture*:

We come then to the following hypotheses concerning the elimination of the share-cropping system. (a) The development of capital markets in which landlords and workers (to the extent that they had capital), could diversify their portfolio meant that the relative importance of share-cropping as a risk sharing management declined. (b) The increasing capital intensity of agriculture meant that either the landlord had to provide strong incentives (the rental system) or had to provide close supervision leading to the wage system. Since there is a natural non-convexity associated with supervision, it was the larger farms which used the wage system. Similarly, since the rental system required the worker to provide the capital, it was the wealthier who became renters, the proper workers becoming landless. . . . [there are three more 'hypotheses'] [p. 252]

14. It is difficult to know to which history of where in what period(s) these 'hypotheses' are meant to refer: Roman agriculture was based on *slave labour*; European feudalism was a system of *serfdom*, and its decline in the West led to a mode of distribution primarily based on rents in kind, but incorporating many of the traditional feudal rights and obligations. In England the emergence of 'gentleman farming' coincided with the expropriation of monastic endowments, etc., and the gradual movement for enclosing 'open-field' lands in the sixteenth and seventeenth centuries. Many factors, including technical progress in agriculture, quickened the pace of this movement in the eighteenth century until the parliament began to enact public and general laws for enclosure. In the process many peasants in various classes ('lease-holders', 'tenants-at-will', 'copy-holders', 'squatters') lost their traditional rights and became 'landless' – for reasons which would take too long to discuss. American agriculture in the 'Northern' States was generally 'homestead type' based on family and casual (wage) labour; and, in the 'Southern' States, it was 'estate type' operated by slave labour – which it took a long and bloody civil war to destroy. At about the same time (1861), *Tsar Alexander II* abolished serfdom in Russia, when *Bismarck* was busy creating the Prussian Junker system, and Italy was about to watch over the bourgeoisification of ownership and technology in its agriculture (shortly after the *Risorgimento*). France had already experienced an unusually egalitarian distribution of land (through the French Revolution) some consequences of which are now felt by her EEC partners because of her insistence on the protectionist Common

Agricultural Policy. Share-cropping is more typical of Eastern tradition and history, where in many areas 'landlords' (until not so long ago) had much less *property rights* than they did *revenue privileges* (cf. the *zamindars* in Moghul India whom the British Act of 1808 settled as 'landlords' – i.e. proprietors). This is an extremely long, complicated (and largely unresolved) story.

15. Finally, the author concludes that:

> The relationship between share-cropping and joint stock companies may best be seen in terms of the early formation of such firms. There are two factors of production 'capital' and 'entre-preneurship'. . . . It is a simple translation of our theory of the contract in agriculture. . . . [p. 253]

II.   Heckscher–Ohlin with Uncertainty

'Production Uncertainty and the Heckscher–Ohlin Theorem' (R. N. Batra, *Review of Economic Studies,* vol. 42 (1975) pp. 259–68) sets out

> to explore the implications of uncertainty in the production function for the validity of the HO theorem and its offspring, the factor-price equalisation theorem. . . . [p. 259].

1. We may recall from Chapter 3 that this is one of the two rival theories of international trade whose naïve theoretical basis has been discussed *ad nauseam* since 1948; and the empirical refutation of whose predictions, in a test by Leontief (1954), has been since christened as 'the Leontief Paradox'. In fact, it has now been largely superseded by its modern variation – the so-called neo-factor theory – which explicitly incorporates 'human capital' as a 'factor of production'.

2. There is a broad similarity between this study and case I above in the choice of 'problem': *they both investigate something in* **uncertain** *conditions*. In fact this is a great new trend in the 'research agenda' of modern neo-classical theory, and we shall come across other examples of it later in this chapter: without having learned much from our theories on the assumption of 'perfect foresight' we are now using mathematics in order to prove that theories which contain little or no real knowledge are also 'true' in 'conditions of uncertainty'. These are the horizons of 'professional scientists' of

the modern technological mass society in quest of 'knowledge'.

3. The author states the assumptions of the Heckscher–Ohlin thereom, and his own model, as follows:

> 1 – . . . two goods . . . produced with the help of capital . . . and labour under conditions of linear homogeneous and concave production functions, perfect competition, full employment, inelastic factor supplies and non-reversible factor-intensities

> 2 – . . . 3 – Producers in the first industry seek to maximise expected utility from profits and are risk-averse . . . all producers have the same utility function . . . . 4 – There is no uncertainty in the second industry and producers there maximise utility from profits. [p. 260]

4. Assumptions in No. 1 are the 'traditional' Heckscher–Ohlin–Samuelson assumptions. Although they are not absoutely impossible to hold together *on purely logical grounds*, they describe a pretty exceptional situation even in the abstract. In particular the assumption of 'non-reversible factor-intensities', in the presence of the rest of the assumptions, is highly restrictive.

5. Assumptions Nos 3 and 4, which are no more 'traditional' but part of the 'new' model, state (*a*) producers in only one of the two industries maximise *expected* utility (i.e. *operate under uncertain conditions*), and they *all* have *the same utility function*; (*b*) producers in the second industry *operate under conditions of certainty* and 'maximise utility, from profits'.

We need not repeat any comments on 'utility' and its maximisation. Let us look at some more specific points: how is it possible for one-half of 'the economy' – i.e. producers in 'the first industry' – to be *uncertain* about the future, and the other half – i.e. those in 'the second industry' – to be *certain* of it (especially as these – 'certainties' and 'uncertainties' – concern future demands, scarcities, prices, technology, etc.). Is this what would happen in (the assumed state) of 'perfect competition' where 'factors' are perfectly mobile, knowledge is costless, there are no technical or institutional barriers, etc., though it could not conceivably happen even in imperfect competition? So far, this refers to the situation in 'one-half' of the world – i.e. one of the two trading countries. Yet exactly the same conditions are assumed to prevail in the other 'half' – i.e. in the second country. So that *both in country 1 and in country 2* the first industry operates under uncertainty and the second under certainty. What is *the meaning* of this? And *all producers have the same utility function.*

There can be no doubt that these 'conditions' are imposed by the mathematics, or no 'proof' will be available.

6. Other explicit or subsumed conditions include no technological differences between the two countries, no land and natural resources, no money, free trade. Even apart from the above observations, it becomes increasingly difficult to believe that these are really two *different* economies (except for differences in 'factor endowments' of which more below).

7. There follows a mathematical 'proof' which we have no doubt of being technically impeccable, mainly for the reason which we have already stated (see point 12 in case I, above).

8. Then, on page 265:

> The discussion . . . must have given an inkling as to the validity . . . of the factor-price equalisation theorem which holds that in the free trade equilibrium, factor rewards are equalised in trading countries. [p. 265]

The theorem about whose 'validity' 'an inkling' has been thus given is the famous Samuelson result – i.e. there would be a single, unique, wage rate (and profit rate) in a freely-trading world – which was so preposterous as it seemed to have sealed the fate of the Heckscher–Ohlin theorem for ever. But we now know . . .

9. However, the restatement of that 'validity' is immediately qualified:

> We will now show that given [our assumption of differences between the physical amounts of capital owned by each of the two countries ['Kh Kf'] factor prices will never be equalised in the two countries when production decisions are made under conditions of uncertainty. [p. 265]

and a proof follows by the aid of Samuelson's original diagram.

10. The reference to the assumption of different *physical amounts* of capital is now worth considering: if one country owns a greater *physical* amount of capital (as opposed to a greater money *value* of

capital) *then there could be only one type of capital – tractors, shovels, skyscrapers, etc. – in the whole world; and that would be so for labour too.* We disregard the 'unrealism', etc. But can 'the two commodities' produced in the whole world by identical capital and identical labour (with no land and natural resources) be really two different commodities *in the general need they fulfil?* A sewing-machine and a tailor may either produce jackets or trousers (assuming Providence will supply the fabric); but surely neither of them could produce *potatoes* with a sewing-machine.

11. That apart; now that – on the new assumptions – 'the factor-price equalisation theorem' has been disproved, a note of caution is added which (we surmise) is meant as a safeguard against the potential displeasure of an important member of our 'invisible college' (this is a fairly direct evidence for some of our conjectures in Chapter 5):

> It is worth pointing out here that even if factor rewards are not completely equalised, one can easily see that the tendency towards factor-price equalisation still remains, provided, of course, absolute risk aversion is decreasing in profits. [p. 266]

12. Finally, it is not clear where this new proof of 'the HO theorem' leaves us with *Ricardo's* (rival) theory of international trade.

III.   Heckscher–Ohlin with Intermediate Products
The article of case II above is immediately followed (in the same issue of the same journal) by another, entitled 'The Heckscher–Ohlin Model and Traded Intermediate Products' (A. G. Schweinberger, *Review of Economic Studies,* vol. 42 (1975) pp. 269–78). It is claimed at the outset that:

> Whether the Heckscher–Ohlin theorem is valid in the presence of produced intermediate products is clearly of considerable importance . . . [p. 269]

Having said enough about this theorem in the previous case we shall maintain silence on this alleged 'considerable importance'.

1. – Part I of the article consists of 'a proof of (the traditional) Heckscher–Ohlin proposition', yet again. Inevitably it is based on

the same old (explicit and implicit) assumptions which we have discussed already.

2 – In part II

> The model is . . . expanded to allow for traded intermediaries. It is again assumed that both commodities are consumed. Each commodity is now also used as an intermediate product in the production of the other commodity. All the other assumptions of the traditional Heckscher–Ohlin model are maintained. . . . [p. 271]

The mathematical proofs, etc., follow as impeccably as in the other cases.

3. Let us examine the theoretical basis of the new model in a little detail: (*a*) it assumes all the 'traditional' Heckscher–Ohlin conditions, including the most important one: the 'two countries are equal in every respect except for factor endowments' (p. 270); (*b*) it assumes that 'both commodities are consumed' in the two trading countries; (*c*) it further assumes that 'each commodity is . . . also used as an intermediate product in the production of the other commodity'.

Assumptions (*a*), (*b*) and (*c*), taken together, seem to pose some *logical economic* – even though, apparently, no *mathematical – problems*. Now, since the model is static, there is no question of growth and accumulaton. But, unless we assume only one period of production (which is not the case, and which would be of no interest at all) then the *given,* but different, amounts of '*capital*' with which the countries start (under assumption (*a*)) *must be reproduceable,* so that the physical depreciation of capital stock could be made good in successive periods of production. It follows that (at least) one of the two commodities produced must be 'the capital good'. But, under assumptions (*b*) and (*c*), the two commodities are both (final) consumer goods as well as intermediate products. Therefore (at least) *one of the two commodities is both a 'capital' good and a final consumer good, and an intermediate product, all at once. Yet there exists no such commodity, not even 'corn', which would qualify for this description: this is a simple example, not just of an unrealistic assumption, but one which has no conceivable counterpart in reality.*

4. Suppose that we give away the above point by thinking that such a product is conceivable in some fertile minds. Now according

to assumption (c) 'each commodity is . . . also used as an inter-mediate product in the production of the other commodity'. This would mean that one of the two commodities is used as 'capital' in the production of itself as well as the other commodity; but it is used as intermediate product in the production of the other commodity only. This, however, seems to be an absurb proposition.

5. The above objections could be met by a further assumption: capital does not depreciate; it lasts for ever and so it does not require periodic replacement either in parts or in toto. Thus capital is entirely distinct from the two commodities produced. There is yet another problem. The two countries begin with different 'factor endowments.' Clearly, intermediate products are also 'factors of production' or they would be just final consumer goods. Therefore, the countries should 'begin' not only with given, but different, amounts of 'capital' and labour, but also with given, and different, amounts of the two produced commodities which are intermediate products and, hence, 'factors of production'. It follows that we have four, not two, factors of production: when the countries begin to trade, they are 'endowed' with given amounts of four inputs: 'capital', labour and the two (intermediate) products. How can then one determine which country is **relatively** more endowed with what input(s)? Even if one country has a greater absolute endowment of all of them measured in physical units, then it would not follow that it has a greater relative endowment in any (one, or two or three) of them (which is indispensable even to the 'traditional' model). Alternatively, if we evaluate these inputs in money terms we would have (at least) three 'factors' to contend with: 'capital', labour and intermediate products. But (i) for such an evaluation one would need to know the distribution of income (and the prices of the two products) which itself is a great unresolved 'puzzle' at present occupying the minds of many prominent economic mathematicians, in a much more 'important' context; (ii) in any case, it would still be impossible to determine the relative endowments with three inputs – unless one aggregates the value of endowments in 'capital' and intermediate products, in which case the 'new' model would be reduced to the 'traditional' one.[3]

Another alternative is to assume that the two countries begin with different physical amounts of labour and 'capital', but equal physical amounts of each of the two commodities. This could only mean that the productivities of capital and labour between the two countries are different; *if so,* since capital and labour are assumed to be homogeneous, *production must be based on different technologies in the two countries* (or, in 'professional' terms, *'the production functions cannot be identical'*). But this is contrary to a crucial assumption of both the 'traditional' and the 'new' models without which there would be *no* model at all. Finally, if we change the assumption of 'a distinct capital good with no physical depreciation', the present problem would (in a slightly different form) still remain; but problems (3) and (4) above would also creep back into the melting-pot.

6. More comments could be passed both on the foregoing 'puzzles' and on the new model's implications for the Rybczinski theorem (which have been discussed in the article). But enough has been said to show that this model is an exercise in pure mathematics and nothing else. It has not proven the 'validity' of the Heckscher–Ohlin theorem 'in the presence of intermediate products', which it has claimed to be *'clearly* of considerable importance . . .'.

IV.   Economic Growth and Uncertainty
'Optimal Economic Growth and Uncertainty: The Discounted Case' (W. A. Brock and L. T. Mirman, *Journal of Economic Theory,* vol. 4 (1972) pp. 479–513) opens with the following remarks:

> The cornerstone of one-sector optimal economic growth models is the existence and stability of a steady-state solution for optimal consumption policies. [p. 479]

1. Therefore, the model concerns an economy with one sector alone: an economy producing a single commodity which is both the capital and the consumption product – that is, *Ricardo's 'corn model'* but with the important difference that – to his credit – Ricardo used this as a parody of a hypothetical capitalist *agriculture alone*; otherwise he would not have tried to extend it to *the whole of the economy.* Ricardo used his model in order to prove 'the existence and stability' of a *static equilibrium* solution; while such contemporary ('growth') models are used to prove 'the existence and stability' of a steady-state [i.e. *'dynamic' equilibrium]*

solution'. Regardless of the amount – or the level of sophistication – of mathematical techniques used, this is clearly no evidence of any real progress in the method and substance of orthodox economic theory (much less economic *knowledge*), a century and a half after Ricardo's death.

2. The introductory remarks continue thus:

The optimal consumption policy is the stable branch of the saddle point solution of the system of differential equations governing the dynamics of the economy. . . . However, the stable branch solution is a knife-edge policy in the sense that any perturbation . . . results in instability and eventual annihilation (this phenomenon is true when Euler conditions are adhered to after the perturbation). Small perturbations might occur due to observation errors or the lack of knowledge of the exact production functions. It seems reasonable to expect that all sorts of human errors influence decision variables. . . . [p. 479]

3. This is a good example of 'the cult of high-sounding language, unintelligibility and ununderstandability' to which we have previously alluded (see Chapter 7). For the above statement could be restated (with some expendable loss of 'rigour') in something like the following: 'these models show that equilibrium growth in a *single-product* economy is possible; that is, such an economy could grow at a rate equal to the rate of increase of labour and its productivity, which will be (ideally) the same as the rate of profit. But the equilibrium would be unstable if human knowledge was less perfect than God's. "It seems reasonable" to expect that this indeed is so.'

4. And a few lines further down:

it should be expected that planners know the future with something less than certainty. Since it seems impossible, in the face of uncertainty of the future, to predict the exact effects of policies which are formulated in the present, it would be comforting to know that it is possible to formulate the model so that the stability properties of optimal capital accumulation paths are

preserved even if under the influence of small perturbations. . . .
[pp. 479–80]

5. It is difficult to guess for whom and to what purpose 'it would
be comforting to know that it is possible, etc., etc.' – for 'planners'
in a *single-product* economy? . . . This is another example of a
piece of substraction which has, and can have, *no counterpart in the
world of reality.*
   6. And later:

If errors or random events are indeed incorporated, optimal
policies will be affected by the expectation of these events.
Under these conditons, it is worthwhile to introduce uncertainty
directly into the process. The deterministic theory would then be
justified on the grounds that it is an approximation of a more
general model. Thus, when the assumptions of the model are
loosened to include uncertainty, the qualitative results are not
radically different. This last statement is a conclusion which may
be deduced from the results of this paper. [p. 480]

7. Two comments: (*a*) There is a note of reassurance for the
establishment that 'the [established] deterministic theory' – i.e. the
same model based on the assumption of perfect foresight – will not
be threatened but 'justified' by the results of this new model; (*b*) this
indeed is the main conclusion of the new model.
   8. And further still:

In dealing in this uncertain context, it is no longer feasible to
maximise discounted integrals of returns [i.e. the sum of future
profits discounted to the present – H.K.] . . . . We maximise the
expected sum of discounted utilities. . . . To be somewhat more
precise, we treat a one-sector model of economic growth and
introduce uncertainty into the model through a random element
in the production function. . . . The criterion is to maximise the
expected sum of discounted utilities. The main emphasis of the
paper is on long-run equilibrium of the economy under the
influence of optimal policies. . . . [p. 480]

9. We shall not pass any more comment on utility and its maximisation, whether *expected,* or 'unexpected', discounted or undis-

counted. It is, however, worth emphasising that the new model 'introduces' *uncertainty* solely by including 'a random element in the production function'. This alone is the basis for the 'originality' of a mathematical model which it has taken over thirty pages of printed material to present. Up to now 'the deterministic model' had assumed that no errors would be made by planners. Now we 'loosen' that assumption *merely* by 'introducing a random element into the production function'. . . .

And when we get to the model itself we discover that 'the [production] function is homogeneous of the first degree in' capital and labour (p. 485); that is, technology is almost perfectly flexible, and there are constant returns to scale. In addition, there are certain constraints imposed on 'the random variable representing uncertainty' which further reduces the realism (if there is any) of the model.

The use of mathematical techiques in economic theory has often followed the development and application of these techniques in other sciences in general, and in mathematical physics in particular. Consequently, many of the 'problems' formulated and analysed in mathematical theory tend to be determined by mathematical techniques which have been developed for the analysis of scientific problems elsewhere; for example, the mathematical techniques appropriate to astrophysical theory and space engineering. That is, whereas in astrophysics it is the problem itself which dictates the development and/or application of certain mathematical techniques, in mathematical economics it is the knowledge of techniques which tends to suggest the 'problem'. For such cases the appellation 'economic *mathematics*' may be more relevant than 'mathematical *economics*'.

V. An Elementary Economic Theory and a Mathematical Description of the Soviet Planning History

'Optimal Growth with a Convex–Concave Production Function' (A. K. Skiba, *Econometrica*, vol. 46 (May 1978)) begins by asserting that the usual assumption of a concave production function in optimal growth models is a 'good approximation to reality' for advanced economies; but 'accurate analysis of growth in certain less developed countries' shows that such a function 'is not always applicable': in this case a 'convex–concave production function' –

i.e. one which displays increasing returns to scale first, and diminishing returns 'at a later stage' – is more appropriate. There-fore the article will 'consider a one-sector dynamic model . . . with a convex–concave production function'. (p. 527)

The model describes a *single-product economy* evolving through *continuous time* whose 'dynamic system' is 'at any moment' *solely determined* by its stock of capital. *Capital does not depreciate. Population and the labour supply are constant.* There is a 'strictly concave and increasing' 'utility function'; and there is a central planner, in complete control of the economy, who intends 'to optimise a certain criterion' *over an infinite time horizon.* (p. 528)

There follow ten pages of 'sophisticated' mathematical analysis, the 'economic interpretation' of whose results is the following: (*a*) If in an underdeveloped country the existing capital stock is below a (mathematically defined) critical level then it may not be worth its while to develop because 'the marginal product of capital is so low' that capital accumulation may take too long to 'pay off'. (*b*) If the capital stock is above this critical level . . . at first increasing returns to scale will make capital so productive as to push up its price and encourage greater investment; but, at a later stage, decreasing returns will reduce the price of capital.

However, the model's analysis, and its conclusions, may be obtained by the use of some elementary principles in neo-classical economic theory: according to 'the laws of return' when a single, homogeneous, variable input (in this case 'capital') is applied to a fixed input (labour), its 'marginal product' would first increase and 'later' diminish. Thus, the author's reference to *returns to scale* is irrelevant for, in this case, 'the scale' is *continuously* altered by *one 'factor' alone* – capital. Given the author's other neo-classical assumptions – such as a 'strictly concave and increasing utility func-tion which, in simpler language, means that 'marginal utility' diminishes but remains positive – it would follow that, as long as 'the marginal product of capital' is rising, 'marginal' additions to present 'utility' will be less than (the discounted value of) 'marginal' additions to future 'utility'; hence a higher premium on investment. In addition, if 'the stock of capital' is very small at 'the beginning', the reverse would be 'true', so that it may not 'pay' to accumu-late. . . . The same simple story may be told in an alternative way: given some well-known assumptions, as long as the rate of interest *goes on rising,* the 'marginal utility' of saving will be higher than the 'marginal utility' of consumption (or, in mystifying terms, there will be a convex–concave transformation curve between future and present consumption). But if 'the consumer' is at the subsistence level, this will not be the case and so it will not 'pay' to 'begin' to save, for he may reach death before 'riching'.

The model is also a covert mathematical description (if not justification) of the history of Soviet planning in retrospect, where 'in the early stage' (roughly 1928–58) the planning price of capital was high and the emphasis was on rapid accumulation. . . . But it is a grotesque description; for it is a purely *mechanistic* model, as if ideas and events had no role in that historic, and tragic, episode; it is a purely historicist 'theory'; and it further generalises from the history of one specific country with an exceptional resource endowment, and in a very special socio-political situation, to all 'developing countries'. The cult of worship of mathematical techniques, unintelligibility, disguising simple ideas in complex forms, and universalising limited theories and experiences – they all seem to have reached a meeting-point in this model.

A BRIEF REVIEW OF SOME OTHER ARTICLES

I.   Heckscher–Ohlin: The Multi-Country Case
The article entitled 'General Equilibrium and the Heckscher–Ohlin Theory of Trade: The Multi-Country Case' (Y. Horiba, *International Economic Review*, vol. 15 (1974) pp. 440–9) purports to generalise the Heckscher–Ohlin theorem to 'a three-country world' with more than two factors of production. It 'solves' the basic problem of determining the relative factor endowments in such a situation by *assuming that there already exists 'factor-price equalisation'*. This, we may recall, was a *conclusion* of the 'traditional' model which was so strange that it nearly led to the latter's downfall. . . . There is hardly any need to comment on the other 'assumptions', analyses and conclusions of this article.[4]

II.   Savings Function and the Rate of Inflation
The most remarkable aspect of a short article entitled 'The Johnsonian Savings Function and The Rate of Inflation: a Correction'

(H. G. Johnson, *Economia Internazionale,* vol. 29 (1976) pp. (87–91) is that, by a few simple algebraic manipulations, it wishes to investigate 'the monetary policy required to maximise consumption per head on "golden rule" lines' under certain conditions affecting the real savings rate (p. 89). There may have been no objection to that had the article not ended with some policy recommendations for *the real world*:

> price stability or deflation may be the optimal policy . . . this may well be the case in less developed countries because . . . the money to income ratio is very much lower in 'developing' than in 'developed' countries. [p. 91]

III.   Liquidity, Risk and Utility

This is a one-page 'Comment' (G. O. Bierwag, *Review of Economic Studies,* vol. 41 (1974) p. 301) on an earlier, three-page 'Note', entitled 'Liquidity Preference and Risk Aversion with an Exponential Utility Function' (E. Glustoff and N. Nigro, the same journal, vol. 39 (1972) pp. 113–15). It begins with the following sentences:

> In a recent, note [the authors] studied a utility function which has the satisfactory property of risk aversion but avoids some of the unsatisfactory properties of the quadratic function. [The authors] concluded that their risk averse function does not allow plunging. . . . Unfortunately there is an error in the . . . derivation which accounts for their conclusion.

In other words, the original authors had tried to solve a problem, but apparently did not succeed because of a purely technical error. Since there is no reply to this 'Comment' by the authors of the 'Note', one may presume that they themselves and/or the journal's editors have agreed with Bierwag's criticism. If the attitude of the academic profession was not such as it is, one wonders whether professional economists would ever spend their time on the solution of little puzzles of this kind, or the discovery of technical errors in the solutions. But, given that such lines of research are encouraged, indeed permitted, by the leaders of the profession, regard for academic success makes it difficult for many, and especially younger academics, to avoid the temptation.

IV   Smuggling and Economic Welfare

In its prefatory remarks the article entitled 'A Theoretical Analysis of Smuggling', J. Bhagwati and B. Hansen (*Quarterly Journal of Economics*, vol. 87 (1973) pp. 172–87) states that:

> In some underdeveloped countries smuggling takes on large proportions and is a major economic problem. . . . It is commonly argued that smuggling must improve economic welfare since it constitutes . . . evasion of the tariffs . . . which, for a small country, would signify a suboptimal policy. We propose to demonstrate in Section I of this paper the falsity of this view, while also investigating the :estrictive conditions under which smuggling may improve welfare. . . . In Section II we . . . show that the achievement of a given degree of protection to domestic importable production, in the presence of smuggling, produces lower welfare than if smuggling were absent. In section III we extend our analysis to the phenomenon of faked invoices. [p. 172]

A later 'Comment' on this article, 'Smuggling and Economic Welfare: A Comment' (H. P. Gray and I. Walter, the same journal, vol. 89 (1975) pp. 643–50), concludes that although the 'analytical framework (used by Bhagwati and Hansen) leaves a great deal to be desired . . . the . . . discussion will surely stimulate a great deal of further thought on this long-neglected topic. . . .'. (p. 650)

In view of what goes, we should perhaps praise the original article for trying to prove that only in certain 'restrictive conditions . . . smuggling may improve economic welfare'. Yet it is depressing to see that 'it is commonly argued that smuggling improves economic welfare'; that this should prompt or provoke abstract analysis to show that this 'belief' is not *generally* correct; that this attempt should be countered by a lengthy 'comment' to demonstrate the limited *theoretical* applicability of the conclusions, ending with the fantastic, though not incredible, prediction that it will 'surely stimulate a great deal of further thought on this long-neglected topic'. Given the great theoretical and practical problems facing economic science and the world economy, we need not elaborate the many significant implications of this one small example for economic theory, economic method, the economic profession, and the Great Technological Societies in which we exist.

There are many more examples of such (growing) tendencies in the choice of 'problems', techniques, methods, assumptions, etc., which can be readily obtained from the outpouring mass of current publications. We can only suggest that the reader (and the critic) see them for themselves.

UNTO THIS LAST: A GENERAL THEORY OF P.I.S.S

In 'The Quantity Theory of Drink: A Restatement' (*Australian Economic Papers* (Dec 1974) pp. 171–7) O. E. Covick has presented an authentic caricature of the substance of orthodox economic theory and method, with a brilliant combination of humour and brevity which – among other things – may simplify the task of some future historians of economics.

The model describes a Normal Boozer as one who never refuses a drink and always buys his round, wishing to maximise a Paralytically Incapable Stationary State, or P.I.S.S. for short. This is a function of different types of drink which he can have, in a 'given evening', with his limited liquidity. Thus, the Normal Boozer maximises his P.I.S.S. function subject to his liquidity, or budget, constraint. Since the process of P.I.S.S. maximisation would involve the condition of Diminished Responsibility, the problem is to discover that *ISOPISS* curve at which 'the Boozer will begin to drop small change on the floor'. However, two leading theorists have postulated that the Boozer maximises 'perceived P.I.S.S.' which would impose some restrictions for a well-behaved P.I.S.S. function. After investigating the first- and second-order conditions for P.I.S.S. maximisation, it turns out that the Boozer should equalise the ratio of the quantities of different drinks divided by their prices to 'the marginal P.I.S.S. of liquidity'. Following a discussion of the conditions of Pareto optimality, and the complications of divergent private rates of time-discount for welfare optimisation, the author studies the macro-economic and policy aspects of the problem. Here opinions diverge between the Quality and the Quantity theorists, with familiar differences on the behaviour of such crucial variables as the elasticity of the Boozer's stomach. This is followed by an analysis of the International Implications of pint devaluation, with the aid of similar concepts and techniques from 'the economists's analytical tool-kit'. In concluding this successful synthesis of modern micro- and macro-theory he states that

> The government should therefore aim at a long-run Drink Policy. . . . It should empower the National Water Board to restrict the supply of water (High Powered Drink). . . .[a] three per cent per annum reduction in the Water Supply will give Britain a seven per cent annum rate of growth of G.N.P. (Gross National P.I.S.S.) with declining involuntary unemployment and no inflation. [p. 176]

In reading this short article John Ruskin's ghost may not be pleased to discover that a century after his own passionate critique of the prevailing orthodox economic theory, it is now possible to write off modern economics in six pages of ridicule.

ANALYSIS OF THE EVIDENCE

The above material tends to support most of the arguments of the previous chapters. In particular:

1.   There is a rising trend among economic theorists to propose ideas which are *not* empirically test*able*. It looks as if, in practice, Positive Economics is virtually non-existent. Let us recall that logical positivism regards untest*able* statements as meaningless noises.

2.   The Kuhnian, and Lakatosian, frameworks are also strictly inapplicable to their case; for – apart from other considerations – Kuhn and Lakatos presume that all scientific 'paradigms' and 'programmes' are inherently test*able,* even though they may not be normally rejected upon refutation.

3.   The precedence of form over content, of technique over problem, of mathematics over economics, is evident.

4.   The ancient preoccupation with 'the existence and stability' of general equilibrium solutions – the ideological *roots* of which have been mentioned in Chapter 2 and elsewhere – seems to be more dominant than at any time in the past. However, it is likely that the more rarified theories (looking for some such 'existence and stability') have less to do with ideological motivations and more

with the use of mathematics (see further, paragraph 12, below). This, at any rate, refutes Blaug's ('Lakatosian') suggestion that the Keynesian Revolution shifted the *hard core* of economic theory away from equilibrium to *dis*equilibrium analysis.

5.   Almost every theoretical model purports to maximise some 'utility function': we are yet to clear up basic problems concerning this 'utility' and that 'maximisation' in the simple static neo-classical consumer theory (see Chapter 3 on marginal utility, 'dis-utility', etc.); but, instead, we assume those problems away and maximise the *expected* utility of share-cropping peasants, of whole 'economies' in growth, of the whole 'world' in trade.

6.   The implicit claims to the *universality* of these theories are also clear: they are supposed to be relevant to everywhere; and they are, therefore, relevant to nowhere: there is hardly any economic, social, technological and cultural *context* in any of them.

7.   Many — and, especially, most of the more mathe-matical – theories are abstractions with little or no conceivable counterparts in the world of reality.

8.   The accent is on analytical puzzles as opposed to substantial problems: for example, contrast the nature of contemporary prob-lems of international economic relations with attempts to formulate 'new models' of a discredited 'traditional' theory of international trade by the force of mathematical techniques.

9.   A reasonable knowledge of (*or* regard for) the history of ideas and events is absent from most of such theories.

10.   The models are generally prescriptive rather than descrip-tive, no matter in what guise they are presented. For they ultimately answer questions such as what certain entities *should do if they wished to attain a certain goal*. However, this fact by itself does *not* make them (any more than it does any other theory) *un*scientific. But there is an in-built ethical bias in so far as most of these theories answer questions pertaining to *general* welfare and efficiency, to the exclusion of many other important problems such as *specific* wel-fare, income distribution, etc.

11.   Thomas Kuhn's acute observation that a clear sign of crisis in a science is a growth in its complexity without a corresponding increase in the content of its knowledge seems to be borne out by the above points.

12.   It is difficult to see much in all this which has a specific

ideological bias in favour of capitalism: there can be no doubt that all neo-classical theory presumes a liberal social framework (although one which is a century too late). Yet even within a liberal framework one can produce correct or incorrect, relevant or irrelevant, serious or grotesque theories. It is likely that the search for equilibrium and its stability, *in its classical origins,* was motivated by ideology: it was intended as an intellectual defence of the *emerging* liberal capitalist society against the dominating remnants of feudalism. But would the capitalist state, class or society now find it 'comforting to know' that the long-term path of steady-state growth in a nondescript, apparently wholly anarchic, single-product economy is stable when a 'random element' is introduced into its 'production function'? We find that hard to believe. We think it more likely that the living capitalist organs would prefer the development of economic theories for the solution of their numerous and important problems which may be vital for their survival.

The only conceivable 'service' rendered by such theories to any capitalist entity is that they do not criticise, attack or threaten it. Yet even that is a necessary outcome of the 'puzzles' chosen, and the methods used for 'solving' them: when a theory has no counterpart in the world of reality, how could it harm (or benefit) that world, or any part of it?

13.   There seems to be some evidence for our tentative remarks concerning the characteristics of the sociology of the (modern) academic profession: overspecialisation; publication for its own sake; the inversion of the concept of originality in research . . . and the role of the 'invisible college' in encouraging these tendencies by preferring the publication of such material, and appointing (or promoting) their producers. With respect to this very last point there is, of course, no *direct* evidence in the foregoing examples. But, since posts and promotions are very strongly influenced by publications (especially, the more mathematical of them, published in 'prestigious' journals), they would automatically imply material success. There are rumours in the (British) economic profession that the publication of three or four (mathematical) articles in some of these journals could earn their author a university chair almost irrespective of age, experience, etc. No doubt this is a caricature of the truth; yet casual observations seem to indicate that it is not too far from it.

CONCLUDING NOTES: A REQUIEM FOR SCIENCE?

Whence knowledge and science; whither man and society? We abandoned our faith in freedom, progress and redemption through God because His self-styled representatives on earth had forsaken Him first. We were left to rely on our own (imperfect) collective reason in the hope of building a better, though still imperfect, human society. Yet we now seem to be completely empty-handed – left, in this hostile universe, with little else than a cult of worship of our new idols which, unlike the more civilised age of paganism, do not even *symbolise* anything higher than themselves: they are filled not with the spirit of long rivers, vast planes or high heavens; they are filled with gasoline, bullets and radioactive material; they do not promise hypothetical fraternity and fertility; they cause real hostility and sterility. We are yet to face the charges of crucifying Faith; and we are busy destroying our own reason.

Professor J. A. Mirrlees has remarked that:

> If anything explains the heat of debates in growth [and capital] theory, it is the difficulty thinkers in the scholastic tradition have in appreciating that, for workers in the scientific tradition, it makes sense to entertain a model and use it without being committed to it; while the scientists cannot imagine why mere models should be the object of passion.[5]

'Scholastic' is a pejorative term describing medieval schoolmen, their predominantly irrelevant topics of discourse and their axiomatic/tautological, and *completely a priori,* methods of conducting them. In myth or in truth it refers to men preoccupied with such questions as how many angels could stand on top of a pin. . . . If this is a correct description of Scholasticism, then *who are the modern scholastics*; those who insist on reason, realism and knowledge, or those who fake them; those who seek solutions to *real problems,* or those who first invent and then 'solve' *imaginary puzzles* once a week? It is hard to know whether or not the medieval scholastics were 'committed to their models'. But it is certain that Galileo, Newton, Lavoisier, Darwin, Einstein, Adam Smith, Ricardo, J. S. Mill, Marx, Keynes and others did not use their own models 'without being committed to them'. There is no point in having useless squabbles on semantics. If the dictionary of modern professional academics would now define the Newtons and the Einsteins of human history as scholastics, and the contemporary schoolmen as scientists, then so be it: let us, then, lament the departure of *that* scholasticism and dread the arrival of *this* science; let us also hope that a new renaissance will, once again, deliver mankind from this revolt against reason, reality and simplicity.

9

CONCLUDING NOTES

This critical study of the foundations of economic knowledge combined an indiscriminate approach to the assessment of ideas and methods with a conscious effort to avoid personal polemics. For we agree with Jevons that 'in science and philosophy nothing must be held sacred'; and with Popper that 'in our ignorance we are all equal'. It follows that we should 'welcome every opinion based on scientific criticism' (Marx).

Science does not 'begin' with, or generalise from, 'observation', nor does it 'end' with conclusions and predictions derived from entirely abstract and *a priori* models. On the contrary, scientific discovery is a *process* whereby the clash of ideas with themselves, and with reality, may result in a greater understanding of both natural and social phenomena. Science rejects dogma; but the most distinctive feature of a scientific outlook is its rejection of *dogmatism*: that is, its rejection of any set of rational or irrational beliefs which are – tacitly or explicitly – held and defended uncritically. It follows that a scientific vision dispenses both with intellectual arrogance and with idealistic perfectionism: whatever is 'unscientific' is not false; whatever is 'scientific' is not true. It is only in their *gropings* that (with different approaches) the scientist and the mystic alike make any progress towards their ultimate goals. For as soon as they delude themselves to have finally *grasped* their objectives, they are certain to miss the opportunity altogether.

If these are the essential characteristics of science, then there can be no significant methodological difference between the natural and the social sciences. What other differences there are – for example, the possibility or impossibility of controlled experimentation; or the relative ease or difficulty of quantification, which, in any case, vary among the natural sciences themselves – are either insignificant or of secondary importance. Besides, while the scientific outlook and vision is – in the above sense – unique; scientific methods are, and should be, diverse: it would be wrong for each and every scientific discipline to adopt and emulate one particular method, or set of methods; on the contrary they should adapt and develop methods which are most appropriate to their own fields of study. For example, while modern economics is obsessed with rigorous logical or mathematical proofs, and computerised 'empirical' studies, without much success; it ignores – often with contempt – the wealth of historical experience, and qualitative evidence at its disposal. Yet, it is likely that a survey of these largely unexplored forests would yield real fruits which may make many a natural scientist sigh in admiration. All roads may eventually end up in Rome; but no single road passes through the entire breadth of the Roman Empire.

The progress of economic knowledge is not seriously affected by such bogus problems; nor by the more real risk of the intrusion of ethical judgements and ideological predilections in allegedly honest and objective theories. It is the preoccupation with little abstract puzzles as opposed to great and real problems; the parochial vision combined with technological formalism; the uncritical commitment to existing theories and methods; the discouragement of alternative approaches and views – it is this attitude which is mainly responsible for the present state of economic science: the ever-increasing complexity of its formal edifice; and the never-ending poverty of its substantial achievements.

If those are the results of a study of the foundations of economic knowledge then they already contain its prospects. Assuming that these results are generally reasonable (i) it would be impossible to know what *would* be done; (ii) it is almost self-evident what *should* be done. Within these two extremes the following remarks seem to be reasonable. In their majorities men do not usually change their views, ideas, methods, prejudices, etc., when these are rationally demonstrated to be false, inconsistent, inferior or whatever. This is particularly true of professional men of intellect, if only because such things are both the means of their livelihood and the sources of their self-esteem. It has been claimed that (in an academic conversation) a leading economist once protested that he could not accept a certain viewpoint because this would be tantamount to a repudiation of his own lifetime's work. Whatever may be the truth or precision of this claim, it is very likely that considerations of this kind play significant roles in the academic (as in any other) *real-politik*. And the world would be a pretty different one – perhaps even a pretty one – had this not been so. Economics is evidently in crisis and the roads out of this crisis are (at least by our reckoning) *apparently* clear: these are, as we said, almost self-evident from the above summary and do not merit an unnecessary repetition. But here, as elsewhere, there is a large gap between available choices and existing constraints: between what freedom of action could permit; and what real barriers to such freedom would forbid; between what economists should do, and what they would do; between scientific revolutions in economics, and superficial readjustments which, as in the past, would probably buy the subject one or two decades of academic peace and comfort.

Yet, even in such difficult cases, ideas and arguments are not wholly worthless. And, at any rate, there is no better alternative available to their holders but to express them, and to demonstrate their uses in practice. There are three very different concepts of idealism: that which claims that all progress is entirely determined by the force of ideas; that which describes a state of self-delusion, a total unrealism or 'wishful thinking'; and that which refers to a commitment to some rational, prescriptive and/or moral principles (or ideals) – and attempts for their promotion. It is this third – non-metaphysical and non-self-deluding – concept of idealism which is relevant to the case in hand. For it always succeeds in realising its own *internal* truth, even when it fails to achieve its *external* objectives. It is an idealism which (together with Spinoza) would *never* have to laugh, nor to weep – for it is able to understand.

NOTES AND REFERENCES

CHAPTER 2

1. See *The Wealth of Nations,* ed. Edwin Cannan (London: Methuen, 1904), book III, chap. 2, where he speaks of the rise of European feudalism as a great catastrophe which might have been 'a transitory evil' had it not been for the *unnatural* laws of primogeniture and entail, which perpetuated the monopolistic ownership of land.

2. In the well-known equation $M = kY$ – where M = money, and Y = money income – let k, the inverse of the velocity of circulation, = unity. Then $M = Y$.

3. See C. E. Ayres, *The Theory of Economic Progress* (1942) (New York: Schocken Paperbacks, 1962), especially chap. 4. Ayres's claim, though it contains a lot of truth, is an exaggeration: in particular classical political economists paid a considerable amount of attention to economic progress and technical change, which, according to Ayres, should be the proper domain of economic analysis.

4. Guy Routh, *The Origin of Economic Ideas* (London: Macmillan, 1977), particularly chaps 1 and 2.

5. There are two related issues here. The first is Ricardo's claim that Smith had confused the 'labour-embodied' and the 'labour-command' concepts of value; the second, that Smith (therefore) abandoned his labour theory of value altogether. The first is a palpable mistake which recently S. Kaushil has claimed to have uncovered for the first time in history, whereas Marx had clearly pointed it out a century earlier: 'Adam Smith nowhere asserts that these were two equivalent expressions . . .' (Karl Marx, *Theories of Surplus Value,* Moscow: Progress Publishers, 1968, vol. II, p. 396) (see also p. 403). Kaushil's own analysis of Adam Smith's value theory leads him to conclude that the latter had *no* labour theory at all even for a 'primitive' society, but a 'three-factor theory'. This is a mistake arising mainly from his lack of distinction between the concepts of use value and exchange value; see S. Kaushil, 'The Case of Adam Smith's Value Analysis', *Oxford Economic Papers,* vol. 25, no. 1 (Mar 1973); and the present writer's 'Adam Smith's Value Analysis – A Comment' (May 1973) (mimeographed). The

second claim that Adam Smith abandoned his labour theory in
favour of a 'cost-of-production theory' or 'adding-up-theory' –
put forward by distinguished authors such as Maurice Dobb, Eric
Roll and Piero Sraffa is due to a confusion between Adam Smith's
theory of *value* and his 'theory' of *distribution*.

6. See *The General Theory of Employment, Interest and Money*
(London: Macmillan, 1961) chap. 3.

7. In his address to the annual conference of the International
Economic Association (1969), Paul Samuelson, the doyen of
Walrasian economics, described Marshall as an 'overhauled'
currency.

8. See, for example, G. L. S. Shackle, *The Years of High Theory*
(Cambridge: Cambridge University Press, 1967).

9. See M. Morishima, *Marx's Economics: A Dual Theory of Value
and Growth* (Oxford: Clarendon Press, 1973).

10. See G. C. Harcourt, *Some Cambridge Controversies in the
Theory of Capital* (Cambridge: Cambridge University Press, 1972);
see, further, Joan Robinson, *Economic Heresies* (London: Macmillan, 1971).

11. Samuelson once observed that 'soft sciences spend time in
talking about method because Satan finds tasks for idle hands to
do'; see 'Problems of Methodology – Discussion', *American
Economic Review, Papers and Proceedings* (1963) p. 231.

12. *Cogito, ergo sum.*

13. In his otherwise excellent analysis of 'A Political Theory of
Property' C. B. Macpherson seems to suggest that the early labour
theories of value intended to justify *all* private property (perhaps
even including *feudal* property). This is highly unlikely of men like
Locke. But, apart from that, the labour theory would logically
exclude all property which was founded on 'usurpation' and perpetuated by 'unnatural' privileges; see his *Democratic Theory: Essays
in Retrieval* (London: Oxford University Press, 1973) p. 130. Note
also that, from this point of view, Marx's labour theory simply
extends the implication of Locke's theory to bourgeois property: if
property not founded, or based, on personal labour is illegitimate,
then bourgeois property is also illegitimate, since – as Marx
argued – it had originated in the *expropriation* of tenant farmers
and artisans by agricultural and industrial enterpreneurs. The historical notion of bourgeois *expropriation* is often confused with its
socio-economic consequence of *exploitation*. Marx's vision of
capitalist development was as follows: capitalist *expropriation* of
yeomen and artisans turned them into wage labourers, which automatically led to the *alienation* of the worker from his product and his
exploitation by his employer.

14. See 'Political Arithmetic', in *The Economic Writings of Sir William Petty*, ed. C. H. Hull (Cambridge: Cambridge University Press, 1899). See also this author's 'The Development of the Service Sector: A New Approach', *Oxford Economic Papers* (Nov 1970).

15. See *The Wealth of Nations*, op. cit., book I, chap. 10, part II.

16. Ibid. book III, chap. 2.

17. See Dugald Stewart's introduction to *The Theory of Moral Sentiments*, Reprints of Economic Classics (London: Kelly, 1965) p. liv.

18. O. H. Taylor asserts that Smith's concept of sympathy is morally objective (these are not his words) since ' "sympathy" ' is an acquisition into one's self – one's own feelings – of a kind of echo or reflection of the other, observed, active person's apparent feelings, which results from a successful, imaginative 'identification' of the self with that other person. I think it is that which a more modern psychological theory calls empathy (see *A History of Economic Thought* (New York: McGraw-Hill, 1960) p. 61. Here is a refutation from Adam Smith: 'Sympathy . . . cannot, in any sense, be regarded as a selfish principle. When I sympathise with your sorrow and your indignation, it may be pretended, indeed, that my emotion is founded inself-love. . . . But though sympathy is very properly said to arise from an imaginary change of situations with the person principally concerned, yet this imaginary change is not supposed to happen to me in my own person and character, but in that of the person with whom I sympathise. (*Moral Sentiments*, p. 456)'. In other words, although 'self-love' may be regarded as the basis for sympathy, because in sympathising with someone else one may be internalising the possible effect of the other person's misfortune on oneself, yet the *feeling* of sympathy belongs to the sympathiser himself. Although the word 'empathy' did not exist at the time it is abundantly clear that Smith's concept is one of sympathy in its full sense and not 'empathy'. F. A. Hayek has asserted that Adam Smith was 'very far from holding such naïve views . . .' as 'the natural goodness of man', the existence of a "natural harmony of interests" . . . (see *The Constitution of Liberty* (London: Routledge & Kegan Paul, 1960) chap. 4, p. 60. Here is a refutation from Smith: '[The landlords] are led by an invisible hand to make nearly the same distribution of the necessaries of life which would have been made had the earth been divided into equal portions among all inhabitants, and thus without intending it, without knowing it, advance the interest of the society . . .' (see *Moral Sentiments*, pp. 264–5). The whole of *Moral Sentiments* is evidence against Hayek's claim but this particular

quotation puts the case most strongly as it extends the beneficence
of the invisible hand to *landlords* as well.

19. See Jean-Jacques Rousseau, *The Social Contract and Discourses,* ed. G. D. H. Cole (London: Dent, 1973).

20. See J. M. Clark *et al., Adam Smith 1876–1926* (Chicago:
Chicago University Press, 1928) – e.g. 'When Smith revised his
Theory of Moral Sentiments he was elderly and unwell. [He may
have] lost the capacity to make drastic changes in his philosophy,
but had retained his capacity to overlook the absence of complete
co-ordination and unity in that philosophy.' In the same volume
Glen Morrow argues that the two books are *consistent!*

21. A. L. Macfie, 'Adam Smith's Moral Sentiments as the Foundation for the Wealth of Nations', *Oxford Economic Papers* (1959).

22. See *The Wealth of Nations,* op. cit., book I, chap. 8, pp. 66–7.

23. See the same passage as in note 22 above, where he says that 'it
would be to no purpose' to pursue the matter any further.

24. See Eric Roll, *A History of Economic Thought* (London:
Faber, 1938) chap. v, P. Sraffa (ed.), *The Works and Correspondence of David Ricardo* (Cambridge: Cambridge University
Press, 1963), vol. I, 'Introduction' (by P. Sraffa). Maurice Dobb,
Theories of Value and Distribution since Adam Smith (Cambridge:
Cambridge University Press, 1973) chap. 2.

25. See *The Wealth of Nations,* op. cit. vol. 2, book V, chap. 1,
part III, art. II. Dugald Stewart was the first critic of Smith's works
to notice the dual impact of the division of labour on society in *The
Wealth of Nations*; see *Moral Sentiments,* op. cit. p. liv. Alfred
Marshall was also well aware of the issue; see his *Principles of
Economics* (London: Macmillan, 1961) book II, chap. 8.

26. Marx introduced the concept of 'absolute rent' *merely* to make
the determination of a *union* rate of profit for the *whole* of a
capitalist economy possible. He found it necessary to do so because
he assumed a lower capital intensity (i.e. lower organic composition
of capital) in the rural sector which would lead to a higher rate of
profit for this sector than for industry. So the landlord collected the
absolute rent, and hence the remaining surplus value in agriculture
resulted in a rate of profit equal to that in industry. But, what if the
organic composition of capital was lower in agriculture, while farming was entirely capitalistic, rather than tenant farming (i.e. there
was no landlord, examples of which can now be found in many
countries of the world, e.g. U.S.A.)? However that may be, the
concept of absolute rent has now been dragged out of its context by
some 'Marxist' sociologists and applied to cases which are, to put it
mildly, startling. See, for example, David Harvey's *Social Justice
and the City* (Baltimore: Johns Hopkins University Press, 1973)

where he confuses the rent of land with the rent of accommodation in cities, and furthermore, triumphantly concludes that the latter is 'absolute rent'.

27. James Mill, *Elements of Political Economy* (London, 1824) p. 8.

28. John Stuart Mill, *Principles of Political Economy*, ed. W. J. Ashley (London: Longmans, Green & Co., 1940).

29. Cited in R. L. Smyth (ed.) *Essays in Economic Method* (London: Duckworth, 1962).

30. See Asa Briggs's review of *The Collected Letters of Thomas and Jane Carlyle (Manchester Guardian Weekly,* vol. 117, no. 11 (11 Sep 1977) p. 22): 'The Saint-Simonians fascinated Carlyle because their "scientific insight" had transformed itself into "Religion"', 'Without religion constantly present in the heart', Carlyle wrote to his brother in 1832. 'I can not see how a man can *live,* otherwise than unreasonably, *desperately.'*

31. A group of frustrated Comtean zealots later tried their 'scientific' hands in the social reorganisation of Brazil with disastrous consequences; a similar group of frustrated Benthamite zealots should take most of the blame for the so-called Indian Mutiny.

32. The idea was of course not wholly novel; in particular, it had been anticipated by Vico, Herder and Michelet. See Isaiah Berlin 'Historical Inevitability' in his *Four Essays on Liberty* (London: Oxford University Press, 1969). See also his *Vico and Herder* (London: Oxford University Press, 1975) and *The Hedgehog and the Fox,* New American Library (1957). See, further, J. A. Schumpeter, *Economic Doctrine and Method* (1912) (London: Oxford University Press, 1954) especially pp. 96-8.

33. Cited in Smyth, *Essays in Economic Method,* op. cit.

34. Routh, *The Origin of Economic Ideas,* op. cit. p. 8. This description of Jones's method is not entirely just. An important element of Jones's approach was his awareness of the historical evolution of social institutions for which (in contrast to Ricardo) he received a round of applause from Marx; cf. *Theories of Surplus Value,* op. cit. vol. 2, pp. 399-403.

35. Schumpeter, *Economic Doctrine and Method,* op. cit. pp. 166-70.

36. E. H. Phelps-Brown, 'The Underdevelopment of Economics', *Economic Journal* (Mar 1972).

37. See this author in *Oxford Economic Papers* (Nov 1970) pp. 362-82, and the references therein.

38. The climatic factor was of course an old idea which had been revived by Montesquieu in the eighteenth century.

39. Cited in Smyth, op. cit. p. 44.

40. See Schumpeter, op. cit.

41. Ludwig von Mises, *Epistemological Problems of Economics* (1933) (New York: Van Nostrand, 1960) p. 13.

42. Ibid. pp. 28–9.

43. Ibid. p. 30.

44. Ibid. p. 200. It is remarkable to observe the great inconsistencies between many arguments of this book and those of von Mises's last publication on this subject: *Theory and History* (London, 1958). Here is a sample from the latter book: 'For the scienes of human action [i.e. the social sciences – H.K.] the ultimate given is the judgments of value of the actors, and the ideas that engender these judgments of value. It is precisely this fact that precludes employing the methods of the natural sciences to solve the problems of human action' (p. 306); 'As soon as somebody . . . tries to prove the harmony doctrine [the opponents of this doctrine] cry out "bias" ' (p. 65); 'All branches of big business cater directly or indirectly to the needs of the common man [p. 119]. . . To the extent that American legislation is successful in its endeavours to curb big business' all are hurt. . . . If the United States had gone as far as Austria did in its fight against big business, the average American would not be much better off than the average Austrian.' (p. 237). However, if the 'arguments' are contradictory, 'the evil intent of the apologetic' (to borrow from Marx) is all too clear and consistent: '. . . our civilisation . . . is safe against . . . foreign barbarians. But it could be destroyed from within by domestic barbarians.' (p. 221). Marx's own words are: 'the evil intent of apologetics': cf. *Capital*, vol. I, Preface to the first edition. Despite popular belief, J. S. Mill is *explicitly* excluded from this reference, and Senior, Longfield, Lauderdale, etc., are *not* mentioned. Later, there is a direct reference to Bastiat in this context.

Notice has just been received of a posthumous essay by L. von Mises entitled *The Ultimate Foundation of Economic Science* (San Francisco: Sheed Andrews & McMeel, 1978). We are as yet unaware of the contents of this new material.

45. See F. A. von Hayek, 'The Trend of Economic Thinking', *Economica* (May 1933) p. 122. Hayek later formulated his methodological ideas in a comprehensive set of three articles entitled 'Scientism and the Study of Society', *Economica* (Aug 1942, Feb 1943 and Feb 1944). These articles were subsequently published in a single volume entitled *The Counter-Revolution of Science* (Evanston, Ill.: Free Press, 1952).

46. L. C. R. Robbins, *An Essay on the Nature and Significance of Economic Science* (London: Macmillan, 1933).

47. von Mises, op. cit. p. 190.

48. Robbins, op. cit. pp. 79–83.

49. T. W. Hutchison, *The Significance and Basic Postulates of Economic Theory* (London: Macmillan, 1938).

50. Hutchison recalls Dobb's 'generous review' of his book (see his 'The Cambridge Version of The History of Economics', *Occasional Papers*, no. 19 (Department of Economics, University of Birmingham, Jan 1974]; but it has not been possible to locate the reference since Professor Hutchison does not remember where it originally appeared. It is of course perfectly consistent for a Marxist economist, such as Maurice Dobb, to have been enthusiastic about the use of empirical and statistical evidence in the study of social and economic problems, especially in the 1930s. Indeed, there can be little doubt that Hayek's, Knight's and von Mises's total opposition to positivism and empiricism had a strong ideological undertone. Alfred W. Stonier's review in *Economic Journal*, vol. 49 (Mar 1939) pp. 114–15, betrays a certain degree of nervousness even although it attempts to give the impression of neutrality. Edmund Whittaker's in *American Economic Review*, vol. 30 (Mar 1940) p. 128, is shorter, a little more generous but not complementary. Frank Knight's, however, is an expression of total horror: see ' "What is Truth" in Economics?' (a review *article*) in *Journal of Political Economy*, no. 1 (1940).

51. Martin Hollis and Edward J. Nell, *Rational Economic Man* (Cambridge: Cambridge University Press, 1975).

52. Ibid. p. 61.

53. Although the authors do not cite his reference, the likeliest evidence for such a claim may be found in John Neville Keynes's *The Scope and Method of Political Economy* (London: Macmillan, 1891; 4th ed. 1917) But Keynes's distinction of fact and value is due to Comtean positivism (which had been accepted by J. S. Mill and others); and his claim that economic method follows a chain of 'induction–deduction–induction' is not logical positivism (which, at the time, did not even exist), because, although logical positivism 'begins' by sense-experience and 'ends' with empirical verification, it rejects induction. In any case what *inductions* were the marginal utility and productivity theories based on?

CHAPTER 3

1. The justification refers to an almost irrational urge to prove that economic theory is a characteristically 'scientific' discipline and, especially, comparable to physics.

2. See A. J. Ayer, *Language, Truth and Logic* (London: Gollancz, 1967) p. 32.

3. The term 'problem-solving' refers to all disciples which purport to extend our knowledge of the physical and social world. It avoids the use of the term 'scientific' prior to a definition for this term.

4. See Harry Johnson's review of *Time on the Cross,* entitled 'Negro Slavery', in *Encounter* (Jan 1975) pp. 56 ff.

5. The clearest statement of this position is found in R. G. Lipsey, *Introduction to Positive Economics* (1963, 1966 and 1971) chap. 1. We reserve judgement on whether this is a correct Popperian interpretation. See 'Popper, Positive Economics, etc.', above, p. 71.

6. Popper does not encounter a similar problem because he does not regard value judgements as meaningless, and he openly describes the criterion of falsifiability as a value judgement. See, further, notes 20 and 21 below.

7. This theory dates back to Ricardo as the basis for his differential theory of rent. It has not been 'derived' from 'direct' empirical observation, but from logical deduction, (perhaps) originally based on casual experience. The crucial point is the definition of 'the fixed factor': with Ricardo this was agricultural land; with Walras it was the (imaginary) 'given stock of productive inputs'; with Marshall it was the (meaningful) given productive capacity of the firm. However, as Joan Robinson has pointed out, the existing institutions, or the state of expectations, may well turn specific or even general labour into 'fixed' factors. See, further, *Economic Heresies* (London: Macmillan, 1971) chap. 2.

8. For a study of empirical cost curves see J. Johnson, *Statistical Cost Functions* (Maidenhead: McGraw-Hill, 1960); P. Sargant-Florence, *The Logic of the British and the American Industry* (1951; 2nd ed.: London: Routledge & Kegan Paul, 1962) and A. A. Walters, 'Production and Cost Functions', *Econometrica,* vol. 31 (1963) pp. 1–66.

9. The case of uncertainty and, with it, the return to the cardinal concept of utility, was inaugurated by J. von Neumann and O. Morgenstern's celebrated *The Theory of Games and Economic Behaviour,* 2nd ed. (Princeton, N.J.: Princeton University Press, 1947). This was followed by a series of articles on the subject, including: F. Mosteller and P. Nogee, 'An Experimental Measurement of Utility', *Journal of Political Economy* (1951); M. Friedman and L. J. Savage, 'The Expected Utility Hypothesis and the Measurability of Utility', *Journal of Political Economy,* (1952); I. N. Herstein and John Milnor, 'An Axiomatic Approach to Measurable Utility', *Econometrica* (1953); and A. Alchian's (synthetic) 'The Meaning of Utility Measurement', *American Economic Review* (1953). Our discussion of this issue specifically refers to Alchian's synthesis.

10. C. E. Ferguson and J. P. Gould, *Micro-economic Theory* (New York: Irwin, 1975) chap. 2, particularly pp. 29–39; J. M. Henderson and R. E. Quandt, *Micro-economic Theory: A Mathematical Approach* (Maidenhead: McGraw-Hill, 1958) chap. 2.

11. Ibid.

12. See P. A. Samuelson, 'International Trade and the Equalisation of Factor Prices', *Economic Journal*, vol. 58 (June 1948) pp. 163–84; 'International Factor Price Equalisation Once Again', vol. 59 (June 1949) pp. 181–97; S. F. James and I. F. Pearce, 'The Factor Price Equalisation Myth', *Review of Economic Studies* (1951–2); A. P. Lerner, 'Factor Prices and International Trade', *Economica* (1952); I. F. Pearce, 'A Note on Mr Lerner's Paper', ibid.; R. W. Jones, 'Factor Proportions and the Heckscher–Ohlin Theorem', *Review of Economic Studies* (1956–7); H. G. Johnson, 'Factor Endowments, International Trade and Factor Prices', *Manchester School*, vol. 25 (Sep 1957) pp. 270–83.

13. W. Leontief, 'Domestic Production and Foreign Trade: The American Capital Position Re-examined', *Economia Internazionale*, vol. 7 (1954); 'Factor Proportions and the Structure of American Trade: Further Theoretical and Empirical Analysis', *Review of Economics and Statistics*, vol. 38 (1956) pp. 386–407.

14. This is not intended as an attack on Leontief, if only because he presented the adverse results of the test with laudable honesty. Indeed, even his interpretation may have been correct. Our criticism is directed against the double standard of Positive Economics which pretends to stringent criteria (and demands them of others on pain of being called 'unscientific') without itself succeeding in observing those criteria.

15. A. W. Phillips, 'The Relation between Unemployment and the Rate of Change of Money Wage Rates in the United Kingdom, 1861–1957', *Economica*, N.S. vol. 25 (Nov 1968) pp. 283–99.

16. For example, see G. D. N. Worswick, 'Is Progress in Economic Science Possible?', *Economic Journal*, vol, 82, no. 325 (Mar 1972) and the reference therein (p. 82) to an early comment by K. G. J. C. Knowles and C. B. Winsten on the Phillips Curve as 'a daring simplification' of a 'complex problem'; see the latter, 'Can the Level of Unemployment Explain Changes in Wages?', *Bulletin of the Oxford Institute of Statistics*, vol. 21 (1959) pp. 113–21.

17. Karl Marx once described the deliberate suppression of truth as a sin against science. The classical Persian poet and writer Sa'adi, tells the story of a man who was thanking God after he had been bitten by a leopard because he had been 'struck not by a sin but by a catastrophe'.

18. See Karl R. Popper, 'Reason or Revolution?' (sec. 8, pp. 298–300) in *The Positivist Dispute in German Sociology* (London: Heinemann, 1976). See also his 'The Logic of the Social Sciences', ibid. pp. 87–104.

19. See his *Positivist Philosophy* (Harmondsworth: Penguin Books, 1972) p. 216.

20. See, for example, K. R. Popper, *Conjectures and Refutations* (London: Routledge & Kegan Paul, 1963) chap. 1. His own theory of 'the third world' or 'World III' (in which he distinguishes between the worlds of physical objects, mental processes and intellectual creations; and further claims a partial autonomy for the world of intellect) is essentially a metaphysical idea; see, further, his *Objective Knowledge* (Oxford: Clarendon Press, 1972) chap. 3. See also 'Scientific Reduction and the Essential Incompleteness of All Science', in *Studies in the Philosophy of Biology* (London: Macmillan, 1974).

21. Popper has explicitly admitted that 'his gospel' – i.e. the rule of falsifiability – is a normative rule, a value judgement, and nothing else. This, if anything, enhances the *logical* status of his position because it makes it clear that such rules cannot be 'positive' and that his own criterion is no exception; see, further, Chapters 5 and 6 on a fundamental clarification of normative statements.

22. As Lakatos himself admits, this is not quite correct, for even then Popper's emphasis was at least as much on a general critical approach to knowledge as on the empirical falsifiability of scientific hypotheses; see his *Conjectures and Refutations*, chap. 1, op. cit. Lakatos attributes the 'invention' of Popper 0 to Ayer.

23. We shall discuss Lakatos's views in greater detail in Chapter 4. See Imre Lakatos, 'Falsification and the Methodology of Scientific Research Programmes', in *Criticism and the Growth of Knowledge* (Cambridge: Cambridge University Press, 1977); see also T. W. Hutchison, 'On the History and Philosophy of Science and Economics', in *Method and Appraisal in Economics*, ed. S. J. Latsis (Cambridge: Cambridge University Press, 1976).

24. Popper regards a scientist's failure to observe basic rules as being almost entirely due to the principle of human fallibility. But this seems to be an exclusively *logical* explanation for such a failure. There could, however, be important sociological and ideological factors involved. See Chapters 4, 5 and 6.

25. See B. Magee, *Popper* (London: Fontana Masters Series, 1973).

26. See Bertrand Russell, *History of Western Philosophy* (London: Unwin University Books, 1961) chap. 29, p. 771.

27. See ibid. chap. 30, particularly pp. 780–1.

28. See L. C. R. Robbins, *An Essay on the Nature and Significance of Economic Science* (London: Macmillan, 1933).

29. See Fritz Machlup, 'The Problem of Verification in Economics', *Southern Economic Journal* (July 1955) pp. 1–21.

30. See T. W. Hutchison's reply to the above article and Machlup's rejoinder to his reply in *Southern Economic Journal* (Apr 1956) pp. 476–93.

31. See Milton Friedman, *Essays in Positive Economics* (Chicago: Chicago University Press, 1953) chap. 1.

32. See E. Nagel, 'Assumptions in Economic Theory', *American Economic Review, Papers and Proceedings* (1963); *Journal of Political Economy* (May 1963) pp. 211–19; A. G. Papandreou, 'Theory Construction and Empirical Meaning in Economics', ibid. pp. 205–10; J. Melitz, 'Friedman and Machlup on Testing Economic Assumptions', *Journal of Political Economy* (Feb 1965) pp. 37–60; T. C. Koopmans, *Three Essays on the State of Economic Science* (New York: McGraw-Hill, 1957).

33. Ferguson and Gould, op. cit., part III, p. 221.

34. ibid. chap. 8, p. 225.

35. P. H. Douglas, 'Are There Laws of Production?', *American Economic Review*, vol. 38 (Mar 1948) pp. 1–41.

36. See his *Economic Backwardness in Historical Perspectives* (Cambridge, Mass.: Harvard University Press, 1962).

37. See Isaiah Berlin, *Four Essays on Liberty* (London: Oxford University Press, 1969) 'introduction', for a forceful demonstration of this point.

38. See *Open Society and Its Enemies* (London: Routledge & Kegan Paul, 1952) vol. 2, where – among other similar statements – Popper writes: 'Marx loved freedom, real freedom [not Hegel's 'real freedom']' etc.

39. See *Theories of Surplus Value* (Moscow: Progress Publishers, 1968) vol. II, p. 121. Lewis S. Feuer has now almost conclusively demonstrated that Marx never offered to dedicate *Capital* to Darwin (see 'The Case of the Darwin–Marx Letter', *Encounter* (Oct 1978) pp. 62–78). But his own claim that Marx was, nevertheless, a Social Darwinist flies in the face of the existing *direct* evidence.

40. See F. A. von Hayek, *Studies in Philosophy, Politics and Economics* (New York: The Free Press, 1967) preface.

CHAPTER 4

1. Thomas S. Kuhn, *The Structure of Scientific Revolutions,* 2nd ed. (Chicago: Chicago University Press, 1970) p. 77.

2. Ibid. p. 79.

3. Ibid. p. 181. See, further, Margaret Masterman, 'The Nature of a Paradigm', in *Criticism and the Growth of Knowledge,* ed. Lakatos and Musgrave (Cambridge: Cambridge University Press, 1970) pp. 59–90.

4. Kuhn, op. cit. p. 208.

5. 'What is precise about Sir Karl's position is . . . the idea of testability in principle. On that much I rely too, for no theory that was *in principle* testable could function or cease to function when applied to scientific puzzle-solving.' See Thomas Kuhn, 'Reflections on My Critics', in *Criticism and the Growth of Knowledge,* op. cit. p. 248.

6. See Kuhn, ibid. p. 237; see also P. K. Feyerabend, 'Consolation for the Specialist', ibid. p. 197–229.

7. R. R. Nelson and S. G. Winter, 'Neoclassical v. Evolutionary Theories of Economic Growth: Critique and Prospectives', *Economic Journal* (Dec 1972) pp. 1237–55.

8. Feyerabend, op. cit.

9. See Kuhn, 'Reflections on My Critics', op. cit. p. 245.

10. See Gerald E. Peabody, 'Scientific Paradigms and Economics: An Introduction', *Review of Radical Political Economics* (July 1971); this issue includes other contributions on the subject.

11. See B. Ward, *What is Wrong with Economics?* (London: Basic Books, 1972). See also A. W. Coats, 'Is There a "Structure of Scientific Revolutions" in Economics?', *Kyklos,* vol. 22 (1969) pp. 289–94.

12. Guy Routh, *The Origin of Economic Ideas* (London: Macmillan, 1975).

13. See Martin Bronfenbrenner, 'The "Structure of Revolutions" in Economic Thought', *History of Political Economy* (1971).

14. See Popper in *Criticism and the Growth of Knowledge,* op. cit. pp. 51–8; see, further, J. W. N. Watkins, 'Against Normal Science', ibid. pp. 25–38.

15. See Paul Feyerabend, 'How to Defend Society against Science', *Radical Philosophy,* vol. 11 (1975) pp. 3–9; *Against Method,* Outline of an Anarchistic Theory of Knowledge, P. F. (London, 1975).

16. Imre Lakatos, 'Falsification and the Methodology of Scientific Research Programmes', *Criticism and the Growth of Knowledge,* op. cit. pp. 91–196.

17. Ibid. p. 135.

18. Ibid. p. 188.

19. See Mark Blaug, 'Kuhn *versus* Lakatos or Paradigms *versus* Research Programmes in the History of Economics', *History of Political Economy*, vol. 7 (1975) pp. 399–433.

20. See *The Theory of Political Economy* (Harmondsworth: Penguin Books, 1970) chap. 8, note on 'The Noxious Influence of Authority' pp. 260–1.

21. See J. A. Schumpeter, *Economic Doctrine and Method* (1912) (London: Oxford University Press, 1954) pp. 184–5. He reports that the followers of Walras and Menger were excluded from university chairs in France and Germany because of their views. We need hardly emphasise that our reference to such odious intellectual persecutions (which have been practised by the neo-classicals themselves since their practical triumph) have no bearing on a purely intellectual evaluation or critique of neo-classical economic theory either then or now.

22. See Alan Coddington's review of T. W. Hutchison's 'Knowledge and Ignorance in Economics' in *Economic Journal* (Dec 1977) pp. 790–2.

CHAPTER 5

1. See Chapter 6 for a more comprehensive discussion of value judgements or normative statements.

2. See, for example, 'Reflections on my Critics', in *Criticism and the Growth of Knowledge,* ed. Lakatos and Musgrave (Cambridge: Cambridge University Press, 1970) pp. 231–79.

3. *The Structure of Scientific Revolutions,* 2nd ed. (Chicago: Chicago University Press, 1970) p. 153.

4. See Keynes's *General Theory,* chap. 12.

5. See Kuhn, op. cit.

6. Although this should be clear both from the preceding and from the following description of 'the democratic nation state', we would emphasise that the use of the term 'democratic' has *no* implication of some ideal type of *political democracy*. It is merely used as a socio-political 'parallel' for technological mass societies (as opposed to all traditional social frameworks) in which, according to significantly varying norms and institutions, there is mass involvement (*and* individual anonymity) in ordinary social and economic processes. This broadly common characteristic must be the (implicit) reason why modern (liberal) political theory speaks of

liberal and totalitarian *democracies*, though this classification itself is subject to further argument.

7. This claim may seem unacceptable in view of the fact that many professional academics now enjoy official tenure, and they have recourse to professional associations and perhaps even the law courts against wrongful dismissals, etc. Nevertheless it is likely to be true: (i) the sense of freedom and security cannot be defined independently from individual psychologies and expectations – it is, ultimately, a *subjective* experience based on objective factors which promote or threaten it; (ii) a contemporary *professional* academic is typically dependent on his appointment, promotions, etc., both for his material living and for his psychological self-respect: he knows that he may not lose his job or tenure except in extreme cases (which do occur); but he also knows that he is likely to forfeit the hope of publishing in learned journals, receiving a fair recognition for his effort, being promoted at the right time, etc., if he decides to assert his full right to intellectual freedom and integrity; (iii) this is reinforced by the fact that the average contemporary academic, rather like the average contemporary desk which he uses, is a 'machine-made' product: his intellectual excellence and, therefore, his psychological endurance and self-reliance is appreciably less than those of his counterparts before the age of mass technological society – he would have little self-respect without *external* recognition. . . . All this refers to a comparison between *contemporary* academics as compared to those in the last decades of the previous, and the earlier, decades of the present century. The case of men like Galileo, Locke, Rousseau and Voltaire is even more obvious. For men like that suffered persecution with smiles on their faces and contempt in their eyes. They were absolutely certain of the value of their convictions and their own intellectual excellence. They did not sell their souls because the souls were great and the price too low.Their sufferings gave them greater – not less – cause fo self-respect and dignity. Their freedom and security was threatened by enemies of intellect not by *ex officio* intellectuals: the intellectual dispute, and the personal animosity, between Voltaire and Rousseau is well known; yet Voltaire invited Rousseau to his home in Geneva to relax from his miserable social and personal conditions; and he violently reacted to the news that Rousseau's books had been publicly burned outside the Sorbonne – Rousseau made a contribution to the fund raised for erecting a statue of Voltaire *in the latter's lifetime*.

8. Mawlavi (Rūmi), the great Persian classical mystic poet, wrote: 'Let me taste the Wine of Reunion, and I shall break down the door

of the eternal prison cell by [my] drunken cries'; elsewhere he wrote: 'Whoever was isolated from his origin, shall seek his reunion with that origin.'

9. See McIntyre's *Marcuse* (London: Fontan's 'Modern Masters' series, 1970).

10. Karl R. Popper, 'Reason or Revolution?' in *The Positivist Dispute in German Ideology* (London: Heinemann Educational Books, 1976) pp. 288–300, sec. 5. See also his 'The Rationality of Scientific Revolutions', in *Problems of Scientific Revolution: Progress and Obstacles to Progress in the Sciences* (Oxford: Clarendon Press, 1975) especially pp. 84–5: 'In recent years, however, it has become fairly clear that affluence may also be an obstacle: too many dollars may chase too few ideas. . . . Big Science may destroy Great Science, and the publication explosion may kill ideas. . . . I may perhaps quote Eugène Wigner . . . who sadly remarks: "The spirit of science has changed." This is indeed a sad chapter. . . .'

CHAPTER 6

1. See his *Capitalism and Freedom* (Chicago: Chicago University Press, 1963) p. 110.

2. For example see L. C. R. Robbins, *Politics and Economics* (London: Macmillan, 1963) p. 19: 'We must certainly hold fast to the idea of a neutral science of economics, a system of generalised description of influences and movements in the world of economic relationships. To have recognized . . . the distinction between positive and normative judgements is one of the achievements of [economic] thought . . . and nothing but confusion could come from any attempt to gloss it over. But the idea that there can be constructed a system of prescriptions which results inevitably from the results of positive analysis can involve scarcely less of a confusion.'

3. W. J. Ashley (ed.), *Principles of Political Economy* (London: Duckworth, 1940).

4. *Epistemological Problems of Economics* (1933) (English edition, New York: Van Nostrand Co., 1960) p. 94.

5. Ibid. p. 35.

6. See L. C. R. Robbins, *An Essay on the Nature and Significance of Economic Science* (London: Macmillan 1933).

7. *Sketch for a Historical Picture of the Progress of the Human Mind,* cited in P. Appleman (ed.), *An Essay on the Principle of Population,* by Malthus (New York: Norton, 1976) p. 7.

8. See Bertrand Russell, *Philosophy and Politics* (Cambridge: Cambridge University Press, 1947).

9. See Herbert Marcuse, *Reason and Revolution,* 2nd ed. (London: Routledge & Kegan Paul, 1955) p. 5.

10. This general description and appraisal of concepts of ideology is, in the first instance, based on primary sources too numerous, and pretentious, to cite. Secondary sources include I. Berlin, *The Hedgehog and the Fox* (New York: New American Library, 1957). W. A. Kaufmann, *Hegel* (New York: Anchor Books, 1966); *From Shakespeare to Existentialism* (New York: Doubleday, 1960). G. Lichtheim, *Marxism* (London: Routledge & Kegan Paul, 1961); *The Concepts of Ideology and Other Essays* (New York: Random House, 1967); *Lukács* (London: Fontana, 1970); G. Lukács, *History and Class Consciousness* (Cambridge, Mass.: M.I.T. Press, 1971); K. Mannheim, *Ideology and Utopia* (London: Routledge & Kegan Paul, 1952). Marcuse, op. cit. J. Plamenatz, *Ideology* (New York: Praeger, 1970; *German Marxism and Russian Communism* (London: Longmans, 1954); *Man and Society* (London: Longmans, 1962) vol. 2; K. R. Popper, *Open Society and its Enemies* (London: Routledge & Kegan Paul, 1952) vol. 2.

11. See Chapter 2, n. 2.

12. *History of Economic Analysis* (London: Allen & Unwin, 1963) chap. 1.

CHAPTER 7

1. See, further, 'Instrumentalism and Positive Economics' in Chapter 2.

2. See, further, 'Of Ideology' in Chapter 6. The concept of historical relativism is further discussed later in this chapter.

3. Needless to say, we are not here concerned with the truth or falsehood of these theories.

4. For example see L. C. R. Robbins, *An Essay on the Nature and Significance of Economic Science* (and references there) (London: Macmillan, 1933); M. Hollis and E. J. Nell, *Rational Economic Man* (Cambridge: Cambridge University Press, 1975).

5. See Robbins, op. cit.

6. For example, see Robbins, op. cit., who seems to argue that because economic theories are not 'historico-relative', they must have universal validity.

7. See, further, this author's 'Adam Smith, Mandeville and Effective Demand' in *The History of Economic Thought* (News Bulletin) (Apr 1977).

8. *Theories of Surplus Value* (Moscow: Progress Publishers, 1968) vol. 2, chap. 17, pp. 502–5.

9. When, in 1933, G. B. Shaw suggested to Keynes to read the work of Marx and Engels (in an attempt to discover the causes of the Great Depression) Keynes replied that he was engaged in writing a book in consequence of which 'the Ricardian foundations of Marxism will be knocked away'! Clearly in 1933 he must still have been totally unaware that he was in fact engaged in criticising a Ricardian theory which Marx had already refuted – largely by arguments similar to his own – many decades ago. It is true that later, in *The General Theory*, Keynes mentions Marx as one of his precursors on the problem of overproduction, but even then he cannot have read Marx extensively on this subject or he would not have grouped Marx with such intellectually insignificant pamphleteers as Silvio Gessel and Major Douglas. This note is not intended as a belated diminution of Keynes's stature and achievements. It is meant, first, as an example to show that even the most serious and original scientists would greatly benefit from a thorough grasp of the history and traditions of their own subject; and, second, as a reminder that ignoring past and present authors for extra-scientific reasons may serve to slow down the growth of knowledge. See R. F. Harrod, *The Life of John Maynard Keynes* (London: Macmillan, 1952) p. 462; and Keynes's *General Theory*, chap. 3, sec. III.

10. Karl R. Popper, 'Reason or Revolution?' *The Positivist Dispute in German Ideology* (London: Heinemann Educational Books, 1976) pp. 294–5.

11. Ibid. p. 293.

12. Hollis and Nell, op. cit.

13. Janos Korni, *Anti-equilibrium* (Amsterdam: North-Holland, 1971).

14. See Arun Bose, *Marxian and Post-Marxian Political Economy* (Harmondsworth: Penguin Modern Economics, 1975) p. 32; see, further, pp. 42–5.

15. Ibid. p. 43.

16. See Joan Robinson, *The Economics of Imperfect Competition* (London: Macmillan, 1933) pp. 281f. For a textbook reference to this problem see C. E. Ferguson and J. P. Gould, *Micro-economic Theory* (New York: Irwin, 1975) pp. 406 and 414–16.

17. Bose, op. cit. pp. 32–3.

18. Ibid. p. 57.

19. Ibid. p. 57; see also pp. 80–1.

CHAPTER 8

1. The following epitaphs precede the text of John Ruskin's *Unto This Last* (1860): 'Friend, I do thee no wrong. Didst thou agree with me for a penny? Take that thine is, and go thy way. I will give unto this last even as unto thee'; 'If ye think good, give me my price; and if not forbear. So they weighed for my price thirty pieces of silver.' Ruskin's essay is a critique of orthodox classical economic theory. See *The Works of Ruskin*, Library Edition (London: Allen, 1905) vol. 18, pp. 5–114.

2. See his critique of Ricardo's theory of rent in *Theories of Surplus Value* (Moscow: Progress Publishers, 1968) vol. 2.

3. The problem of determining *relative* factor-endowments in a multi-input situation has led another author *to begin with an assumption which the Heckscher–Ohlin model 'proves' as a conclusion*; see, further, 'Heckscher–Ohlin: The Multi-Country Case', p. 200.

4. See above, 'Heckscher–Ohlin with Uncertainty', p. 189, which confirms 'factor–price equalisation' as a *valid conclusion* of the Heckscher–Ohlin theorem without uncertainty; *but refutes that validity* when there is 'uncertainty in the production function'.

5. Quoted in G. C. Harcourt, 'The Cambridge Controversies: Old Ways and New Horizons', *Oxford Economic Papers*, vol. 28, no. 1 (Mar 1976) p. 25; for the original statement see 'Introduction', in J. A. Mirrlees and N. H. Stern (eds), *Models of Economic Growth* (London: Macmillan, 1973) p. xxi.

INDEX

Page numbers in **bold type** indicate whole chapters or sections. 'p' means *passim* (here and there), scattered references. Alphabetical order: word-by-word.

EEC (European Economic Community,
'The Common Market')   188
Effective Demand   14, 15–16
'Eighteenth Brumaire of Louis
Bonaparte' (Marx)   87
Einstein, Albert (1879–1955)   50,
159, 180, 207, 208
Eliot, T. S.   151
Empire, Britain's age of   15
empirical
criticism   67
knowledge   169
methods   169–70
testability   72
tests   73; tools of   70
empiricism and empiricists   19, 31–2,
32, 48, 51, 70, 85 bis, 99
practical counterpart of   172
empiricism and historicism   157
'Encyclopedists, The' (French
sociologists)   31, 32
Engels, Friedrich (1820–95)   86;
quoted   41
English Revolution, The (1642–8)
11, 32, 97
Enlightenment, The (Renaissance,
15th-century)   125
equilibrium, economic (see also
disequilibrium)   11, 16 bis
28, 68, 103, 111–12 p, 144, 162
164, 165, 191
and capitalist market-mechanism
172–8
and the Law of Diminishing Returns
56–7
conditions for   24
dynamic and static   195–6
general theory of   15, 24, 27 bis, 28,
57, 58, 60–1
stability of   15, 21
Equilibrium, General, and the H–O
Theory of Trade (Horiba)   200
Essay on Profit (Ricardo)   74, 185
Essays on Positive Economics
(Machlup)   79
European Economic Community
(EEC, The Common Market)
188
'European Soul, The'   38
Evans-Pritchard, E. E.   87
evidence, factual and empirical, in
economics   32

Evolutionary Theory of Growth versus
Neo-Classical Theory of Growth
(anonymous article quoted)   101
expenditure: for investment and for
consumption   6
expressionism, paradigm of   97
Extra-logical Factors, Influence of
114–16

Fable of the Bees (Mandeville, 1714)
16, 160
Fable of the Fox and Hedgehog   132
factor–price equilibrium theorem
188–9, 191, 192 see also
equilibrium
facts, scientific 'processing' of, to
form theories   139
faith: in progress and in tradition   126
falsifiability, falsification(ism) (see
also verifiability, verification)
54, 55, 72, 73 bis, 97, 106, 107–8,
109, 110, 113
falsificationism
naïve   106, 110
sophisticated   106, 110
Al-Farabi: The Excellent City   22
Faraday, Michael (1791–1867)   126,
154
farming, capitalist   21
farming, 'gentleman' (in England)
188; see also agriculture
fatalism, 32; see also determinism
'fellow-feeling' (among human beings)
21
Ferguson, C. E., and Gould, J. P.
quoted   82 bis
feudalism, European   21 ter, 87–8, 188
agriculture under   188
paradigm of   97
Feuerbach, Ludwig Andreas (1804–72)
86 bis
Feyerabend, P. K.   106 bis
Fisher, Allan, G.   16, 37, 165
foreign exchanges: purchasing-power-
parity theory of   105
foreign trade   10, 12, 13, 14; expansion
of   10
Fourier, François M. C. (1772–1837)
25
Fox and Hedgehog fable   132
'free trade'   11, 14, 24
a universal panacea   24

prices, relative, determination of   15, 111
Prince, The (Machiavelli, 1532)   76
Principles of Political Economy (Steuart, 1767)   179
production, capitalist–industrial system of   25–7
  absence of harmony in   25–6
  concentration of   27
  four possible reactions to discovery of lack of harmony in   25–6
  Marx on   163, **174–5**
Production, Theory of   22
'Production Uncertainty and the Heckscher–Ohlin Theory' (R.N. Batra), *article discussed*   189–92
productivity, rate of increase of   16
professionalism and vocationalism 125, 132 *bis*, 133
professionalism in all scientific and intellectual pursuits   **119–23,** 155
professions
  academic, *see* academic profession
  disciplinary   121
  'Professor Clark's Economics', Veblen's critique of   17
profit   15, 22–3
  falling rate of (theory)   13, 89
  uniform rate of (*impossible*)   24, 27 *bis,* 28
Profit, Essay on (Ricardo, 1815)   174, 185
Programmes, Paradigms, etc., *see* ECONOMIC KNOWLEDGE, DEVELOPMENT OF (Chapter 4) **91–113**
promotion, academic and publication **120–1**
property
  bourgeois   20
  feudal   21, 23
  forms of   88
  ownership of   88
  private   21, 22
  views on (economists' and philosophers')   21
PROSPECTS AND RESULTS (Chapter 9)   **209–11**
prosperity, greater (the main aim of economics) – but whose prosperity?   31
Proudhon, Pierre Joseph (1809–65)   25
  Marx's polemic against   86

psychoanalysis, Freudian (and others) 114
psychologism   29
psychology, behavioural (social)   5
psychology, individual and social   114
public spending (a general panacea)   6
publication, and academic promotion 120–1
'publicity explosions'   166

'Quantity Theory of Drink, The': A Restatement (O. E. Covick)   203–4
quantity theory of money   11–12, 81, 105 *bis*

racism (racialism)   102
radicals
  and Kuhn's theory   100,102 *bis*
  and revolution   101
Rational Economic Man (Hollis and Nell)   44
'rational faith' (faith in reasoning)   32
rationalism and rationalists   19, 48 *bis*
  faculty of reason   19
Rayleigh, Lord   118
realism, paradigm of   97
reality and appearance, Plato's (and the author's) conception of   149, 150–1
reason, faculty of   19
Reason and Freedom, the kingdom of (Hegel)   129
reason and freedom among academic scientists   171–2
reductionism, methodological and substantive   74
Reflexions (Turgot, 1766)   161
relativism, historical   160
Renaissance, the European (15th-century)   125, 132
  another   134
rent   23 p
  absolute (Marx)   27
  differential (Ricardo)   13
'rentier, euthanasia of the'   16
Republic, Plato's (4th century B.C.)   22
'Requiem for Science, A',   **207–8**
RESEARCH, CURRENT: SOME EVIDENCE FROM (Chapter 8)   **184–208**
for details see 'UNTO THIS LAST'
research, emphasis in   146
research agenda   147, 155–6, 175, 177